SEVEN
DIRTY
WORDS

SEVEN DIRTY WORDS

◇　◇　◇　◇　◇　◇　◇

The Life and Crimes of
George Carlin

JAMES SULLIVAN

DA CAPO PRESS
A Member of the Perseus Books Group

Designed by Jeff Williams
Set in Adobe Garamond by the Perseus Books Group

Library of Congress Cataloging-in-Publication Data
Sullivan, James, 1965 Nov. 7–
    Seven dirty words : the life and crimes of George Carlin / James Sullivan.
      p. cm.
    Includes bibliographical references and index.
    ISBN 978-0-306-81829-5 (alk. paper)
    1. Carlin, George. 2. Comedians—United States—Biography. I. Title.

PN2287.C2685S85 2010
792.7'6028092—dc22
[B]
                                                                    2010000583

First Da Capo Press edition 2010

Published by Da Capo Press
A Member of the Perseus Books Group
www.dacapopress.com

Da Capo Press books are available at special discounts for bulk purchases in the U.S. by corporations, institutions, and other organizations. For more information, please contact the Special Markets Department at the Perseus Books Group, 2300 Chestnut Street, Suite 200, Philadelphia, PA 19103, or call (800) 810-4145, ext. 5000, or e-mail special.markets@perseusbooks.com.

10 9 8 7 6 5 4 3 2 1

For Jim Sheehan,
who taught his kids the most offensive words are *shut up*.

CONTENTS

◇　◇　◇　◇　◇　◇　◇

I have believed all my life in free thought and free speech—up to and including the utmost limits of the endurable.

—H. L. MENCKEN

WARM-UP

YOU HAD TO LAUGH.

In twentieth-century America, he went looking for the sublime and found only the ridiculous. How could any thinking person see it otherwise? Born on the eve of World War II, he lived the Atomic Age up close, working on bomber jets while serving in the U.S. Air Force. He experienced the cultural upheaval of the 1960s from its epicenter, and he lived long enough to experience the absurd excess, and the inevitable, colossal hangover, of the end of the American century.

It's called the American Dream, he said, because you have to be asleep to believe it. In his lifetime, laughter seemed like the only sane response. So George Carlin set about studying it and creating it. For fifty years he may well have produced more laughs than any other human being.

He also rubbed his share of people the wrong way. If he hadn't, he wouldn't have been doing it right. Carlin knew that comedy is meant to shock. Funny doesn't happen without a sense of surprise. And audacity—the courage to say what you mean—is critical to the art of making people laugh. Whether speaking truth to the powerful or telling fart jokes, comedians, by their very nature, deal in taboo.

Comedy bends the rules. Humor, wrote an early scholar of American popular culture, is "a lawless element." Every comedian is "a scofflaw," wrote another, "who could be charged with breaking and entering—with breaking society's rules and restrictions, and with entering people's psyches."

George Carlin was a natural born transgressor. He saw where the line had been drawn, and he leaped. If he spotted a sacred cow—God, country, children—he went cow-tipping. Raised on Spike Jones anarchy and Beat Generation rebellion, he heard it every time he got into hot water, with the nuns and priests, the owner of the corner drugstore, his commanding officers: "What are you, a comedian?"

Yes, he was. Wholly devoted to the craft, he made every kind of comedy his own. Some comedians do self-deprecation. Some do surrealism. Some do political humor or dick jokes, impressions or observations. Carlin did it all. He questioned everything, from the existence of God and the authority of government, to the military and the police, to the accuracy of the phrase "shelled peanuts": "If you're clothed, you have clothes, so if you're shelled, you should have shells." "Every comedian does a little George," Jerry Seinfeld wrote in the *New York Times* upon Carlin's death. "I've heard it my whole career: 'Carlin does it,' 'Carlin already did it,' 'Carlin did it eight years ago.'"

Carlin often said there were three main elements to his comedy: the "little world" of everyday experience ("kids, pets, driving, the stores, television commercials"); the big, unanswerable questions, such as race, war, government, big business, religion, and the mysteries of the universe; and the English language, with all its quirks and frustrations ("lingo and faddish trendy buzzwords and catch phrases and Americanisms"). In fact, that covers just about everything under the sun.

Just as no topic was off-limits for Carlin, no style of comedy was beyond his grasp. He was equally enamored of hokey puns ("My back hurts; I think I over-schlepped") and sly brainteasers. ("If crime fighters fight crime and firefighters fight fire, what do freedom fighters fight?") He did street corner insults and Zen non sequiturs. He changed voices, made sound effects, whistled, sang, stuck out his tongue and blew raspberries. He was an outstanding physical comedian, too, with enough rubbery faces and herky-jerky gestures to do an entire set in mime.

Many comedians have distinctive voices, but only a few are fortunate enough to develop one that's never been heard. George Carlin's voice was unmistakable. In his younger years he had the mellow, quizzical tone of a perpetually amused pot smoker. Later it aged into a hard-earned rasp. Throughout his various stages, this one-of-a-kind voice—quintessential New Yorker, representative hippie, reflexive contrarian—spoke for a nation of dissatisfied idealists and for himself alone.

Timing is essential to comedy, and Carlin's personal timing could not have been more precise. "The comic comes into being just when society and the individual, freed from the worry of self-preservation, begin to regard themselves as works of art," wrote Henri Bergson in his famous essay on laughter. Born during the Golden Age of Radio, Carlin devoted more time to reading *Mad* magazine (established 1952) than to his Latin and algebra lessons. The stand-up comedy rebirth of the 1950s, when performers including Lenny Bruce, Mort Sahl, Shelley Berman, Jonathan Winters, and Dick Gregory demolished the old order of vaudevillian shtick, gave his early career its context. And Carlin was at that crucial age of transformation—thirty-three—when he found he could no longer ignore the lure of the countercultural revolution. Comedy, as the proud autodidact knew better than anyone, is a constant voyage of discovery.

Picking up the baton from the martyred Lenny Bruce, he remade stand-up, once the trade of strip-club flunkies in cheap tuxedos, for the rock 'n' roll crowd. He took it to theaters, turning the art of the joke into a concert event. Then he brought his provocative routines into the home, rejuvenating his career with an association with HBO that would last three decades. Some comedians can stretch a half-hour's worth of one-liners to last a lifetime. Carlin wrote an hour of new material for each HBO show, roughly every two years. Younger comedians are awestruck by the sheer vastness of his productivity. No one else came close.

For most comics, stand-up is a means to an end. In the 1980s, ten solid minutes got more than a few their own sitcoms. In the age of television, Carlin was a rare creature—a comedian for whom stand-up comedy was the mountaintop. "I found out that it was an honest craft, and in fact, that art was involved," he said.

Like a master craftsman, Carlin worked with words. He held them up to the light. He inspected them, rubbed them, and whittled them. He worshipped them, in a way that he felt precious few products of the human mind deserved to be worshipped.

His most famous routine, "Seven Words You Can Never Say on Television," branded him as a vulgarian, a foul-mouthed comic who worked "dirty." But the routine was much more than mere titillation. It was an airtight example of Carlin's belief in the one thing he truly believed in—the power of reason. Why, exactly, are these few words—out of 400,000 in the English language—off-limits? Who are they hurting, and how? When Carlin reserved the right to use the whole language, he sparked a debate about censorship that brought his seven magic words—*shit, piss, fuck, cunt, cocksucker, motherfucker,* and *tits*—into the halls of the Supreme Court. Decades later, his questions are more relevant than ever in our media-saturated culture.

In his later years, the unruffled hippie became known for a certain irascibility. As he pointed out, laughter is our response to injustice. ("The human race has one really effective weapon," said Mark Twain, "and that is laughter.") The old shpritzers who played the Catskills told zingers about their mothers-in-law. He took the longer view. His targets were the massive institutions that supposedly have civilized the species.

To Carlin, American mediocrity was a real disappointment. We've sold our souls, he said, for cheap thrills and false beliefs. In his later years he cranked up the volume on his rants, writing darkly comic pieces about the fate of humanity. "I prefer seeing things the way they are," he said, "not the way some people wish they were." He became a kind of oracle of disaster, finding black humor in school shootings a few years before Columbine and in horrific calamities just before the planes hit the World Trade Center, and even presupposing the government bailouts of 2009 ("The Fund for the Rich and Powerful").

Like a doctor searching for a swollen gland, he pressed on any subject that made people sensitive. At various times in his career it was the

Catholic Church, bodily functions, the sanctity of children, the emptiness of our sense of entitlement. Many casual observers thought he grew angry in his later years. To Carlin, it was just an extended comic exercise: How far could he go? Comedy was a constant intellectual challenge, an endless reevaluation of received wisdom and group thinking. He genuinely liked individual people; it was their collective beliefs he couldn't stand. "No matter how you care to define it," he once said, "I do not identify with the local group."

"How he stood above and apart from the world . . . observing the human comedy, chuckling over the eternal fraudulences of man!" another wicked American humorist once wrote of Mark Twain. "What a sharp eye he had for the bogus, in religion, politics, art, literature, patriotism, virtue!" When Carlin learned that he was to be honored with the Mark Twain Prize for American Humor—five days before his death, as it turned out—much was made of the comparison between the comic and the writer for whom the award was named. But Carlin had at least as much in common with H. L. Mencken, originator of the above quote, the iconoclastic journalist who saw the rampant misuse of the English language as an all-too-perfect symbol for the dismayingly low standards of his culture. "No one ever went broke underestimating the intelligence of the American people," Mencken famously put it.

Few things, Twain felt, are as rare in American life as the act of a man speaking freely. Our constitutional commitment to free speech is a wonderful idea, in theory. In practice, however, we can speak freely only so long as we are willing to keep our most uncompromised thoughts to ourselves. Unequivocal free speech, Twain argued, is "the privilege of the dead." The living are much too paralyzed by the potential social costs to dare utter "unpopular convictions."

In a society inescapably inundated with evasions, false promises, phony manners, fine print, and outright lies, George Carlin never failed to say what he meant. "Just when I discovered the meaning of life," he joked, "they changed it." If the meaning of life is laughter, he changed it himself.

1

HEAVY MYSTERIES

◇ ◇ ◇ ◇ ◇ ◇ ◇

The kid had a mouth on him, and he knew it. Young Georgie Carlin, a scrawny, buzz-cut New York City boy in striped shirts and rolled-up jeans, had predicted his professional life almost to the letter. Required to write a self-portrait in Sister Nina's fifth-grade class, he had confidently explained that he would become a radio announcer, an impersonator, a stand-up comedian and, finally, an actor.

Now, barely into his twenties, he was in Boston, working as a board announcer at an easy-listening radio station. He read promos and sponsorships, patched through the various programs of the NBC radio network, and hosted an after-hours show featuring the "beautiful music" of Frank Sinatra and Nelson Riddle. It was here that Carlin met Jack Burns, a fellow radio newcomer with whom, within a year, he would appear on *The Tonight Show*, doing comedy.

Boston was Carlin's second city in radio. He'd broken in three years earlier while serving as a radar technician at Barksdale Air Force Base outside Shreveport, Louisiana. Hired in 1956 by an upstart rock 'n' roll station with the call letters KJOE, he spun records on his own drive-time showcase, *Carlin's Corner.* (He had his own zingy jingle: "*George, Carlin,* is on the air/The coolest record man anywhere!") Although the Boston gig had a lower profile, it was in a bigger market. Each night at a quarter to seven the city's archbishop, the stentorian Richard Cardinal

Cushing, led the rosary for fifteen minutes, just before NBC's *News on the Hour*.

One night Cardinal Cushing went on the air from his remote location with some spontaneous comments about the Little Sisters of the Poor. By the time he began praying the rosary, he'd fallen behind schedule. At 6:59 the cardinal was just midway through the Fifth Sorrowful Mystery of the Rosary. Carlin was on the edge of his seat, panicking about the news. There was only one thing to do. At seven o'clock on the nose, he pulled the cardinal's feed and cut to the broadcast: "The NBC News, brought to you by Alka-Seltzer."

Within minutes the phone rang in the studio. "I want to talk to the young man who took off the Holy Word of Gawd," boomed Cardinal Cushing. Carlin, alone in the studio, nervously admitted he was that young man. Then he did something he wouldn't do again for as long as he lived: He "hid behind the government," as he recalled years later. He explained to the imposing clergyman that he was bound by law to follow the program log from the Federal Communications Commission. If he didn't accommodate a network newscast and its paying advertisers, he could lose his job. It was the first, and decisively the last, time that George Carlin would take the side of the FCC. In the morning the station manager backed his junior staffer, telling the archbishop's office he'd done the right thing.

The exoneration was short-lived. Weeks later Carlin took the station's mobile news unit for the weekend and drove to his native New York to score some weed.

It was a fireable offense, and fired he was. So much for a career in Boston. It wasn't the first time, and it wouldn't be the last, that he felt trapped by expectations. A decade after his apprenticeship in radio, just as he was becoming a prime-time television personality and nightclub headliner, he threw away his burgeoning success to pursue a seemingly quixotic vision of himself as a voice of the oozing counterculture. Throughout his performing life Carlin had run-ins with the tipsy crowds and heavy-handed moguls of Las Vegas, where top-shelf comedians could make big money in steady engagements as long as they played nice. When he finally landed a sitcom of his own, in the mid-1990s, he couldn't wait to get the hell out of it. Groucho Marx famously joked that he wouldn't join any club that would have him as a member. Carlin wasn't joking. Catholic school, the Boy Scouts, the Air Force, the chummy world of network television—it didn't take him long to recognize that his natural vantage point was from the outside.

HIS CAREER WAS BORN at age thirty-three, when he realized that his work was his life, that comedy could be more than just clowning: a calling. It was born during his first appearances on *The Tonight Show, Merv Griffin*, and *Ed Sullivan*; it was born on the stage of the Café Au Go Go in Greenwich Village, where Lenny Bruce had been arrested for saying the word *cocksucker*. Or it was born at age thirteen, when he discovered the skewed analytical benefits of smoking marijuana, or when Brother Conrad helped the budding voice artist purchase a primitive Webcor tape recorder, or even earlier than that, when his mother instilled in her second son a lifelong reverence for the dictionary.

In truth, his actual birth was a mistake. George Denis Patrick Carlin was conceived during a period of separation for his parents, a slick-talking newspaper advertising salesman named Patrick Carlin and an executive secretary named Mary Bearey. Patrick Carlin, the national advertising manager for the *Sun* newspaper, the conservative broadsheet then in head-to-head competition with the *New York Times* and the *Herald Tribune*, had previously worked at a couple of Philadelphia papers and done a stretch at the *New York Post* as well. He was an accomplished after-dinner speaker who won a nationwide Dale Carnegie public speaking contest in 1935. Throughout his life, George Carlin kept the mahogany gavel his father had been awarded in the contest. "He had a real line of shit, boy. He could talk your donkey's ear off," Carlin recalled. The winning speech, given two years before the birth of Patrick Carlin's second son, was called "The Power of Mental Demand."

Patrick Carlin, born in 1888 in Donegal, Ireland, was seventeen years older than Mary Bearey. They were married in 1930, and their son Patrick was born one year later. Though the man of the house was making good money during the Great Depression, averaging a thousand dollars a week in commissions (for three years in a row, he was the leading newspaper ad salesman in the country), he and his young bride fought bitterly over Mary's "lace curtain" aspirations and Patrick's prodigious drinking. Within a few years they were separated. By chance they met again in the summer of 1936. Patrick Carlin convinced his estranged wife to accompany him for the weekend to Rockaway Beach, in Queens, where they checked into their old getaway, Curley's Atlas Hotel and Baths, along the oceanfront. There, as George Carlin often noted, the baby was conceived.

Mary contemplated having an abortion, going so far as to schedule an appointment for a D&C with a doctor in Gramercy Park. She'd been to see that doctor before; his code name, according to Carlin, was "Dr. Sunshine." But fate, and superstition, intervened: Gazing at a painting on the wall in the waiting room, Mary became convinced she could see a likeness of her own mother, who had died six months earlier. "Let's get out of here, Pat," she said. "I'm going to have this kid."

The impending birth of George Carlin brought on a short-lived reconciliation for the couple. But Patrick's drinking was too much for Mary to take. "The Irish call it the curse," Carlin said. "My mother called him a street angel and a house devil." Two months after the delivery on May 12, 1937, Patrick Carlin arrived home at the family's Riverside Drive apartment, having made his usual stop at an Upper Broadway watering hole en route. In the course of their latest argument, Mary wondered aloud why she should bother to set out crystal and fine china at dinnertime, if her husband was just going to stumble in three sheets to the wind every night. Enraged, Patrick Carlin took a tray of his wife's place settings and chucked them out an open window.

Mary Carlin gathered up her boys and fled down the fire escape. Making their way through the back lots out to Broadway, they piled into a Packard owned by one of Mary's brothers and headed out of town. When they returned, mother and sons moved from apartment to apartment in the neighborhood, trying to avoid confrontation with the boys' father. "We ran for four years," said Carlin. "I saw the fear in her when the doorbell would ring." With four brothers living nearby and occasional escorts from sympathetic beat cops, Mary felt safe enough from physical harm, though she could not escape her husband's intimidation.

He bid the boys a quiet farewell on one last visit; according to Carlin, he sang an emotional version of "The Rose of Tralee," the traditional Irish ballad about the "lovely and fair" Mary, who won her beloved not with her beauty alone, but with "the truth in her eyes ever beaming."

The young son understood from an early age that he took great pleasure in entertaining people. As a toddler he learned a few surefire attention-getters from his mother, who worked as secretary to the president of an advertising association, demonstrating the new dance craze called the Big Apple or mimicking Mae West ("Why don't you come up and see me sometime?") for her friends in the office secretarial pool. When he was old enough, Carlin began sneaking onto the subway to meet his mother after work, where his impromptu performances for her colleagues sometimes earned him a dinner at the Automat in Times Square. "I noticed that this process of doing something for people pleased them, and you gained some feeling of approval from it," he said. Approval, attention, applause, approbation: "All these *A*s that I never got in school, I got for acting out for people."

Patrick Carlin died of a heart attack in 1945, when his youngest son was eight years old. It isn't difficult to infer that his father's absence helped shape the son's lifelong skepticism about authority figures. "The thing is, I never really had issues with my father because I was so young," he once said. "My brother hates his guts. I hate him by proxy, but I also love him by proxy."

Almost six years older than George, brother Patrick was often out carousing. When Patrick came home at night, the younger Carlin sometimes lay in bed listening to his mother chastise him. Pat, Mary would say, was just like his father. Georgie was different. He had sensitivity. She vowed to "make something" of her youngest. From a young age Carlin recognized that he would have to contend with Mary Carlin's smothering instinct. "I had to fight her off," Carlin recalled. "And it made me stronger."

With their mother working long hours—earning "a man's salary," she said—Carlin and his brother were often on their own in the apartment in which the family eventually settled, on 121st Street. Grant's Tomb lay two blocks to the west. Morningside Heights, ensconced alongside Spanish Harlem to the east and the main economic artery of black Harlem, 125th Street, was an ethnically eclectic neighborhood, "wonderfully alive and vibrant," as Carlin recalled. "Cubans, Dominicans, Puerto Ricans, blacks, and Irish." In warm weather the smells of spicy cooking and the sounds of imported music hung in the air. The area was also home to an impressive array of institutions, including Columbia University, the Manhattan School of Music, the Union Theological Seminary, and the Jewish Theological Seminary of America, all of which earned it the nickname "the Acropolis of New York." Carlin and his Irish friends preferred to call the neighborhood "White Harlem," which sounded tougher than Morningside Heights.

With Patrick out on the streets, George would fix himself a simple dinner, a hamburger or some spaghetti, and exercise his considerable imagination with the radio and his comic books and magazines. Far from being lonely, he had lifelong blissful memories of this youthful independence. Answering a question about when and where he was happiest, he once replied, "Home alone after school, before my mother got home from work." Like thousands of kids his age at the time, he devoured the humor magazines that were becoming big business by the late 1940s. *Ballyhoo* was a groundbreaking parody magazine for kids, packed with advertising spoofs that prefigured the content of dozens of wisecracking titles to come. Another favorite, *Thousand Jokes*, was a monthly collection of single-panel gag cartoons. Carlin's Aunt Aggie worked for William Randolph Hearst's King Features Syndicate, the newspaper company that produced *Puck*, the weekly funny pages. Each week she brought her nephew the insert that would run four weeks later. His insider status gave him great leverage on the playground, where he convinced gullible schoolmates that he could predict the storylines of their favorite comics.

He dog-eared a copy of *Esar's Comic Dictionary*, a collection of punning definitions by the humorist Evan Esar. In the author's world, a cynic was "a man bored with sinning"; faith was "the boast of the man who is too lazy to investigate"; and freedom was "the ability to do as you please without considering anyone except the wife, boss, police, neighbors and the government."

Then there was *Mad*, the legendary sarcastic omnibus magazine, which Carlin started reading in its original comic book format. "Humor in a Jugular Vein," read a banner on the cover of the debut issue in August 1952. With its direct appeals to kids' inherent skepticism, *Mad* "was magical, objective proof to kids that they weren't alone," wrote the *New York Times* on the magazine's twenty-fifth anniversary. "There were people who knew that there was something wrong, phony and funny about a world of bomb shelters, brinkmanship and toothpaste smiles." Another admirer wrote that the magazine gave the writer and countless peers

a way of thinking about a world rife with false fronts, small print, deceptive ads, booby traps, treacherous language, double standards, half truths, subliminal pitches and product placements. . . . It prompted me to mistrust authority, to read between the lines, to take nothing at face value, to see patterns in the often shoddy construction of movies and TV shows; and it got me to think critically in a way that few actual human beings charged with my care ever bothered to.

The radio gave Carlin another world in which his mind could roam. He was enthralled by the adventures of *The Lone Ranger*, and he became a big fan of *Fibber McGee and Molly*. Broadcast on NBC at 9:30 on Tuesday nights, the show was a ratings champion by Carlin's grammar-school years. Jim Jordan and his wife, Marian Driscoll, played the title characters, the scheming, yarn-spinning knucklehead McGee and his ever-patronizing companion. Another popular program, *The Aldrich Family*, prefigured the family-oriented situation comedies of television, following the mild misadventures of young Henry Aldrich and his chum, Homer Brown, who closed each show by singing a jingle from their sponsor, Jell-O. "That was my family, the people on the radio," Carlin recalled. "No cousins, no grandparents."

Henry and Homer were archetypes of the classic all-American boy, soon to be seen on television's *Leave It to Beaver*. They were mischievous, but well-meaning. As the critic John Crosby once noted, radio's fictional boys, despite their propensity for mischief, were much too timid to ever amount to anything. "There aren't any Huck Finns in radio," Crosby wrote. Each week the Henrys and Homers and Oogies (Judy Foster's pubescent suitor, played by Richard Crenna, in *A Date with Judy*) "get into one jam after another, always by accident, never by design. . . . They never *try* to get into trouble."

Much more attractive to Carlin's already wicked sense of humor was the more sophisticated humor of radio's variety hosts—former vaudevillian Fred Allen, the deadpan improvisational duo Bob and Ray, and the acid-tongued Henry Morgan. The latter was a cantankerous New Yorker who delighted in mangling sponsors' pitches, for instance, accusing the makers of Life Savers of defrauding their customers out of the candy centers. Between such irreverent ad-libs the announcer played satirical records, many by the comic bandleader Spike Jones, whose City Slickers orchestra was famous for its zany arrangements, with toilet seats, bicycle horns, cap guns, and other props adding to the galloping irreverence. Morgan had a true devil-may-care attitude that earned him the admiration of fellow radio personalities such as Fred Allen and Jack Benny. But it also hastened his exile from the business. "I grew up thinking it was American to be outspoken," he wrote in his 1994 autobiography. "I've since learned it's un-American. If I was bringing up a kid today, I'd teach him to nod."

Just as he toyed with advertisers, Morgan couldn't deliver a simple weather forecast without mocking the format. "Snow, followed by little boys with sleds," he'd report, or "Dark clouds, followed by silver linings." Morgan's irreverence had a clear impact on one listener: Years later, Carlin introduced his own version of a subversive meteorologist to the stoner generation. "Tonight's forecast: dark," Carlin's most enduring stock character, Al Sleet, the Hippie-Dippy Weatherman, said countless times in his dope-addled drawl. "Continued dark throughout most of the evening, with some widely scattered light towards morning."

Fred Allen, bow-tied and erudite lampooner of American convention, was another of the young Carlin's exemplars. Unlike most of his gag-dependent counterparts, Allen was a writer first, a comic second. The man of whom James Thurber once said, "You can count on the thumb of one hand the American who is at once a comedian, a humorist, a wit, and a satirist," the Boston-bred Allen mixed verbal gymnastics and gentle put-downs with parodies of topical events and the mass diversions of the day, most notably his own medium, radio. "He took generous and regular swipes at mawkish soap operas, treacly kiddie shows, noisy quiz programs, talentless amateur hours, insipid husband-and-wife chatfests, banal interviewers, and mindless commercials," wrote Gerald Nachman in *Raised on Radio*. Not coincidentally, the host of the hour-long *Town Hall Tonight* was forever grappling with censors, who objected to many of the three-dollar words Allen so loved, such as *titillate* and *rabelaisian*. The watchdogs routinely required him to change references to potentially offended parties, including cockneys, hucksters, rodeo fans, and other targets of the announcer's exasperated wit. "Fifty percent of what I write ends up in the toilet," Allen complained.

Allen was one of the earliest radio celebrities to mine the daily news for satirical commentary, featuring segments called "Town Hall News," "Passe News" (a takeoff on the Pathe newsreels of the day), and "The March of Trivia" (which alluded to *The March of Time, Time*'s long-running newsreel series). For much of his career—from childhood, actually—Carlin created his own mock newscasts: "In labor news, longshoremen walked off the pier today. Rescue operations are continuing." Those routines, delivered in the clipped nasal tone of an off-the-rack newscaster, typically featured the additional talents of the Hippie-Dippy Weatherman and a rat-a-tat sportscaster the comedian called Biff Burns. Carlin borrowed that character, subconsciously or otherwise, from a character of the same name in the repertoire of Bob and Ray.

Bob Elliott and Ray Goulding—like Fred Allen, Boston natives drawn to New York, around 1950—brought the understated, off-the-cuff humor they'd developed as announcers on WHDH to the NBC network, where they became nationally beloved figures. The pair's comedy took the wind out of radio's insufferable windbags, from the exhausting sportscaster Burns to the self-important critic Webley Webster, to Elliott's standby, the hapless newscaster Wally Ballou. "Our original premise was that radio was too pompous," Elliott explained.

For Carlin, the nuanced send-up comedy of such vintage radio programs was complemented by the more lawless humor of other period entertainers to whom he was drawn. "I was a hip kid," he joked. "When I saw *Bambi* it was the midnight show." There were the Marx Brothers, of course, with their constant peppering of rectitude. Like many of his classmates, Carlin also got caught up in the national craze for Dean Martin and Jerry Lewis, whose convulsive physicality and audacious pranks seemed like a reaction to the insanity of the Atomic Age. Such wild men "represented anarchy," Carlin recalled. "They took things that were nice and decent and proper, and they tore them to shreds. That attracted me."

At the dawn of network television, Carlin often went downstairs to a neighbor's apartment to watch "Uncle Miltie," Milton Berle, on *The Texaco Star Theater*. Fascinated with the new medium, he sometimes traveled to the RCA Building in Rockefeller Center to walk in front of the closed-circuit cameras in the showroom, where visitors could watch themselves in real time on television screens overhead. Mary soon purchased a TV console for the Carlins' apartment.

The kid made time for Jackie Gleason's parade of characters on *Cavalcade of Stars* and on Sundays for *Toast of the Town*, the original name of *The Ed Sullivan Show*. Even better, however, was the short-lived *Broadway Open House*, the prototypical late-night variety show starring veteran comedian Jerry Lester, "The Heckler of Hecklers," whose trademark was twisting his glasses into uncomfortable angles on the bridge of his nose. The show also featured accordionist Milton DeLugg and a vapid bombshell known to viewers as Dagmar. With its antic mix of vaudeville routines and slapstick gags, "That one really got my attention," said Carlin. "I never missed *Broadway Open House*." One of the guests during the show's short run was a twenty-four-year-old comedian named Lenny Bruce.

All of this input worked on the young boy like an electric shock. He took the gags into his classrooms and onto the streets, where he found an eager audience. By telling jokes he was discovering his innate gift for language. Mary recognized it and introduced him to the dictionary, encouraging him to look up a word whenever he was unsure of its meaning, a habit he retained throughout his life. Carlin often said his parents had heightened instincts for storytelling: "Both of them could hold the center stage in any room." With his mother's professional colleagues and then the neighborhood children rewarding his affinity for the spotlight, he found himself drawn to performing "like a flower [to] the sun. . . . I had some tools for it from my genetic package, but now the environment was inviting me to develop them."

Carlin could trace his love of words to his mother's father, a retired New York City cop, a man dedicated to self-improvement who, during his off-duty hours, liked to copy the works of Shakespeare in longhand. As a boy Carlin was also intrigued to learn about his namesake, his mother's troubled brother George Bearey, who insisted on being called "Admiral" and once took his clothes off on a trolley car. "I was impressed, not that he was an admiral, but that he was nuts," he said.

Carlin's youth would soon become a lengthy experiment in tweaking authority. It didn't take long for him to recognize that he had no use for the practices of the Catholic Church. He traced the realization back at least as far as his first communion, when he was disenchanted to find that he felt nothing—no transcendence, no oneness with God, no miraculous visitation, as he'd been led to believe he would. Maybe, just maybe, these church people were clinging to beliefs they couldn't prove.

He attended grammar school at Corpus Christi School on West 121st Street, a progressive Catholic school that would paradoxically instill in the young student just the inquisitive tools he needed to reject the religious education he was in line to receive. Founded in 1907, the school was run by the Dominican Sisters of Sinsinawa, Wisconsin, who had been invited to New York by Father George Barry Ford, the second pastor of Corpus Christi, in 1936. His church had a reputation for encouraging liberal thinking, particularly because of its association with the writer and activist Thomas Merton, who was baptized there while a graduate student at nearby Columbia University. The pastor was a disciple of the educational reformer John Dewey, who was a professor of philosophy for years at Columbia's Teachers College, just across the street. Father Ford "talked the diocese into experimenting in our parish with progressive education," Carlin later explained in a routine called "I Used to Be Irish Catholic," "while whipping the religion on us anyway, and seeing what would happen."

Classrooms at Corpus Christi were unorthodox for the time, with movable desks and relaxed seating arrangements. Classes were coed, and there was no uniform requirement. There was also no formal grading system, and the students were encouraged to ask questions of all kinds. The setting served Carlin well. Years later he would often acknowledge the role the nuns of Corpus Christi played in shaping his mindset. (Several priests and nuns, including Father Ford, are sincerely thanked in the liner notes to his 1972 album *Class Clown*. "This album would not have been possible," Carlin wrote, without their "loving help.") "The church part and the neighborhood part were typical, but the school was not," he told his audiences. The students at Corpus Christi had so much freedom, in fact, "that by eighth grade, many of us had lost the faith. Because they made questioners out of us, and they really didn't have any answers."

To Carlin, the church's solemn rituals seemed laughable. As one historian has noted, since medieval times the Catholic Church has "frowned on laughter. To laugh was to mock heaven, by creating a kind of heaven here on earth." Of course, trying to suppress his giggling only made Carlin laugh more. The cosmic uncertainty of it all—the "Heavy Mysteries," as Carlin called them—naturally led the emerging disbeliever to the roots of absurdity. Why are we here? What is the point? Who makes the rules, and what are they for?

Mary began sending her boys away to camp during the summer, to get them out of the city. Carlin spent eight weeks each July and August at Camp Notre Dame, a Catholic boys' retreat on Spofford Lake in southwestern New Hampshire. Opened by a group of New York area priests in 1900 as Camp Namaschaug, the compound of cabins and cottages was purchased in 1939 by John E. Cullum, a grammar school principal from North Bergen, New Jersey. Known as "Uncle Jack" to a succession of nephews who attended Camp Notre Dame, Cullum was a devout Catholic who expected the boys—200 or so of them each summer—to climb out of their cots at sunrise every morning to attend mass, before breakfast. The camp was run with military precision, with regular bugle calls—"Reveille" at sunup, a mess call at mealtime, and "Taps" at day's end.

Athletics were strongly emphasized, with the campers playing baseball, basketball, volleyball, and other organized sports. They swam every afternoon and took part in track and swim meets on the weekends. They rowed, canoed, and hiked; at night, they sat around bonfires. Saturday nights were reserved for a talent show, with campers concocting singing groups, playlets, magic acts, and other amateur performances. At the end of each season boys were honored for excellence in various categories, including drama. Dave Wilson, a camper from Hoboken who was four years older than Carlin, was the perennial drama winner as the director of comic skits, which earned him the nickname "Wacky." Carlin, meanwhile, opted to go it alone, delivering comic monologues and shaggy-dog stories. "I don't know whether he got them from radio, or what," recalls Leo Cullum, a nephew of Uncle Jack's who attended the camp from 1948–1959. "But he was very good. He had your attention. He was known around the camp as a funny guy. You'd hear his name dropped around the camp—'George Carlin, George Carlin.'"

A sense of humor was imperative at the camp, says Cullum, a longtime *New Yorker* cartoonist who began his career as a gag writer for the black-humor illustrator Charles Addams. "There were a lot of funny people, a lot of mocking and jibing. It was kind of a survival mechanism—being a good 'ragger,' we called it." After a few summers, Carlin finally unseated Wacky Wilson, winning the drama award, for which he received a medal embossed with the masks of comedy and tragedy.

Throughout his life the medal remained one of his two most treasured possessions. (The other was an autograph he got from the saxophonist Charlie Parker, outside the New York nightclub called Birdland, when Carlin was fifteen.) For Carlin, the medal affirmed his strongest instinct—that he belonged on the stage.

Whether or not he belonged in Catholic camp was another question. An aspiring shutterbug, Carlin was caught shoplifting film for his camera at a grocery store in town. "He left under a cloud," recalls Cullum. "My uncle packed him up on a bus and sent him back to the city." True to form, however, Carlin did not begrudge the camp director. In later years, after he'd made a name for himself, he sometimes returned to Camp Notre Dame to visit John Cullum.

In New York the boy found himself increasingly attracted to trouble. Though Catholic school and summer camp had been Mary's idea of instilling structure and discipline in her mischievous son, it was becoming abundantly clear they weren't the solution—that there might be no solution. "That was her big thing—'the boy has no male supervision at home,'" Carlin remembered. "As if that's gonna help." At ages twelve and thirteen he was hanging around the parks, drinking beer, talking about girls—"debs"—and running with classmates in would-be street gangs. They had jackets with gang names: "the Riffs and the Condors and the Beacons and the Corner Boys and the Lamplighters and the Chaplains and the Bishops."

Carlin claimed that in 1951 he and his friends began to experiment with marijuana, then a little-understood drug that appealed primarily to musicians and coffeehouse types. For city boys just entering their teens, it was a secret doorway to a forbidden world. For Carlin, the high let him dig deeper into a comic mind that was finding silliness in every facet of daily life. The mellow, goofy high stripped Carlin and his friends of their latent aggression: "In one semester, in shop class, guys went from making zip guns to hash pipes," he joked.

By then he was flirting with real delinquency. After getting caught stealing money from a locker room during a basketball game in seventh grade, Carlin was sent to a parochial school in Goshen, New York. Playing up his big-city sophistication on the playground, he showed two gullible classmates a bag of "heroin"—actually, colored erasers. The administrators sent him back to Corpus Christi, where he was told he would have to repeat a term before he could graduate. Carlin pleaded with the administration to let him graduate with the students he'd known since first grade. The nuns made him a deal: Write the year-end play, and you may graduate on time. "It was called 'How Do You Spend Your Leisure Time?'" Carlin told *Playboy* in 1982. "Once again, I was rewarded for my cleverness, my show-business skills."

Carlin's mother enrolled him in Cardinal Hayes High School, a Catholic boys' school for middle-class families who couldn't afford the city's more expensive private schools. Tuition was five dollars a semester when the school opened on the Grand Concourse in the Bronx in 1941. Carlin's brother had preceded him at Cardinal Hayes, graduating in 1948. "Going to Hayes was absolutely the coolest thing you could do coming out of eighth grade," Carlin recalled years later. He looked up to Patrick: "He could dance good, he could fight good, he could talk his ass off on the corner. And he went to Hayes. . . . My brother even claimed you could make out better if you went to Hayes."

Hayes had a championship marching band, and Carlin joined it as a trumpeter. He'd had a subscription to *Down Beat* from the age of twelve; like so many city kids of the time, he was also a big fan of the R&B vocal groups of the pre–rock 'n' roll era. He chose the trumpet, he said, because there happened to be one in the family apartment: "I think my brother stole it at the St. Patrick's Day Parade." ("I really wanted to play a stringed instrument, but they told me the yo-yo was out," he joked at a Hayes reunion years later.) He lasted one year in the band, marching but never blowing a note. "My reasoning was, people can see me marching, but no one can hear me not playing." He did, however, participate enthusiastically in the football chants, especially enjoying the ones that threatened mild profanity: "Block that kick, block that pass/Knock that quarterback on his—rip, rip, rip, rap, rap, rap, Hayes High, Hayes High, clap, clap, clap!"

For Carlin, Hayes was the beginning of the end of his formal education. He dreaded taking the crosstown 149th Street bus to get there in the morning. "I was one of those guys who didn't try too hard in school," he explained. Again and again, he heard the same cliché from the priests: "You have a good head, but you're not using it."

"And they'd smack you on the head just to get it started for you," he joked.

Always trying to make his classmates laugh, he found himself increasingly assigned to detention hall with Father Stanislaus Jablonski. "Jabbo," as the students called him, was a strict disciplinarian, otherwise known as the Mean Dean or the Sinister Minister. Jablonski, a New York City fixture who would be appointed monsignor by Pope John XXIII in 1961, had a calm resolve that was so recognizable to generations of Hayesmen that one alumnus, who went on to work in television, suggested the father's colorful name for a character on *Hill Street Blues*.

Mary Carlin's exasperation with her son's rebellious behavior only made him more inclined to misbehave, and he began to spend days at a time away from home. "She had it all worked out," he remembered. "I would attend a nice college, then get a job in advertising," like the men she knew professionally. Utterly uninterested in that path, Carlin ignored his mother and her psychological warfare—her "black moods, silent treatment, and martyrdom." "The older I got, the more apparent it became that my mother was losing control over me," he recalled.

Carlin was expelled midway though his sophomore year at Hayes. In an otherwise undistinguished year and a half, he'd managed to frequent the dean of discipline's office so often that he was no longer welcome at the school. Thirty years later Carlin was the unlikely guest speaker at a Hayes event, the school's first annual Alumni Association Hall of Fame Dinner, honoring Jabbo. Before the ceremony, the two men got reacquainted. "I remember you, Carlin," said Father Jablonski. "You sat near the wall."

"The sum and substance of my career at Hayes—I sat near the wall," Carlin said with a nudnik laugh when he took the stage. "The better to conceal my nefarious activities."

Acknowledging the only discipline that could hold his attention, Carlin applied to two of the city's performing arts high schools, but was turned down by both. He briefly attended Bishop Dubois, another Catholic high school, located on 152nd Street, before transferring to George Washington, the secular public school in the Fort George neighborhood of Washington Heights, in the shadow of Yankee Stadium. Though famous George Washington alumni included Harry Belafonte, Maria Callas, Henry Kissinger, and Alan Greenspan, Carlin was not destined to number among them. In six months of nominal attendance at the school, his routine absences made him a nonentity. By his count, at the height of his truancy he missed sixty-three consecutive school days. He was just trying to hold on until his sixteenth birthday, when he could legally drop out. Which he promptly did.

2

CLASS CLOWN

After the supportive atmosphere of Corpus Christi, George was ill-prepared for the disciplinary tactics of Catholic high school. Rote education held no interest for him. Working up a decent impression of Cagney or Bogie, however—well, that was worth studying. While bouncing from school to school, trying to hang on until he turned sixteen, Carlin met a teacher named Brother Conrad, who told his students he could get them cameras and other electronic equipment with his clergyman's discount. Brother Conrad was a bit of a hustler, Carlin recalled. The class clown already had a camera, but could he get his hands on a tape recorder? Mary Carlin had promised her younger son a gift for completing his studies at Corpus Christi. Carlin told his mother that's what he wanted—a tape recorder.

He thought of it as a training tool, infinitely more useful than his Latin textbooks. Carlin's state-of-the-art, reel-to-reel tape recorder—"big as a Buick," he joked—was one of the earliest commercially available models, made by the consumer electronics pioneer Webcor, the Webster-Chicago Corporation. He quickly became adept at recording himself doing mock radio broadcasts, commercial parodies, and other comic bits. "I'd do little playlets about the neighborhood," he recalled. "I'd make fun of the authority figures—the shopkeepers, the parents, the priests, the policemen." Friends of his older brother began asking

Patrick to bring Georgie to their parties, to entertain with his tapes. His career in comedy was already underway.

He was in a headlong rush to get on with the transition to adulthood and out from under his mother's suffocating expectations. For one thing he was engaged, however briefly, to a neighborhood girl named Mary Cathryn. Shortly after quitting high school, Carlin decided to enlist in the Air Force. Not quite a decade into its existence, the Air Force was considered the country club of military service by many enlistees. Rather than train to storm a beachhead or engage in hand-to-hand combat in some godforsaken jungle, Carlin reasoned that he'd rather "fly over the area, drop some bombs, fly home, take a shower, and go out dancing." Though military life held no attraction for him, with the draft looming he figured he would enlist early, put the service behind him, and then use the G.I. Bill to train for a career in radio. (A regular listener to radio Hall of Famer Martin Block on WNEW's *Make Believe Ballroom*, Carlin had been thinking for some time that he might be cut out to pursue a similar career, introducing the hits of the day on the air.) Seventeen-year-old George Carlin—his mother signed his enlistment papers—was assigned to be a radar technician with the 376th Bombardment Wing's Armament and Electronics Maintenance Squadron, working on B-47 bombers at Barksdale Air Force Base in Bossier City, outside Shreveport, Louisiana.

The duty was not particularly captivating, and Carlin soon began looking for extracurricular activities to occupy his time. He heard about a local Shreveport playhouse that was auditioning for a new production of Clifford Odets's *Golden Boy* and decided he'd try out. Joining the cast at the Shreveport Little Theater, he met another aspiring actor, a local man named Joe Monroe. Monroe was part owner of a Top 40 "daytimer" radio station (which went off the air at sunset, then a common practice), a thousand-watt channel at 1480 on the AM dial known as KJOE. When the fresh-faced New Yorker mentioned his eagerness to break into broadcasting, Monroe took him down to the station. He asked Carlin to have a go at reading news reports from the ticker tape machine. Already working to tone down his New York accent, the linguistically inclined kid from Morningside Heights "read it off like nothing," recalls Stan Lewis, a well-known music distributor and record-store owner from Shreveport known as Stan the Record Man. Lewis was good friends with Monroe, bringing the latest rhythm and blues releases to his station and playing poker with him once a week. Lewis soon befriended Carlin, who often hung around the Record Man's shop, listening to the newest records by Stan Kenton and other favorite jazz artists. Hired for weekend duty at KJOE for sixty cents an hour, Carlin read promotional copy and filled in whenever a disc jockey was absent.

Carlin's military future was considerably dimmer. He was in near-constant trouble, not only with his superiors, but with local law enforcement as well. He has claimed that he was once stopped for riding in a car with two black enlistees. (In a 1974 interview he said that he was "a voluntary nigger. I gravitated toward the urban blacks rather than the rural rednecks.") They smoked three joints in their cell. He was also tossed in a jail cell for causing a disturbance at the Stork Club, a combination supper club and strip joint out on the Bossier City strip, where the Barksdale airmen were known to blow off more than a little steam. "He called early one morning, I'm talking post-midnight," says Jeff Stierman, whose father, Vern, a fellow announcer on KJOE, had become a good friend of Carlin's. The elder Stierman had to bail out his young friend. "George had had a few too many," says Stierman's son. "He was being somewhat obnoxious, I think, making a nuisance of himself. The cops were called, and he was hauled off."

At the Air Force base, seventy men in Carlin's squadron had an experimental function: They were guinea pigs in an ongoing medical inquiry into the spread of infectious diseases in barracks living. "They would plant cultures in our throats once a week and study the spread," Carlin once explained. "So we got out of a lot of duty." Despite the easy duty, he couldn't help but chafe when confronted by his superiors. "When I ran into hard-nosed sergeants and section chiefs and even COs," he said, "I would tell them to go take a flying fuck. You get court-martialed for that."

Carlin's radio work was sanctioned by his commanding officer, who arranged for an off-base work permit for the young malcontent, figuring he'd be of some use as a goodwill ambassador to the local community. But Carlin did his best to undermine the assignment. As a DJ he enjoyed some of the perquisites of the job, accepting pizzas and boxes of donuts from distributors trying to get their records played. On the air one weekend he began drinking a fifth of liquor he'd just received as a gift. According to Stan Lewis, who was listening at the time, the drunker Carlin got, the more he joked about life at Barksdale. Some minutes later the last record ended, and the needle stayed in the groove, leaving dead air. Lewis called the studio—no answer. "I thought he'd gone to the bathroom," he says. He called Joe Monroe, who hustled down to the station, where he learned that Barksdale MPs had hauled Carlin out of the studio and down to the guardhouse.

By Carlin's own count, he was court-martialed three times and slapped with "numerous" Article 15s for minor offenses. On the night the Brooklyn Dodgers beat the New York Yankees to win the World Series in 1955, Carlin was with his Strategic Air Command unit on a training mission in England. He'd been a Dodgers fan from childhood. Though both the Yankees and the New York Giants played in the Bronx, Carlin instinctively rooted for the unlikely team way over in Brooklyn. The perennially successful Yankees were a "boring, arrogant" team whose fans were "dull-spirited, overbearing twits," as he once wrote in a *New York Times* article about his love of baseball. The Dodgers, by contrast, were a motley crew affectionately known as "Dem Bums," a team that had integrated baseball by adding Jackie Robinson to its roster in 1947. To Carlin, the Dodgers were "colorful, reachable, human . . . and definite underdogs."

On the night the team clinched the Series victory, Carlin celebrated by getting drunk on cooking wine in a small town near the barracks. "When my tech sergeant expressed his displeasure with my actions— not to mention my noise level—I replied in a manner that he didn't consider in strict accordance with military protocol," Carlin recalled. "I told him to go fuck himself. To be honest, I don't think my salute was up to standards, either."

There were plenty of other opportunities for him to express his displeasure with military service. During a simulated combat drill at

Barksdale that December, Carlin, cold and tired, slipped away from his guard duty post. "I left my gun on the ground and went up into the crawlway of a B-47, smoked a joint, and went to sleep," he said. The judge told him he'd been inclined to lock him up, but because it was Christmastime, he let him off.

The offenses continued to pile up. In July 1957 Carlin was given a general discharge under honorable conditions—not a dishonorable or bad-conduct discharge, but one that nevertheless implied considerable behavioral issues. In a letter to "Airman Third Class George D. Carlin," his commanding officer, Lt. Col. Edward E. Matthews, described his decision "to have you eliminated from the Air Force as unproductive." The officer cited several incidents: his failure to report for guard duty, a driving-while-intoxicated charge in February, a reckless driving episode the previous November, and "Disrespect to Air Policeman, Failure to obey a lawful order by an Air Policeman and Disobeying a direct order from an Officer" on June 24, 1955. Carlin was also reminded of the numerous times he'd been chastised about his personal appearance, the condition of his room, and "drinking alcoholic beverages to such an extent that you could not control your actions."

While he was busy misbehaving his way out of the Air Force, Carlin was also expanding his role at KJOE, where he took over the afternoon drive-time shift. As a modest nine-station market, Shreveport radio was deeply competitive. When Carlin arrived, KJOE had a commanding fifty-two share, meaning the station could claim more than half of all listeners in the area. But KEEL, another AM Top 40 station, was in hot pursuit, with incoming owner Gordon McLendon vying for the loyalty of the city's young rock 'n' roll fans. McLendon, known as the "Old Scotchman," was already something of a nationally known figure in radio, having been instrumental in the development of the Top 40 format. The founder of the Liberty Radio Network, which pioneered national baseball broadcasts, McLendon would later establish the country's first all-news station, WNUS, in Chicago. He had come to Shreveport after learning that Monroe had been secretly monitoring KLIF, McLendon's influential station in Fort Worth, and directing his disc jockeys to program their broadcasts accordingly.

Though Carlin's stint in Shreveport was relatively brief, he was a real asset to KJOE. With Monroe taking the morning shift and Vern Stierman covering the midday slot, Carin brought up the rear, before the station went off the air at sundown. *Carlin's Corner* made him a bona fide local personality, with listeners tuning in to hear the latest songs from the Everly Brothers, Johnny Mathis, Elvis Presley, and the rest of the era's chart regulars. "Stick around," he'd implore his listeners. "Good things happening here on *Carlin's Corner*." A born motor mouth, he was more conversational, more easygoing than the unctuous boilerplate announcing types he later played in his act. "His voice was different—it didn't sound like a straight announcer, the Tommy Turntables of the day," says Howard Clark, a hard-partying fellow Shreveport radio novice who was later noted for his tag line—"This is Howard Clark, high at noon"—on San Francisco's KFRC. "He was very warm, one-on-one sounding, rather than those standoff-ish announcers. That was very intriguing to me."

Carlin moved in with a friend from the Air Force, Jack Walsh, a Georgia native who had been a navigator in the Strategic Air Command. Walsh, like Carlin and Monroe, had been involved with the theater group, and Carlin began telling his roommate that he should look for work in radio. Walsh, a bright, well-spoken man who shared Carlin's affinity for jazz and comedy, soon got a job at KRMD, a twenty-four-hour Shreveport station. Though Walsh was five years older than his roommate, he was evidently less schooled in the ways of the streets. According to his widow, Dot Walsh, Jack once asked Carlin why his "cigarette" smelled the way it did. The two bachelors arranged a warning system for each other: If there was a tie hanging from the doorknob of their apartment, the other roommate had a girl inside and needed privacy.

Walsh, who went on to gain some renown in Atlanta on radio station WAKE—under the alias Stan "The Man" Richards, he was inducted into the Georgia Radio Hall of Fame—played a significant role in the development of his roommate's comic sensibility: He turned Carlin on to Lenny Bruce. One night he brought home a copy of

Bruce's conceptual first album, *Interviews of Our Times*, pressing his roommate to listen to it.

Despite his youth, Carlin was not a big fan of the new rock 'n' rollers he was playing on KJOE. He preferred the jazz and vocal music he'd loved in New York. "I grew up with real rhythm and blues," he said. "I hated when the whites took over the music. . . . I just had that little cultural divide, where I was more of a black-music person and I was playing this hybrid of black music and country that came to be called rock 'n' roll." Unquestionably, though, he recognized the new cultural groundswell as a powerful social force—"nothing short of a revolution. You could sense that and feel that, especially in the white South."

One of those revolutionary figures, Elvis Presley, was well-known to the Shreveport audience, where he'd made his national break-through in 1954 on the *Louisiana Hayride*, a live country music broadcast for flagship station KWKH. Oddly, Carlin's biggest moment of Shreveport infamy involved the music of the blues-loving poor boy from Tupelo, Mississippi. In early 1957 Stan Lewis received a routine shipment of promotional records from RCA. Along with several new releases, the box contained one wayward copy of Presley's latest recording, "All Shook Up," not quite due for release. Realizing instantly that he had a piece of vinyl gold on his hands, Lewis took it down to his buddy Monroe's station, where Carlin became the first disc jockey in the country to play the song, which would become Elvis's seventh number one. After this broadcasting coup Carlin, not yet twenty, was featured in the nationally syndicated news. McLendon was incensed, demanding that Lewis, who serviced all the local stations, tell him why he'd given the record to KJOE.

Although he was becoming a popular personality at KJOE, now that he was no longer in the Air Force, Carlin had no need to be in Louisiana. He packed up and returned to New York, enrolling in the Columbia School of Broadcasting. It took him all of two weeks to realize that he already had more than enough on-the-job training at KJOE to learn everything the school could teach him about broadcasting. He quit and headed right back to Shreveport, where he would stay for another year.

In radio, the typical objective for on-air talent was to keep moving into larger markets. Homer Odom, an acquaintance who later managed the Bay Area's KABL for McLendon, offered Carlin a job with Boston's WEZE, a "beautiful music"-style station and a network affiliate that broadcast NBC soap operas such as the long-running *Young Dr. Malone*. Carlin went up to Boston and took a job running the board—unglamorous duty that he justified by reminding himself he'd moved into a bigger radio market. It was here that he had his run-in with Cardinal Cushing. Spinning popular balladry and orchestrated pop songs by Perry Como, Tony Bennett, and their ilk in his part-time role as an after-hours disc jockey, the devoted R&B fan bridled. "I had to play that and keep a straight face and make believe I liked it," he remembered. After three months he knew he was in the wrong place. When Carlin took the news van to New York, the furious station manager tracked him down at his mother's apartment. There'd been a prison break at the new maximum security facility in Walpole that they should have covered. Prison breaks happen all the time, Carlin argued; they could cover the next one. "They thought that was a poor attitude for a professional," he recalled. Sure enough, when he returned with the truck, he was unceremoniously relieved of his job.

The one bright spot of Carlin's short stay in Boston was his instantaneous rapport with a WEZE newsman and Boston native named Jack Burns. Born in November 1933, Burns was almost four years older than Carlin. The two men shared an attitude toward the military: Burns, who spent his teen years living the peripatetic life of his father, an officer in the Air Force, realized he was no serviceman as soon as he enlisted in the Marine Corps in 1952. After serving as a sergeant in Korea, he gladly took his discharge and headed back to Boston, where he studied acting and broadcasting at the old Leland Powers School of Radio and Theater in Brookline.

Jeremy Johnson, an aspiring actor who'd done a hometown Bob and Ray–style radio show with a partner before enrolling at the Powers School, met Burns there and quickly became a friend and drinking buddy. They first became acquainted on the set of a student-run radio comedy—"variety stuff," recalls Johnson, like Fred Allen's *Allen's Alley*, primarily consisting of mock interviews with outlandish characters. "We used to go to parties together and drink—quite a bit, actually," says Johnson. One time, after passing out on the floor and staying overnight, Johnson woke up and saw his friend still snoozing. He staggered to his feet, stood over Burns, and woke him up by putting the fear of God into the hung-over acting student: "I am omnipotent!" he boomed. "I am omnipresent!"

After graduating from Powers, Burns spent some time in New York, studying acting at Herbert Berghof's studio and performing in an off-Broadway production of *Tea and Sympathy*, the controversial Robert Anderson play about an effeminate young man, originally directed on Broadway by Elia Kazan. Soon, however, he was back in Boston, where he took a job as a radio newsman. By the time Carlin arrived at WEZE, Burns was the station's news director. Carlin, the newcomer, moved into an apartment with Burns and another roommate. While the New Yorker was jeopardizing his own livelihood in radio, Burns was establishing himself as a bona fide newsman, interviewing Senator John F. Kennedy and his wife, Jackie, and traveling to Havana to interview Fidel Castro. "I was staying at the Hotel Nacional de Cuba in Havana and it was . . . well, I really believe life is like a B-movie without the music," Burns once recalled. "The blonde told me she was working with anti-Castro forces and she needed to use my telephone because hers was bugged. Fantastic! People with beards running around, carrying guns. The last I saw of the blonde was when they dragged her and the phone from my room. Somebody suggested it might be time for me to return to the States."

After Boston, Carlin quickly landed on his feet. He heard from a Shreveport acquaintance who'd become a sales manager at KXOL, a competitor of McLendon's KLIF in the Dallas-Fort Worth market. "Anybody who came to Dallas-Fort Worth knew that was the place to be in radio," says "Dandy" Don Logan, a fellow Shreveport radio personality who spent some time in Texas himself. "It was a real hotbed for DJs. They had a lot of what they call 'six-month wonders.'" Media figures who would become nationally recognized, such as CBS news-man Bob Schieffer, game show host Jim McKrell, and *The Price Is Right* announcer Rod Roddy, were all products of the Dallas-Fort Worth radio scene around Carlin's time. Starting in July in the seven-to-midnight slot, Carlin took to calling it the "homework" shift, tak-ing dedication requests from young lovebirds and peppering his banter every Friday night with the all-important high school football scores. "Developed great rapport with teenage listeners by not putting them on," he wrote a decade later for an early press kit.

In between spinning new songs from singers such as Connie Francis, Bobby Darin, and Freddy "Boom Boom" Cannon on *The Coca-Cola Hi-Fi Club* (later known as *The Teen Club*), Carlin began extending his comic premises on-air. KXOL was a popular station with local advertis-ers, known for its brisk in-house production of ads and jingles. The DJ who preceded Carlin each afternoon once did an entire hour so packed with commercials that he had time to play just one song, Carlin recalled, "and it still sounded like pure entertainment." But during the evenings Carlin had relatively few commercial obligations, and he used the time to his advantage. "It was nice—the log book wasn't very crowded, so you could have a little fun," he recalled years later, in a tribute to the station. "It was so relaxed, in fact, that one night I did two whole hours in a British accent. Apparently, no one thought anything of it. . . . It was a chance to express my goofy self at night."

"Everything George said was funny," recalls Pat Havis, then a Fort Worth resident, a twenty-year-old divorcee and mother of a baby daughter, living on odd jobs and listening to her favorite DJ at night while she did the household chores. "He helped me laugh at myself, and everything in general." Though a newcomer to Texas, Carlin was quickly established as an asset for KXOL. His name was prominently featured in ads on benches at bus stops across the city, says Havis. One of Carlin's recurring bits, the "Hippie-Dippy Weatherman," depicted a gently addled hippie character years before the long-haired, glassy-eyed hippie archetype came into mainstream usage. (The term *hippie*, gen-erally presumed to have been adopted by Beat Generation hipsters in reference to their younger collegiate followers, was not yet widely recognized, though by some accounts it had been used on the radio as early as 1945 by Stan Kenton, one of Carlin's musical heroes.) Carlin's Weatherman sounded as though Maynard G. Krebs, Bob Denver's absent-minded, bongo-playing jazzbo on *The Many Loves of Dobie Gillis*, had taken up meteorology. Adopting the deliberate, bemused voice of a chronic stoner (without making explicit references to marijuana), the disc jockey offered absurd parodies of weather reports, just as Henry Morgan had a decade earlier.

Within a matter of weeks, Carlin's career took a serendipitous turn. Arriving unannounced at the station one day was Jack Burns, his short-term Boston roommate, who explained that he was en route to Hollywood, hoping to give the entertainment industry "one last chance at me." He had an idea that he might become the next James Dean, Carlin recalled. By sheer coincidence, one of the station's newscasting positions had become available the day before, and Carlin convinced his friend to take it, at least temporarily. Badly in need of new tires for his car, Burns accepted, and he immediately began delivering five-minute news broadcasts during Carlin's evening program.

They took a place together at the Dorothy Lane Apartments in Fort Worth's historic Monticello neighborhood, and their conversations picked up where they'd left off in Boston. Mostly they talked about the things that made them both laugh. Comedy in America was undergoing some radical changes at the time. Mort Sahl was already established as the next generation's politico humorist, an off-the-cuff cold war commentator with a trademark newspaper tucked under his arm. His grad-student analyses of global politics and the American system were a wholesale shift from the broad gags of Gleason and Uncle Miltie. The jokes of the new comedians were crafted for insiders—campus current events connoisseurs and coffee shop intellectuals. "If things go well, next year we won't have to hold these meetings in secret," Sahl joked. His humor had a whiff of grad school about it, as he ad-libbed lofty barbs about fleeting political role-players and policy communiqués.

Other comics were bringing Freudian analysis and frank talk about the sorts of things previously reserved for private company onto the spartan stages of San Francisco's legendary hungry i in North Beach and its big-city counterparts in Chicago and New York. Many guardians of good manners felt affronted, just as the new comedians intended. Lenny Bruce, the onetime strip-club emcee, was fast becoming "the most successful of the new sickniks," as *Time* magazine declared in a July article on comedy's emerging emphasis on previously *verboten* subjects such as sex, race, religion, and morality. The Compass Players, a group of improvisational comics with ties to the University of Chicago, opened their permanent theatrical home, the Second City, in 1959. One of their alumni, Shelley Berman, debuted his neurotic humor that year on the album *Inside Shelley Berman*, for which the "onetime Arthur Murray dance instructor with a face like a hastily sculpted meatball," as one writer put it, won the first-ever comedy Grammy award. And a husky Ohioan named Jonathan Winters, a "roly-poly brainy-zany" whose mountainous head seemed overstuffed with caricatures, had recently become a regular on Jack Paar's *Tonight Show*, bewildering viewers with his loony menagerie of ordinary people, all nearly as bizarre in their own way as the manic-depressive who channeled them.

For two sharp-witted young men who shared a predilection for subversion, the comedy renaissance of the late 1950s was at least as thrilling as a run-in with a mysterious blonde in Castro's Cuba. Unlike the old Borscht Belt burlesque men, who were more or less interchangeable—bellyaching, as Carlin often noted, about middle-of-the-road indignities such as crabgrass, "kids today," wives, and mothers-in-law—the new wave of comics "began to emerge with significant identities of their own. Shelley Berman couldn't do Mort Sahl's act. Mort Sahl couldn't do Lenny Bruce's act. They were just different." What each of these men did was to challenge authority, the establishment, "the country itself. We were drawn to that."

Up to this point Carlin, still only twenty-two, had been effectively apolitical. Though he'd begun questioning the church's authority from a young age, he'd grown up blindly accepting his mother's belief in the strict jingoism of newspaper commentators such as Walter Winchell and Westbrook Pegler. Pegler, a featured writer for the sensation-minded

Hearst syndicate, was a Roman Catholic sometimes accused of anti-Semitism, a prominent foe of labor unions, communism, and Franklin Delano Roosevelt's New Deal. "In my home Westbrook Pegler and Joe McCarthy were gods, and I picked up a lot of that," Carlin once explained. For him, Burns "opened the door" to political enlightenment. "I began to realize that the right wing was interested in things and the left wing was interested in people, that one was interested in property rights and the other was interested in human rights. I began to see the error of what was handed to me through the Catholics, through the Irish-Catholic community, through my mother, through the Hearst legacy in our family."

Burns recognized an opportunity to affect Carlin's unexamined way of thinking. "At that time George was fairly conservative," he later told the writer Richard Zoglin. "I always had a progressive agenda. I thought it was the duty of an artist to fight bigotry and intolerance. We had long, interesting conversations, good political discussions." They also, by Carlin's account, spent plenty of time sitting around the apartment in their underwear after their radio shifts, drinking beer (Jax, or Lone Star), listening to long-playing comedy records, and watching Paar on *The Tonight Show*. Their "comedy affinity," as Carlin put it, naturally led to the makings of an act together, as they impersonated the voices on the comedy albums they spun endlessly and improvised mock interviews, Bob and Ray style, with a repertoire of oblivious blowhards.

By the time they felt ready to go public with their act, Burns and Carlin had developed a stable of wrongheaded, inflexible stock characters of the kind that would later achieve infamy with *All in the Family*'s Archie Bunker. As local radio personalities, the pair went from fantasy comedy duo to actual stage time almost literally overnight. The place to be in Fort Worth in 1959 was the Cellar, a basement-level "coffeehouse" just opened beneath a hotel at 1111 Houston Street. Serving vodka and whiskey on the sly in paper cups, the Cellar was the open-mike playroom of Pat Kirkwood, a race car driver who, according to local legend, won the room in a poker game, and Johnny Carroll, a true rock 'n' roll lunatic who was good friends with rockabilly star

Gene Vincent and had once been signed by Sun Records. Thrashing at his electric guitar while seated behind a drum kit, stomping on the kick drum and the high-hat pedal, Carroll was a howling, overstimulated one-man band. Fueled by Desoxyn tablets hidden in a metal ashtray stand, the rockabilly wildcat ran the club as an anything-goes showcase, paying amateur dancers with booze and frequently giving the stage over to "King George Cannibal Jones," an eccentric junk percussionist named George Coleman who later recorded as Bongo Joe. "You must be weird or you wouldn't be here," read one scrawl on the blackboard-style wall of the club.

Into this den of iniquity Burns and Carlin brought their makeshift comedy team, performing excessively raunchy routines—"dirty, filthy things," as Carlin himself admitted. Some took the form of imaginary interviews with their television hero, the silly sophisticate Paar, which they often sprang on each other in the apartment: "How did you two meet?" Burns, playing Paar, would ask Carlin, representing the duo. "Well, I was fucking Jack's mother, and. . . ." Other sketches, deliberately steamrolling into the realm of bad taste, would within a year end up on the duo's only album together, including a manic routine that proposed a mail-order "Junior Junkie" kit for "hip kiddies" from those lovable corrupters of children, Captain Jack and Jolly George. (Besides the "U.S. Army Surplus 12cc hypodermic needle" and other supplies, they joked in aggressively gruff voices, the first 250 buyers would also receive an eight-by-ten glossy of Alexander King, then a *Tonight Show* regular who'd written a book about his struggle with morphine addiction.)

Burns and Carlin were long gone by the time the Cellar was forced to move to a new location in late 1960, after a fire. The new venue, one of several that Pat Kirkwood opened across Texas, from Houston to San Antonio (always on Pearl Harbor Day), would become notorious as the place where several of President Kennedy's Secret Service agents congregated on the night before the assassination. Lee Harvey Oswald, Kirkwood claimed, worked as a dishwasher at the short-lived Cellar in San Antonio for two weeks before committing his crime, and his killer, Jack Ruby, a fellow nightclub proprietor, was known to the Cellar's owner as "a Jewish wannabe hoodlum and speed freak who was like all the other joint owners from here to Casablanca."

Kirkwood knew how to build a legend and how to keep it in business when the goings-on attracted an inordinate amount of unwanted attention. "All policemen, all reporters, all pretty girls, all musicians, all doctors, all lawyers, and all our personal friends come in free and get free drinks forever," he instructed his staff, which typically consisted of a small pool of waitresses often clad in bras and panties and a couple of ruthless, no-nonsense bouncers. Though he welcomed eccentricities of all kinds, Kirkwood nevertheless instituted several iron-clad rules—"no troublemakers, no queers, no pimps, no blacks, [and] no narcotics." The cover charge was a dollar, unless a member of one of the offending groups appeared at the door, in which case the doorman would point to the sign claiming the cover was actually a thousand dollars.

With one bare red bulb constituting all the lighting the place could muster, jazz tapes playing over the speaker system in the absence of live entertainment, and many customers sitting on pillows on the floor, the original Cellar, Carlin recalled, was "pre-hippie, but definitely post-beatnik." For a New Yorker, the idea of hipsters in dark shades gathered in a dank hovel, addressing each other as "daddy," was a bit musty by 1959. Several years too young to have participated firsthand in the bohemian renaissance of the early 1950s in New York and San Francisco (Jack Kerouac was born in 1922, Allen Ginsberg in 1926), Burns and Carlin were sufficiently removed to see it through the filter of popular culture. By 1959 that meant Maynard Krebs and sensational pulp novels and movies about promiscuous young people in black turtlenecks—the "beatniks," as *San Francisco Chronicle* columnist Herb Caen had labeled them a year earlier. Though the comedians were undoubtedly drawn to the freaky, arty underground and the footloose freedom the Beats represented, beatniks were an easy target by 1959.

In Fort Worth, however, the freewheeling vibe of the Cellar was unprecedented. With a clientele made up largely of return customers who came back night after night, eager to see what kind of fresh debauchery Johnny Carroll could rustle up, Burns and Carlin were obliged to think fast on their feet. "We became very inventive and creative," said Carlin. In one "vignette," as Burns labeled it on the act's album, the pair skewered what was by then the universally familiar caricature of the Beat Generation—the angry poet, railing against inhumanity with excessive use of the adjectives "naked," "dirty," and "stinking." Haphazardly crediting Kerouac and "Arnold" Ginsberg for inspiring the archetype, Burns played the shrill performance poet Herb Coolhouse, the fertile mind behind the epic verse "Ode to a Texaco Restroom on Alternate U.S. 101 South." Carlin, sucking greedily on an imaginary roach and talking in a wise guy's nasal clip, identified himself as Coolhouse's sidekick, Amos Malfi, a "fairly salty bongo player."

The comedy team had bigger, more mainstream ambitions. After several months pinballing among the KXOL studio, the Cellar, and the bachelors' apartment in Monticello, the two friends packed their meager belongings and headed for Hollywood. On the air Carlin told his listeners that he and his newscaster were hitting the road as soon as he signed off. Hearing that, listener Pat Havis drove over to the station and parked in the deserted lot. As Carlin walked out of the building and got in his car, she stood there forlornly against her bumper and watched him leave.

Heading west in Carlin's new Dodge Dart Pioneer, the partners listened to the KXOL signal as long as they could, until it faded into the night sky over west Texas. In a salute to his departing colleagues, "Captain" Mike Ambrose, the overnight disc jockey, played Marty Robbins's "El Paso," then a Top 10 hit, several times during the hour after Carlin signed off. It was February 1960. The pair felt sure they were destined for stardom.

Earle Fletcher, KXOL's station manager, had heard such plans before. He was annoyed; he'd just spent a good deal of money having fan club cards printed for the host of the *Hi-Fi Club*. "A lot of people, young boys like yourself, have left to go to Hollywood," he told Carlin. "Between you and me, most of them came right back."

BURNS AND CARLIN had $300 saved up. Their plan was to live off that until they could round up some nightclub appearances in Los Angeles. They were determined not to fall back on menial labor. "We're not gonna park cars, we're not gonna wash dishes, we're not gonna wait tables," Carlin recalled them saying to each other. "We're gonna do the comedy." In Los Angeles they went straight to Dean Martin's place, Dino's Lodge, which they recognized from *77 Sunset Strip*. The popular detective series featured a character named "Kookie" Kookson, a valet parking attendant and street-smart informant whose rock 'n' roll slang and constant hair-combing made actor Edd Byrnes a teen idol.

The newcomers immediately blew some of their savings hanging around Dino's and the Brown Derby, hoping to spot someone famous. They were soon panicked to find that someone had lifted the rest of their cash from a drawer in their new apartment. Hastily canvassing for emergency jobs in radio, they dropped in on an R&B station with the call letters KDAY, then located on Vine Street in Los Angeles. As it happened, the station was looking for a new morning-drive comedy team. Burns and Carlin auditioned, were offered the job on the spot, and began punching the clock two weeks later.

Originally owned in part by Gene Autry, the "Singing Cowboy," KDAY was "the leading Negro and foreign-language station this side of Chicago" by 1953, when it was sold to the owners of the *Santa Monica Times*. In the spring of 1960, just after Burns and Carlin's arrival, the fifty-kilowatt station would become the new home to disc jockey Alan Freed. According to Bob Dye, then KDAY's chief engineer, Freed's hiring marked a period when the station's owners were "trying anybody and everybody to make the station go"—including the new morning team. At the time, KDAY was experimenting with a playlist that relied heavily on doo-wop, which was enjoying a modest resurgence in popularity following the tumultuous emergence of rock 'n' roll in the mid-1950s. (Carlin, of course, was a doo-wop fanatic, going back to his days on the street corners in "White Harlem.")

Freed was a legend on his way down, a nationally recognized promoter of rock 'n' roll from Cleveland—credited with popularizing the term—who had become persona non grata in the New York market following a series of scandals. His short-lived network television program was canceled in 1957 when the teenage black singer Frankie Lymon danced on air with a white girl, infuriating many of ABC's Southern affiliates. Two years later he was named a primary defendant in the government's case against "payola," the music industry's kickback system for getting new records played on the radio. Freed had come to KDAY at the invitation of program director Mel Leeds, his former boss at the Manhattan station WINS. On the air Freed pounded on his trademark telephone books and clanged his cowbells, gamely trying to re-create his famous exuberance for the youth music he'd helped popularize just a few years earlier.

In their three brief months at KDAY, Burns and Carlin went by an alias, the Wright Brothers. The station promoted them as a hot new thing in town, taking out full-color ads in *Variety*. The partners did scripted comedy on-air, for which they scoured the topics of the day and wrote furiously. "We were insane," Carlin remembered years later, "and it was a funny show, but we had to open the station at six a.m., which was a drag. Sometimes we'd be as much as fifteen minutes late, all hung over, so we'd break in like, '—oudy today, chance of drizzle in the late afternoon,' so the listeners would just assume there was something wrong with their radios." It was a ploy they borrowed from Bob and Ray, whose bumbling newscaster, Wally Ballou, had an unbreakable habit of starting to talk a beat before his microphone went live.

The brief KDAY gig was just enough to get the partners' feet in the door of the LA nightclub scene, the goal they'd set for themselves when they left Texas. Years after they quit the station, Carlin requested that his star on the Hollywood Walk of Fame be placed outside the former KDAY studio.

In May they took a weekly engagement at Cosmo Alley, a quintessential Beat coffeehouse in Hollywood. The waitresses wore black tights and long hair combed down their backs; some of the customers wore stereotypical berets. The club was opened in 1957 by Herb Cohen, later known as an artist manager of Frank Zappa, Tom Waits, and many others. Cohen had previously managed the Los Angeles outpost of the Purple Onion, and he and the actor and folk singer Theodore Bikel had partnered in the opening of the Unicorn, the first folk café of its kind in Los Angeles when it opened on Sunset Boulevard in 1955.

For Cosmo Alley, Cohen took over a room that had been an Armenian restaurant—"sort of a back room to the Ivar Theater," he says. "When they moved up to Sunset, I took over the space." Named for the side street it was on, Cosmo Alley was on "a narrow street with nothing else on it. No big entrance, just a door. You couldn't find it. There was no front to it." The mystery of the place, of course, was what drew people in. When 150 people were in the room, it was packed. Cohen took down the plaster walls, exposing the original brick, and had the overhead pipes painted—"very sparse, very industrial, which is what I wanted it to look like. At the time, it was very hip. It was black and dark, candles, very intimate."

In addition to folk and jazz music, Cosmo Alley featured comedy, and the trendy club attracted a Hollywood clientele—Marlon Brando, Dennis Hopper, Peter Fonda. The place had a caged mynah bird, and one headliner, Lenny Bruce, labored for weeks to teach the bird a short phrase: "The pope sucks."

At Cosmo Alley, Burns and Carlin put in their own hard work, fine-tuning the routines they'd conceived in Texas and developing several more. One bit was about Edward R. Murrow interviewing a bigoted senator, and another was about a boxing palooka ("Killer" Carlin) with a voice like a rusty saw blade. They also had Carlin's uncanny impersonation of Bruce doing one of his own earliest recorded bits, "Djinni in the Bottle." Their humor was biting, often flirting, as in the "Capt. Jack and Jolly George" routine, with outright tastelessness. But the two comics were also working out their social consciences. "We took positions," Carlin recalled. "We did jokes about racism, about the Ku Klux Klan, about the John Birch Society, about religions. . . . We felt connected to that sort of movement that was starting then": comedy about "values, the world, and, in a lot of cases, self."

Not that they drew much in the way of a following. "They were booked when there was time available, when I couldn't get Maya Angelou [then a calypso singer] or Lenny Bruce or the Limelighters," says Cohen. "The act was not great. If you heard Lenny Bruce once, you were mesmerized. If you heard Mort Sahl, it was so unique, it was brilliant. . . . I'm not trying to denigrate what they did. It's just that they weren't in that category yet. I have this visual image of them in suits. It was a very straight comedy act. I'm not saying it wasn't good—it just wasn't anything special."

Still, their introduction to Hollywood could hardly have been more propitious. They quickly picked up an agent, a Tinseltown operator named Murray Becker, who'd been a road manager with Rowan and Martin, future hosts of NBC's zany, lava-lamp-style sketch comedy show *Laugh-In*. Dan Rowan and Dick Martin were already familiar to a national audience by 1960, having alternated with Jerry Lewis and Dean Martin as weekly hosts of NBC's *Colgate Comedy Hour*. Hired to assemble a summer replacement for *The Dean Martin Show* in 1966, the duo parlayed that success into *Laugh-In*, which would debut in January 1968.

KDAY was another "sundowner" station, going off the air each night at dusk. Its offices were used after hours by various freelance characters circling the entertainment industry—song pluggers, mostly, and managerial types. Burns and Carlin took advantage of their access to the building, rehearsing their act in the studio. Becker was one of the hustlers working the angles in the station hallways. He watched the two comics from the Northeast tinkering with their act and announced that he wanted to become their manager. "He didn't have a lot of connections," Carlin recalled. "He was just a really dedicated guy. He really cared about us." And he was encouraged that the comedians, although intentionally confrontational, could also work "clean," as necessitated by their new radio gig. "That was big. 'They work clean,' he'd tell people."

Becker started pushing his new clients, and he soon cut a small-time deal with Herb Newman, owner of the independent, locally based Era Records. For a $300 advance, Burns and Carlin hastily recorded their act one night at Cosmo Alley. Era had scored a surprise number one pop hit back in the spring of 1956 with Gogi Grant's cinematic ersatz Western, "The Wayward Wind," written by Newman, and the label would soon have its biggest hit with Chris Montez's "Let's Dance."

Comedy albums had been a reliable niche market since the advent of long-playing records in the late 1940s, with "party" albums by raunchy comics such as Redd Foxx, Moms Mabley, and the classically trained, sexually outrageous comedienne known as the "Knockers Up" gal, Rusty Warren, reaching devoted customers through under-the-counter transactions. By 1960 recordings by the new wave stand-up acts were becoming bona fide mainstream hits. Berman's debut, *Inside Shelley Berman*, was the first comedy album officially awarded a gold record, and the stuttering Chicago straight man Bob Newhart would soon be named Best New Artist and presented with Album of the Year honors at the Grammy Awards for his own debut, *The Button-Down Mind of Bob Newhart*, which beat out Elvis Presley and the cast recording of *The Sound of Music* to top the Billboard charts. Still, no one had illusions of a chart-topping comedy record coming from the two upstarts in skinny ties at Cosmo Alley. The idea was to use the release as their calling card for future nightclub and, ideally, television bookings.

Era did not actually issue the album until 1963, the year after the team broke up. To capitalize on the success of Hugh Hefner's Playboy Clubs, the label took the liberty of releasing the record as *Burns & Carlin at the Playboy Club Tonight*. The hit-and-miss track listing was a representative sample of the pair's green act, featuring "Mothers Club," in which Burns portrayed a series of blueblood society ladies in falsetto, and "War Pictures," a half-baked Hollywood send-up, as well as "Killer Carlin"; the beatnik bit; the satire of Edward R. Murrow's interview program, *Person to Person*; the "Capt. Jack and Jolly George" routine; and Carlin's Bruce and Sahl impersonations. The verbose liner notes, perhaps written by Becker, were typeset on the back of the record jacket in the shape of a womanly hourglass figure.

"The world has known many teams—Adam and Eve, Stanley and Livingstone, Sears and Roebuck, spaghetti and meatballs," read the punch-drunk copy. For those not yet hip to the latest addition to this "lustrous list," the anonymous writer pointed out that Burns and Carlin were comedians, "and twice as funny as most. Because there are two of them." Their style was described as "not sick but definitely ailing humor"; their minds were "more unbuttoned than buttoned-down." Jack Burns, the copy helpfully noted, "is not George Burns, although this wouldn't be such a bad idea for an aspiring young comic." In his formative years, Carlin "learned how to play one-old-cat, teased girls, [and] survived a case of adolescent pimples" before joining the Air Force. In a canny bit of foreshadowing, the team's brief career at KDAY was noted primarily for the disc jockeys' good fortune at having "escaped the attention of the Federal Communications Commission long enough to jolly up goodly portions of early-rising Los Angeles, including Murray Becker," who "concluded that they had a much bigger potential than competing with time signals, freeway reports, and stomach tranquilizers."

Becker, who had served in the U.S. Navy with Lenny Bruce, invited the comedian and his wife, Honey, to Cosmo Alley to see the act that featured a guy doing a spot-on impression of Bruce himself. Becker was also acquainted with Sahl's manager, Milt Ebbins, a Rat Pack insider with connections to the Kennedy clan, and he put in calls to get Sahl into the room as well. Both avant-gardists soon made the scene. Sahl was stunned to see that this newcomer, Carlin, had perfected an impression of him, nailing the Canadian-born humorist's clipped, articulate delivery, his sudden expulsions of laughter, and his habit of segueing to a new idea by saying "Right. Onward."

"He had a great ear," says Sahl. "He had the cadence down. Like any good impression, it was revealing. I'm not that conscious of what I'm doing—I was busy doing it. He got it down because he listened to the records." After catching the act, the established comic pronounced his protégés "a duo of hip wits."

Though legend has it that Bruce was equally impressed, Sahl is somewhat skeptical. "Lenny was terribly competitive," he recalls. "He said repeatedly to me, 'The teacher's grading on a curve. If there's one *A*, I want it. I don't want to share it with the others.' I told him the country is starving for laughter and there's room for plenty of *A*s." By most accounts, however, Bruce was even more effusive in his praise for Burns and Carlin than his counterpart was. His presence at Cosmo

Alley was not lost on his young admirers. "We didn't know the legendary quality of this encounter at the time," said Carlin, "but we knew how important he was to us and what he represented. . . . I heard *Interviews of Our Time*, and I was changed forever."

The "sickest" comic contacted agent Jack Sobel, who was with General Artists Corporation (GAC), then a chief rival of the William Morris Agency in the world of entertainment bookings. Get these boys signed, Bruce recommended. Sobel responded immediately, sending a telegram to GAC's West Coast office: "Based on Lenny Bruce's rave reaction, hereby authorize the West Coast office to sign Burns and Carlin to exclusive representation contract in all fields."

After just a few months in Hollywood, mere weeks into their showcase at Cosmo Alley, Burns and Carlin had a manager, a performance recording in the can, the imprimatur of the two most highly regarded progressive comedians of the day, and an agency. GAC, which had grown out of the big-band-oriented Rockwell-O'Keefe booking agency, primarily handled pop singers by the early 1960s: Connie Francis, Tony Bennett, Perry Como, Frankie Avalon. Despite an aversion to the newfangled rock 'n' roll, the agency would soon beat out even more skeptical agents at William Morris to sign a British outfit called the Beatles to their first American performing deal.

When GAC arranged for Burns and Carlin, its newest clients, to open for the cabaret singer Bobby Short in Chicago, the duo eagerly hit the road in the Dodge. In Oklahoma they drove through a driving summer rainstorm. When it passed, the two comics saw a double rainbow over the horizon. "We felt that was an omen," Carlin said.

After the engagement at a jazz room called the Cloister Inn, Burns and Carlin picked up a few more dates around the Midwest. In Dayton, Ohio, then part of a bustling Midwestern nightclub circuit established during the heyday of big band swing, they performed at a hip new venue called the Racquet Club. Located in a sleek, modern facility, the place was a members-only club with tennis courts, a pool, and a dining room. It also had a tiny performance space, open to the public, in which customers could see the pool lights through plate-glass windows behind the entertainers. Operated by a recent University of

Dayton graduate named Bill Brennan, who married into the locally well-known Huber construction family, the Racquet Club was envisioned as a younger, more happening alternative to Suttmiller's, a much larger, more traditional showroom across town. The place, says Shane Taylor, a local promoter who was friendly with Brennan, might have held a hundred people on a particularly packed night. "I'm talking about squeezed," he says. "A table for four became a table for eight." The club featured comedy (including Dayton native Jonathan Winters and Lima, Ohio, housewife turned comedienne Phyllis Diller), jazz singers (Mel Torme), and vocal groups (such as the Four Freshmen and the Crosby Boys, Bing Crosby's sons, who had one of their first engagements at the Racquet Club). At the time, Brennan's place had an electric air about it: "When you walked in, you felt like the music was being played for you," recalls Taylor. "You walked in clicking your fingers."

In this lively setting Carlin began flirting with the hostess, a local resident named Brenda Hosbrook. "Brenda and I clicked on all levels right away," Carlin later said. They went out together every night that he and Burns were in Dayton, and they called and wrote each other while Carlin was on the road.

Burns and Carlin made their way to New York, where they and Becker were scheduled to meet some of the agents in GAC's headquarters. Two of the New York agents, Peter Paul and Shelly Schultz, took the act to see Bob Shanks, the talent coordinator at *The Tonight Show*. For Burns and Carlin, it was almost laughable. Half a year after leaving Fort Worth, where they'd sat in front of the television in their underwear, joking about the crude things they'd say to Jack Paar if they were ever invited onto his show, here they were, actually auditioning for it.

Paar had taken over NBC's *Tonight Show* from original host Steve Allen in 1957 following a brief, unsuccessful attempt with a different format. The casually conversational Paar, a native of Canton, Ohio, who called his own show "a night light to the bathroom," had a natural rapport with his audience and the camera, and he loved to feature comedy on the program. Jonathan Winters, the brainy improv duo of Mike Nichols and Elaine May, and a very young Carol Burnett were just a few of Paar's many comedic guests. Atypically for those early years of television, with its stone-faced announcers and farcical vaude-villians, Paar wore his considerable emotions on his sleeve. Prone to hysterical fits of laughter, he was also unafraid to shed tears if he was upset or feeling sentimental. "Being natural, being yourself, being honest is very hard work," he said on a retrospective program decades after quitting *The Tonight Show*, leaving the franchise to his successor, Johnny Carson. "I'm not an actor. All I am is what I am."

What he was, among other things, was a facile storyteller with a particular love for language. One night in February 1960, Paar told a joke on the show about a cultural misunderstanding over a "W.C." At NBC, the Standards and Practices department determined the joke to be too risqué for broadcast, and they preempted that portion of the show, replacing it with news coverage. Paar was outraged. The next day the press—not aware of the content, the mild double-entendres, of the joke, aware only that it had been cut—claimed the host had said something "obscene." Eliciting an admission from NBC's president that the joke was harmless, Paar asked for permission to air the edited segment, to let the audience judge for itself, but he was denied. That night he addressed his audience. He'd spent a sleepless night, he said, "wrestling with my conscience," and he'd decided to quit *The Tonight Show*. Like Fred Allen on radio, who once had to defend a joke about a woman who could have found a better husband in a cemetery (the S&P man felt the quip might offend cemetery caretakers), Paar was exasperated by the seemingly constant struggle with his own com-pany's watchdogs. "There must be a better way of making a living than this," he said. NBC, he said, had been wonderful to him, "but they let me down." With that, Paar walked offstage, leaving his flummoxed sidekick, Hugh Downs, to improvise the rest of the show.

Less than a month later, Paar returned to the show without missing a beat. "As I was saying . . . ," he said as he began his monologue.

Burns and Carlin were enamored of Paar—his wit, his morality, and the genuine appreciation for comic risk-taking he shared with both his predecessor, Steve Allen, and his successor, Carson. Their choice of material for their first shot at the show was serendipitous.

They'd been doing impersonations of NBC's nightly news team, Chet Huntley and David Brinkley, for some time. More recently, they'd added Vice President Richard Nixon and Senator John F. Kennedy—both men having just been nominated by their respective parties to run for the presidency—to their growing repertoire of public figures. At first it was Burns, the Bostonian, who did Kennedy, with Carlin taking on Nixon, hunching his shoulders and puffing his cheeks, as dozens of comics would do in the 1970s. They soon switched, however, when it became apparent to both men that Carlin's version of JFK was even more accurate, and funnier, than Burns's.

As young, blithe, and matter-of-fact about their rapid ascent as they were, Carlin's stomach churned during the audition. After being told they'd earned a spot on an upcoming show, the elated trio of Burns, Carlin, and Becker discussed their plans as they rode the elevator from Studio 6B down to ground level at 30 Rockefeller Plaza. Burns had something to attend to at home in Boston; he was headed out of town to thumb a ride up I-95. Becker was going to stop in the office of the network's legal department to fill out some paperwork. Gesturing in succession to his two young funnymen, he barked out their respective marching orders: "You go to Boston. You take a shit. I'll go to the legal department." It was a moment about which Burns and Carlin would never tire of reminding each other.

3

ATTRACTING ATTENTION

I t seemed too good to be true. Less than a year after fantasizing about it, Burns and Carlin were about to appear on *The Tonight Show*.

Maybe it *was* too good to be true. As it happened, Paar wasn't hosting the night they were scheduled. The guest host was Arlene Francis, whose work on a pioneering daytime women's show called *Home* led *Newsweek* to call her "the first lady of television." Bob Shanks, then a young talent coordinator and writer on *The Tonight Show*, figures Paar must not have been eager to have the act on his show. The guest hosts typically got the B-list, he says.

Shelly Schultz was the GAC agent booking television appearances, introducing new talent such as Phyllis Diller, whom Paar loved. He has another theory—that the show's writers slotted Burns and Carlin on a night when Francis was the guest host to shake up a dull program. Francis, Schultz recalls, "was deadly. They would have put them on to give the show a lift." The *Tonight Show* writers, he says, were reluctant to book untested comic acts on nights when Paar was hosting, because the host could be brutal. "They put up a big grid a couple weeks ahead of time," recalls the former agent, who worked for *The Tonight Show* from 1962 until 1970. "They listed all the people who were submitted for those days, and they tried to put together a show that would be cohesive. They were all scared shitless of putting comedy on, because

Paar was allegedly a comedian. . . . Paar was very hands-on, and he could make your life miserable." If an act bombed, Schultz says, "He'd say, 'Who's responsible?' He made everybody crazy."

Burns and Carlin went on with the Kennedy-Nixon bit. "It was very current and timely, a month before the election," Carlin recalled. "I think that's how we got the job." In their dark suits and Brylcreem, they seemed like fine young gentlemen. "My mother would say, 'You look reasonable,'" Carlin recalled.

They may have looked reasonable, but for a moment they felt euphoric. It was, however, a brief moment. For the next year, other than an unmemorable spot on Hugh Hefner's short-lived syndicated program *Playboy's Penthouse*, the agents at GAC had no luck returning their young comedy team to television. In Chicago, where Mort Sahl was playing Mister Kelly's, he bumped into Murray Becker at Eli's Delicatessen. Sahl says he and his best friend, the late Herb Sargent (who later became a writer and producer for *Saturday Night Live*), "made every effort to get 'em going." He convinced his San Francisco friend Enrico Banducci, the avuncular, beret-wearing proprietor of the hungry i, the experimental nightclub, to give the team a trial run. Without a lot of high-profile gigs, they did more than their share of "one-nighters," corporate parties for salesmen's associations and other business groups.

They played the Tidelands in Houston, where Bob Newhart had recently recorded his *Button-Down Mind* album. They did the Crystal Palace in St. Louis, the Embers in Indianapolis, the Casino Royal in Washington, D.C., and Freddie's in Minneapolis. They played Storyville in Boston's Kenmore Square, where Billie Holiday and Dave Brubeck had recorded. Many of the club dates they landed, though, fell short of glamorous. "Some really great toilets," Burns recalled wryly. Drinking on the job, they sometimes found themselves challenging hecklers to step out into the alley. At a cinderblock club outside Akron, they took the stage on the first night of a weeklong engagement, to discover that their audience consisted solely of the softball team sponsored by the bar. "They had their cleats on, and their uniforms," Burns recalled. "And George and I are up there doing political satire." Five minutes into the set, with the room barren of laughter, one of the ballplayers got up, strode over to the jukebox, and punched a few buttons. Show over. The owner pulled the act aside and threatened to take the week from them if they didn't cut the jokes about government agencies. "Don't you work dirty?" he demanded. So they went out to a Woolworth's and brought back a few ridiculous props—a yo-yo and a fright wig—for the second show. Burns, addressing his partner as "Georgina," asked him how he was feeling. "Pretty shitty," Carlin replied. "And we just started doing crap jokes for about fifteen minutes," Burns said, "and that got us through the week."

In Dallas Carlin stopped in to pick up some shirts he'd left at a dry cleaner. While the attendant dawdled, police officers suddenly materialized and ordered Carlin up against the wall. Burns was rounded up, too, and the partners were detained at the local precinct. It turned out to be a case of mistaken identity: Carlin had a newspaper clipping in the pocket of one of his shirts that described a stickup by two armed men in Chicago. On a tip from the cleaner, the cops were convinced they'd found the perpetrators. The comedians were released when they explained they'd saved the page because of the story on the other side of the police log.

Sahl, a good friend of Hugh Hefner, helped the team make their way onto the Playboy Club circuit, the fast-growing network of lounges dedicated to the magazine's bon vivant lifestyle of sports cars, fashionable accessories, and smart-set entertainment, with chicks on the side. "*Playboy* itself and I personally were very interconnected with what was going on in the clubs and the comedy scene in Chicago in the late 1950s," says Hefner, who first became interested in publishing a magazine as an aspiring cartoonist. "We did profiles on almost all the major new comedians who[m] *Time* magazine lumped together and called 'sick' comedy—Lenny, Mort, Jonathan Winters, Shelley Berman, [Don] Rickles." During the 1960 presidential campaign, the magazine sponsored a mock candidacy by the manic stream-of-consciousness comic "Professor" Irwin Corey. "We did a promotion with him at what was called Bughouse Square, a park on the Near North Side of Chicago," says Hefner. Corey joined the soapboxers in Washington Square, well known as a haven for free speech, to announce his candidacy.

After John Kennedy was elected, Hefner received a call from the new president's father, Joseph Kennedy. He was planning to be in Chicago and wanted to have dinner with the celebrity magazine publisher. "I didn't know him," says Hefner. "We had dinner together at a restaurant at the Drake [Hotel], right across Michigan Avenue from the Playboy Club. After dinner I took Joe Kennedy and the rest of our party up to see a show at the club." Burns and Carlin were on the bill. "They did a parody of President Kennedy," says Hefner, "and Joe Kennedy was not amused. It was my first experience with Carlin managing to not amuse certain people. I, of course, was distressed, because it was very funny."

Between the grueling cross-country driving, the girl in Dayton, and the nagging feeling that he should be doing stand-up on his own, Carlin soon realized his heart wasn't in it. "We didn't work very hard, and the act wasn't growing," he said. "I think that was mostly my fault, because after we split up, Jack became a tireless writer with Avery Schreiber and with Second City. I just never wanted to sit down and make up new routines, and I became a bit of a drawback to him. I guess I was subconsciously saving myself for my own act." On June 3, 1961, he married Brenda Hosbrook in her parents' living room in Dayton. They honeymooned in Miami, where Burns and Carlin were booked into the Playboy Club. Carlin's mother invited herself for a visit with the young couple.

During one layover with Brenda in Dayton, while Burns was on the East Coast, the owner of the Racquet Club, Bill Brennan, asked Carlin for a favor. The folk trio Peter, Paul, and Mary had to cancel two nights of shows when Peter Yarrow fell ill. Carlin agreed to fill in, performing amended versions of the team's act and a few things he'd been working on for himself. Flying solo, he made the audience laugh. He could feel that he was ready to do this on his own.

In March 1962 Burns and Carlin mutually agreed to part. On the last day of a two-week run opening for Vic Damone at the Living

Room, they split up, celebrating late into the night at the Maryland Hotel. Burns enrolled in improv classes at Second City. Carlin kicked off his solo career at the Gate of Horn, the cramped folk music club where Odetta and Memphis Slim, among others, had cut live albums. He was booked as the opening act for Peter, Paul, and Mary.

For the rest of the year Carlin and Brenda stayed on the road in the Dart, wearing a groove between the Hosbrook home in Dayton and Mary Carlin's apartment in the old neighborhood. The new groom caught his first solo break when Sahl filled in one week in June as a guest host on *The Tonight Show*. Paar had left the program for good in March, and his replacement, Johnny Carson, was contractually obligated to fulfill his contract as a game show host before taking over in October.

Sahl, the brainy progressive, was at odds with the decision makers at *The Tonight Show* all week. "I put George on and Woody [Allen], and NBC didn't want either one of them," he says. Allen, who had been writing comedy for *Tonight*, Ed Sullivan, Sid Caesar, and others since he was nineteen, had debuted his neurotic stand-up persona the previous year. "I had a hell of a time getting them booked," says Sahl. "I also put on Ella Fitzgerald with a mixed trio, and they didn't want that, either." Sahl, a Kennedy insider who occasionally wrote lines for the president's speeches, had Carlin do his Kennedy impersonation. Stages were packed at the time with comedians doing Kennedy impressions; Vaughn Meader, the New Englander who would achieve great fame spoofing the president, was about to record *The First Family*, his ubiquitous, Grammy-winning album. Carlin's own Kennedy was by then well-honed; he dropped and added *R*s like a good Boston Brahmin—"We must lowah the quoter of sugah from Cuber."

On the show that night, Carlin slipped his fingers in and out of his suit pockets, setting his jaw and hunching his shoulders, emulating the stiff posture of the president with the chronically bad back. He led with a joke about the Kennedy clan's well-known nepotism: "On behalf of the attorney general, the joint chiefs of staff, the members of the Supreme Court, and the rest of my family. . . ." Sahl attests that Carlin did well on the appearance, though no one at NBC would admit as much. "They'd lose their position of aggression if they did that!" he sputters.

Despite Sahl's endorsement and an appearance on CBS's long-running *Talent Scouts* program, Carlin was unable to muster much career traction over the next two years. Still represented by Becker and GAC, his gigs were typically unexceptional and sometimes downright pathetic. He played the Exodus in Denver, the Colony in Omaha, the Living Room in New York, and four Playboy Clubs that had unfulfilled contracts with Burns and Carlin. A run at the Copa Club in Cleveland was canceled midweek, his first true flop. In Indianapolis he landed a prime booking at the Embers, but his subversive attitude did not go over well with the well-heeled audience. "I can remember doing the supper show," Carlin said. "That means there are still dishes on the table. Stone silence," for an excruciating half an hour.

At one point he managed to finagle an audition as a writer for Steve Allen's syndicated Westinghouse show, but he squandered the opportunity. "It wasn't a case of the staff missing out on something. I simply wasn't ready," Carlin years later told the host, who hadn't been at the playhouse on Hollywood's North Vine Street for the tryout. Allen, too, felt he'd missed an opportunity: "Since I have always been able to detect true funniness at a range of at least a thousand yards," he wrote, "George's career might have been accelerated, without the year-and-a-half delay, if only I had been present when he came to our theater." Later, when Carlin began appearing on Allen's programs, the admiration was mutual. "Steve was an instant fan of his because he was so bright, and so well organized," says veteran comic Bill Dana, who was a writer and talent scout for Allen before striking out on his own with a deadpan alter ego named Jose Jimenez. "George was an expert at getting a complete knowledge of what he wanted to say, and then backing it up in so many delightful ways."

In December 1962, while he was playing the Chicago Playboy Club, Carlin, Brenda, and a folk-music friend, a member of the Tarriers, attended one of Lenny Bruce's performances at the Gate of Horn. Up in the balcony the beer was flowing as Carlin watched his idol's set. Just as the comic launched into a bit about a marijuana bust, two undercover Chicago police officers stood up. "Show's over, ladies and gentlemen," one of the cops announced. The club's piano player and saxophonist kept playing, archly providing a cool-jazz soundtrack to the bust. Alan Ribback, who had opened the club with music impresario Albert Grossman (best known as Bob Dylan's mercurial manager), was escorted outside, along with a *Swank* magazine writer and, eventually, an underage female. Arriving officers began the tedious process of checking all IDs before the patrons were allowed to leave. Carlin and his companion kept drinking. "I was good and juiced by the time they got to us," Carlin recalled, "and we purposely waited to be almost the last people, just to watch all this going on."

When it was Carlin's turn to produce identification, he wise-cracked, "I don't believe in IDs." That was enough to get him pinched for disorderly conduct. The arresting officer "sorta grabbed me by the collar of [my] suit and the baggy pant of my ass and bum-rushed me down the stairs," Carlin recalled. Knowing that his wife was waiting in the lounge near the front door, he hollered over his shoulder, "Tell Brenda I'm going to jail!"

In custody he encountered the comic he'd just been watching perform. How did Carlin get himself arrested? Bruce asked. "I didn't want to show them my ID," replied the man who owed his career to Bruce's recommendation. Bruce, even more familiar with the sensitivities of law enforcement than the habitually reckless junior comic, was amused. "You schmuck!" he teased.

Bruce's performance, including his onstage arrest, was recorded by *Playboy*, which was planning a feature story on the comic at the time. Hefner, working late at the Playboy Mansion, missed the show. "Shel Silverstein, one of my closest friends, who was living in the mansion at the time, was in the audience that night, and he came back and told me that Lenny had been arrested," Hefner says. "In the days that followed, I gave Lenny my lawyer to defend him, and I gave him a necktie to wear. He didn't own any ties." Like many of Bruce's fans, Hefner maintains that it was the comedian's contempt for the Catholic Church—his signature bit "Religions, Inc." in particular—that made him a target of law enforcement. They went after the drug talk and the four-letter words only because they were prohibited by the First Amendment from acting against his religious satire. "It remains for me unreal that it would be possible for someone to be arrested in the middle of a nightclub act, appearing in front of a completely adult audience," says Hefner. "Chicago was a very Catholic city at the time. One of the cops said to him, 'As a Catholic, I'm offended by you,' and *Variety* picked up that quote. So it was very clear what was going on there."

Carlin paid close attention to Bruce's snowballing legal troubles as he went on with his own solo career. Brenda was often on the road with her peripatetic husband, laughing loudly from the back rows to boost his morale when the reaction of the crowds, especially for the late-night sets, left something to be desired. They traveled as far afield as Regina, Canada, and Fort Lauderdale, Florida, so that Carlin could play small coffeehouses. At the Sacred Cow in Chicago, he had to compete with a brawl in the audience while he was doing his act. The club folded that week, during his run.

There were days when Carlin's career seemed to be bottoming out. Walking with Brenda on Rush Street during one of their many layovers in Chicago, he blurted out his uncertainty. "Do you think anybody's ever going to recognize me on the street?" he asked his wife. "Oh, yeah," she said. "Someday everybody's going to know your name."

In June 1963 the couple had a daughter, Kelly. Carlin called his old Shreveport roommate, Jack Walsh, to tell him the news. (The last time they'd seen each other, Walsh told his buddy he'd named his own daughter Kelly.) The Carlins had had difficulty getting pregnant for some time, and Brenda was diagnosed with a "tipped uterus." Carlin often joked that their participation in a limbo contest at one of the Playboy Clubs tipped his wife's uterus back just enough so that she could conceive.

With the baby in tow, life on the road quickly became untenable. In early 1964 the Carlins took an apartment in Mary's building in Morningside Heights. Having earned just $11,000 the previous year and spent most of it on the road, the comedian decided the prudent thing to do would be to focus his energy on New York, where he could boost his reputation with steady nightclub work and, with a bit of luck, draw the attention of the network talent bookers, whose shows were still based in the city.

The nightlife in Greenwich Village was teeming with bohemia, as it had been for decades. Since the arrival of the neighborhood's first espresso machine in the 1930s, coffeehouses had sprung up in what seemed like every other doorway, attracting a chess-playing, enlightenment-seeking, policy-debating clientele. Three decades later, many of these meeting places were luring customers by promoting events catering to the youthful folk-revival crowd.

By 1964 Bob Dylan, the Village folk scene's most visible representative, had become a national phenomenon, with versions of his songs performed by Peter, Paul, and Mary and his onetime girlfriend, Joan Baez, introducing the shy guitarist's thorny music to the mainstream. Aging radicals and self-serious campus philosophers rubbed elbows in the cafés and dive bars of Bleecker Street and the surrounding neighborhood with thrill-seekers from the outer boroughs and stifling small towns across the country. Folk mainstays such as Dave Van Ronk, Phil Ochs, and Fred Neil shared the stages at the Gaslight, Café Wha?, Gerde's Folk City, and Bitter End with such future pop stars as Jose Feliciano, John Denver, and Emmylou Harris.

The neighborhood was crawling with creativity. At the Village Vanguard, Max Gordon's long-running jazz room on nearby Seventh Avenue, contemplative musicians such as Bill Evans and John Coltrane settled in for long residencies. The Vanguard, the Gaslight, and other clubs had featured plenty of spoken-word acts during the heyday of the Beats. By 1964, however, the spoken-word acts were more apt to be angling for laughs.

"Greenwich Village was a way of looking at the world," says comic actor Larry Hankin, who, with his odd-duck style, opened for the Blues Project during the band's long residency at Café Au Go Go. "I would imagine it was like Montmartre when the Impressionists were there."

The daytime show at Café Wha? was "an extravaganza of patch-work," Dylan recalled, "a comedian, a ventriloquist, a steel drum group, a poet, a female impersonator, a duo who sang Broadway stuff, a rabbit-in-the-hat magician, a guy wearing a turban who hypnotized people in the audience, somebody whose entire act was facial acrobatics." Musicians working the Village included a ukulele player and distinctive falsetto vocalist named Tiny Tim and a one-of-a-kind everyone knew as Moondog, a blind poet who played bamboo pipes and whistles in "a Viking helmet and a blanket with high fur boots."

Weird was the norm in the Village, and the comedians represented it well. In his oversized spectacles and checked newsboy cap, a local legend named Stanley Myron Handelman made self-deprecation an art form. Bill Cosby, a student athlete from Philadelphia, broke in at the Gaslight in 1962 with an imaginary conversation between Noah and the Lord. David Frye, who did uncanny impressions of movie stars (George C. Scott, James Mason), liked to warm up in the bathroom before his sets. Sitting in a toilet stall one night, he startled a customer with his steady stream of familiar voices. "What kind of place you running here?" the disturbed patron asked the owner.

Another newcomer, raised by his grandmother in the brothel she ran in Peoria, Illinois, was a jittery young man named Richard Pryor. He made his Village debut at Manny Roth's Café Wha? in 1963. Soon he was opening at the Village Gate for Nina Simone, who rocked the quivering comic like a baby to calm him down before his set each night. "In 1963, the Village was alive," Pryor recalled. "Full of cats similar to me. A bunch of hobos looking for work."

Carlin dove right into this cacophony of voices. He began by plying his trade at a handful of hootenannies, the folk crowd's quaint name for an open mike night, at Café Wha? and the Bitter End. Across the street from the Bitter End was a red canopy advertising the entrance to Café Au Go Go. Down a flight of stairs and behind a full-length curtain, the good-sized room (capacity 350) featured a semicircular stage surrounded by butcher-block tables, with benches lining the walls. Murals depicting show folk hung on the brick walls. When Carlin first appeared at Café Au Go Go, the club had just been the target of a sting operation, with the New York district attorney's office bagging the man who was butting heads with law enforcement officials across the country—Lenny Bruce.

The bleary-eyed Bruce had first been arrested for his use of language in October 1961, at Art Auerbach's Jazz Workshop in San Francisco's bohemian North Beach neighborhood. Onstage, he'd joked about his first gig in the city, just across Broadway at a small, dreary hideaway popular with gays and lesbians called Ann's 440. "What kind of a show is it?" he'd asked his agent. "Well, it's not a show," his agent replied. "They're a bunch of cocksuckers."

Officer James Ryan had been assigned by his superior, Sergeant James Solden, to monitor the comedian's performance at the Jazz Workshop. Ryan notified the sergeant about the use of the eleven-letter word; in between sets. Solden then approached Bruce and informed him he was going to jail. The police force was trying to clean up North Beach, he explained, and an entertainer using a word like *cocksuckers* was, he felt, part of the problem. Solden told the comedian he couldn't envision "any way you can break this word down. Our society is not geared to it."

"You break it down by talking about it," Bruce replied.

Bruce had endured a number of arrests for drug possession in Philadelphia and Los Angeles by the time he arrived in the Village for ten nights of shows at Café Au Go Go in late March 1964. His third night at the club was attended by a license inspector named Herbert S. Ruhe, a former CIA agent in Vietnam, who frantically jotted phrases in a notebook as Bruce performed—"mind your asses," "jack me off," "nice tits." Ruhe's findings were just the sort of evidence District Attorney Frank Hogan was looking for. Hogan, an Irish Catholic moral crusader with close ties to Cardinal Francis Spellman, had been instrumental in bringing obscenity charges against Edmund Wilson's 1946 story collection *Memoirs of Hecate County*. Hogan ordered four plainclothes vice-squad officers to attend Bruce's next show, while he searched for a prosecutor on his staff who would be willing to take the case. Using a small wire recorder concealed on one of the officers, the patrolmen made a barely audible recording. They took the transcript to a grand jury, which authorized the arrest of Bruce and Café Au Go Go owner Howard Solomon on charges of violating Section 1140-A.

"But that's prostitution," Bruce protested the following night, as the officers intercepted the comic and the club owner in the dressing room just before the ten o'clock set. Don't get technical, one of the officers countered, "It's one of them numbers." Now facing charges, Bruce defiantly fulfilled the rest of his commitment at the club, forging onward with his off-color jokes: He spelled out the offending words.

At Café Au Go Go, Carlin joined the pool of Lenny's disciples, taking as little as $5 a night, sometimes just a burger, to keep the crowd occupied between musicians' sets. Weekends were better, when he could make as much as $65 opening for a headliner like the pianist Bill Evans. Carlin set up shop in the club, working a total of ten weeks in 1964. Ochs, the rabble-rousing topical songwriter, was a regular. Jazz saxophonist Stan Getz introduced the New York audience to his new quartet at the club, recording an album there featuring the Brazilian singer Astrid Gilberto. With a piano onstage, Howard Solomon asked Bob Golden, a session guitarist who could play some fair piano, to sit in whenever special guests dropped in to try their hand at a song or two, which was often. "Just about anybody called a celebrity on the New York scene was there," says Golden. "Liz Taylor and Richard Burton, people like that. I was the house band."

After taking the stage at the café a few times, Carlin approached the piano player, who was evidently friendly with the owners and seemed to know most of the performers. "George came up to me and said, 'I've been listening to you play, and you're pretty good, and I know you're making ten times as much as I am,'" Golden recalls. "'But I know I'm ten times a better comic than you are a pianist'—which, of course, was very true—'so how about becoming my manager?' It was a life-changing moment for me."

By this time Murray Becker was out of the picture. By some accounts, he'd gotten cold feet when Carlin was nearly pinched in Chicago for possession of marijuana. Years later one of Carlin's friends briefly took on Becker as his manager. "You can be the next George Carlin if you listen to me," Becker told him. "He had good things to say about

George every step of the way," claims the comic, "but it was said with onion breath. George abandoned him, was the way he said it."

Golden, frustrated by the studio sessions he'd been getting, jumped at the chance to take on a new challenge. He thought this Carlin fellow was good, that he might be going places. "I was looking for something else to do with my life," he says, "and he seemed to feel I knew my way around. He sensed that I could be helpful." Ironically, Golden's father had been all too familiar with Carlin long before his son and the comedian first met. The elder Golden owned a drugstore on 112th and Broadway, in Carlin's neighborhood. When Bob mentioned the name of his new client, his father groaned. "He knew him as one of these reprobates who would come into his store late at night to scam drugs," claiming he'd lost his prescription, Golden says with a laugh. To Golden's father, giving up a promising career as a musician in favor of managing a two-bit comic with a hankering for mood-altering substances sounded like a lousy career move. "Needless to say," says Golden, "after a few months of seeing George on TV, and then when George started doing *The Ed Sullivan Show*, that was a complete validation."

At the time, however, the comedian was closer to food stamps than to Ed Sullivan's stamp of approval. His idea was to develop a bit that would convince talent scouts he had one piece of material that was sure to go over well on the box. "Hunks," they called them. Carlin, recalls Larry Hankin, who shared a manager with Woody Allen in those years, was better suited to television than most of his peers in the Village. Unlike those (like Hankin) who worked without a net—just "rapping," with little preparation or forethought—Carlin fine-tuned his most promising routines, shaping them with an eye toward a four-minute spot in front of the cameras. "He had an incredible sense of the absurd," says Hankin. "His characters were amazingly funny bozos." Like Cosby and Allen, both of whom did time in the Greenwich Village clubs, Carlin was "*in* the Village, but not really *of* the Village," says Hankin. "They had to go through there to see what was going on, but they were doing TV material. I don't remember anybody else who could get on TV doing what they were doing in the Village, except those three."

But television bookings were the ticket to lucrative headlining gigs, and none of the new wave comics was immune. "They all act like big non-conformists," complained old-schooler Joey Adams, a traditional Borscht Belt comic, to *Time* magazine, "but they're all aiming to get on the Ed Sullivan or Steve Allen show." Professor Irwin Corey, who was already fifty by 1964, was more sympathetic to the new breed, who so evidently had been influenced by the uncertainties of the cold war. A madcap wordsmith who was blacklisted in Hollywood for his ties to the American Communist Party, Corey, like the truly outlandish Lord Buckley, a self-made aristocrat with gargantuan appetites and an unchecked id, was a kind of spiritual forefather to the next generation of satirists. "The future seems so precarious," he said, "people are willing to abandon themselves to chaos. The new comic reflects this."

For the better part of two years Carlin scraped by in New York. Golden found him occasional work outside the city—taking fifty bucks to play Brown's Hotel in the Catskills, for instance. He went over well at another jazz club in Boston, Paul's Mall; bombed at a New York bistro called the Sniffen Court Inn; took a quick trip to Bermuda to play the Inverurie Hotel. Still, Café Au Go Go was his real incubator.

For Carlin, a high school dropout who possessed a lively, inquisitive mind, the electric surge of ideas in the Village was intoxicating. "I wasn't very well-educated, but I saw this beautiful stream of intelligent comedy coming out of those people"—Newhart, Cosby, Nichols, and May—"and it really got to me," he said. At Café Au Go Go, he befriended an unlikely stockbroker named Bob Altman, a high-IQ, deep-reading dope smoker who'd been owner Howard Solomon's roommate at the University of Miami.

"I'd hang around the club 'cause I could fuck the waitresses," says Altman, a discursive firecracker who later had a lucrative, if short-lived, career as a campus comic known as Uncle Dirty. "I'd tell them, 'I know the owner. I'll get you a better station.' George was funny. He was brilliant. He smoked pot, and I smoked pot. Plus I had access to a car. When he had a gig out of town, I'd drive him." Carlin sometimes brought Brenda and Kelly over to Altman's place to scrounge up something to eat: "He was broke, really bust-out." Altman frittered away many nights with Carlin and his old friends from the neighborhood at the Moylan Tavern, playing darts and bumper pool and introducing his friend to the ideas of such radical spiritual thinkers as G. I. Gurdjieff and P. D. Ouspensky. Carlin especially liked the French psychologist Emil Coue's notion of autosuggestion: "*I* equals *W* squared, where *I* is the imagination and *W* is the will," explains Altman. "It shows you how powerful the imagination is."

Altman also turned Carlin on to a new book by Arthur Koestler, author of the anti-Stalinist novel *Darkness at Noon*. Called *The Act of Creation*, the book explored the author's theory of human ingenuity, the ability to integrate previously unrelated ideas. Jokes, as Carlin was well aware, are rooted in incongruities. To Koestler, scientific discovery, mystical insight, and "The Logic of Laughter," as he named his opening chapter, can each be traced to the unique human ability to make cognitive connections. The author designed a triptych showing a continuum from jester to sage to artist. "Jester and savant must both 'live on their wits,'" he wrote, "and we shall see that the Jester's riddles provide a useful back-door entry . . . into the inner workshop of creative originality." By falling into dream-states or finding other ways to transcend our stagnation, Koestler argued, we can achieve a "spontaneous flash of insight which shows a familiar situation or event in a new light, and elicits a new response to it."

All this was heady stuff for a young man plumbing the recesses of his imagination in search of his own sense of humor (and smoking considerable quantities of funny cigarettes to get there). Years later Carlin recalled studying Koestler's triptych:

> The jester makes jokes, he's funny, he makes fun, he ridicules. But if his ridicules are based on sound ideas and thinking, then he can proceed to the second panel, which is the thinker—he called it the philosopher. The jester becomes the philosopher, and if he does these things with dazzling language that we marvel at, then he becomes a poet, too.

But it would be some time before Carlin allowed himself to think in terms of wisdom and poetry. For the time being, he was committed to writing unapologetically silly material with no pretenses and potentially broad appeal. Much of it was variations on the characters he'd devised years before on the radio—the absurdist newscaster and his goofy sidekicks in the sports and weather departments. Closer to home, he had created a glib, speed-talking Top 40 disc jockey named Willie West, spinning records for a fictitious station, "Wonderful WINO," with Carlin adding his own a cappella jingles and mock pop tunes.

On the night before New Year's Eve, Carlin taped an appearance on another talent show, *On Broadway Tonight*, hosted by the veteran crooner Rudy Vallee. The program aired on the first of January 1964, a harbinger of good things to come in the new year. Coincidentally, it was a summer replacement for *The Danny Kaye Show*, hosted by Carlin's boyhood hero.

As a student Carlin had been enamored of the comic actor Kaye, who became famous for his dazzling propensity for flawlessly delivered, tongue-twisting song lyrics. When Carlin was ten years old, his hero starred in *The Secret Life of Walter Mitty*, an early Technicolor release based on a short story by James Thurber. Mitty is a harried, absent-minded book editor who escapes the stresses of his job and home life through a hyperactive imagination, daydreaming himself into increasingly fantastic scenarios. Kaye, who developed his talent for communicating by contorting his face and singing in gibberish during an extended vaudeville tour of Japan and China in the mid-1930s, was known for such nonsense songs as "Bloop Bleep," "The Frim Fram Sauce," and his rendition of Ira Gershwin and Kurt Weill's breakneck "patter song," "Tchaikovsky and Other Russians." One of his most familiar hits, in 1950, was "I've Got a Lovely Bunch of Cocoanuts," and he made Cab Calloway's scatting "Minnie the Moocher" another signature song, often leading audiences in exuberant call-and-response sing-alongs.

Carlin delighted in Kaye's rubbery faces and vocal gymnastics, knowing that he had a similar knack for both. "Anything that was challenging verbally I liked," he said. And Kaye "was incredibly adept verbally. He did funny accents, funny faces. All those things appealed to me." From a young age he looked at Kaye's career—the Catskills, radio, stage, films, and, eventually, television—as the model for his own ascent in show business. The way he figured it, if he succeeded as a comedian, Hollywood would have no choice but to make him a comic actor.

But Carlin's boyhood enthusiasm for his favorite performer cooled considerably after a personal episode. Knowing that Kaye was scheduled to make an appearance at Radio City Music Hall, the young fan waited in a doorway on a cold, misty day to ask for an autograph. When a cab pulled up and Kaye hopped out, he strode briskly past the kid holding the pen. "Not even an 'I don't sign autographs,'" Carlin recalled. "That was a crushing moment." Years later, when Carlin was established as a comic celebrity and had an opportunity to meet his onetime hero, he didn't have the heart to tell him about the snub. "That was my gift to him," he said.

In 1965 Carlin was still dedicated to the goal of breaking into Hollywood. His "responsible agent" at GAC—the one who coordinated the client's career and saw to it that the agency's various departments (television, film, nightclubs) kept his best interests in mind—was a veteran in the nightclub department named Peter Paul, who did his best to keep the young comedian busy. In the new year Carlin played five more weeks of bookings at Café Au Go Go. He also did two stints at another Chicago club, Mother Blues, in the city's folkie Old Town neighborhood, and he was invited for return engagements at Paul's Mall in Boston and the Inverurie in the Bahamas. Other gigs were not so notable. At a place called the Blue Dog in Baltimore, he performed without a paying soul in the audience.

Still, he was getting plenty of laughs most nights. He'd been honing one hunk in particular, "The Indian Sergeant," which was emerging as his surefire crowd-pleaser. The premise involved an Indian warrior who called his troops to order like an army drill sergeant. Carlin introduced the bit by noting that classic Westerns typically spent an hour and a half showing the cowboys getting ready for the climactic Indian attack, but never showed the Indians preparing. "It was a standard fish-out-of-water gimmick, the thing that Bob Newhart was doing so well then," he once explained. "The idea was that if the Indians were good fighters, they must have been organized, and military organization means N.C.O.s." Carlin's Indian sergeant addressed his troops in one of the born mimic's favorite, and most natural, voices—a posturing Bronx baritone that mangled the word "loincloth" as *lernclot'*. The braves, the sergeant reported, were performing their drills admirably: "Burnin' settlers' homes—everybody passed. Imitatin' a coyote—everybody passed. Sneakin' quietly through the woods—everybody passed, except Limping Ox. However, Limping Ox is being fitted for a pair of corrective moccasins." He then made a few scheduling announcements: "There'll be a rain dance Friday night, weather permittin'."

In May Carlin landed an audition for a new syndicated talk show set to premiere in July, *The Merv Griffin Show*. Having broken into show business as a singer, the host first found fame as the featured vocalist on popular bandleader Freddy Martin's 1949 hit version of "I've Got a Lovely Bunch of Cocoanuts," which inspired Kaye's own version a few months later. Before he got into television, Griffin had a brief film career, including an appearance in a 1953 musical (*So This Is Love*), in which he and costar Kathryn Grayson shared a then-controversial open-mouthed kiss. After hosting several game shows, the affable Griffin lent his name to a short-lived daytime talk show for NBC in 1962. Three years later he launched what would become his long-running syndicated show for Westinghouse Broadcasting. Most affiliates ran the show in the afternoon, though it was seen in some markets in prime time or in a late-night time slot opposite Carson's *Tonight Show*.

Bob Shanks, the former *Tonight Show* talent coordinator, had joined the Griffin program as a producer. When Peter Paul urged him to take a look at this new comic, Carlin, Shanks agreed. "I had sort of forgotten George from *The Tonight Show*," says Shanks, though his memory was refreshed when they were reintroduced in his office. On cue, Carlin performed "The Indian Sergeant" for his private audience. "I was falling out of my chair," says Shanks. "I booked him right away."

Carlin became one of *The Merv Griffin Show*'s earliest guests, along with another smooth-shaved product of the Bleecker Street scene, Peoria's Richard Pryor, who sometimes did impromptu improv sketches with Carlin when they introduced each other at Café Au Go Go. "It was a gift to me to have both Carlin and Pryor walk in," Shanks says. With the nightclubs beginning to move away from folk and comedy in favor of British Invasion–style rock 'n' roll, Shanks felt fresh comic talent was becoming tougher to find: "I was looking hard for new comedians, and suddenly these two geniuses appear."

"The Indian Sergeant" went over so well with both Griffin's audience and the host himself ("Oh, Lord," says Shanks, "he loved him") that Carlin was invited back for regular weekly spots. In all, he did sixteen appearances with Griffin in 1965, and four more the following year. The success led directly to a high-profile booking at Basin Street East, one of the few midtown jazz clubs then still thriving in the decline of the bop era. He opened for Herb Alpert and the Tijuana Brass, who were "hot as a pistol then," he recalled. "I didn't get a lot of attention, but I didn't care." Carlin's first few appearances on the Griffin show included encore performances of "The Indian Sergeant." At first he was reluctant to do it again, but Shanks convinced him not to worry about overexposure: "I told him, not everyone watches the show every day. That's the reason they repeat commercials. If we ask you to do a routine, then do that. They want to hear it again—it's funny."

Carlin also scored with several segments mocking the various conceits of television advertising—detergent and aspirin companies grandly exaggerating their significance in the daily lives of American families. "Our young Irish friend George Carlin is about to bite the hand that feeds us all," Griffin said, introducing the comic at one taping. Carlin, Griffin claimed, had recently done his commercial jokes for a group of advertising copywriters. They cried, he said, but only from laughing so hard.

Standing in front of the set's glittering curtain in an extra-skinny tie and a sharkskin jacket two sizes too big, a small spit curl dangling over his forehead, Carlin looked as though he was pledging a fraternity as he worked the Griffin audience. The commercial bits gave him a golden opportunity to showcase his growing repertoire of stock media characters—hale-fellows-well-met, pursed-lipped housewives, apple-cheeked little

Jimmys at the dinner table—and his Jerry Lewis-like ability to screw his facial muscles into the daffiest expressions. In a prim, motherly voice, Carlin teased his audience by alluding to a bit of blasphemy, mouthing the middle word in the phrase "for Christ's sake." Then he took a moment to imagine what would have happened if the marketers had instead hired a profane longshoreman to vouch for the aspirin company. The censors would've needed to erase so many words from the guy's commentary, Carlin said with an impish grin, there would hardly be any sentence left at all: "Well, when I get a _____ headache the _____ ____," he rasped, lapsing into a Tourette's-like string of staccato consonants and hiccups. It was the first nationally televised flirtation with four-letter words for the man who would become comedy's most widely recognized authority on the subject.

Already he was reaching his hand into the snake-charmer's basket. On another Griffin appearance, Carlin got big laughs when he joked about the fact that many cough syrups contained codeine, "a class-B narcotic referred to by junkies as Pepsi-Cola." Yet he was also eager to please. Invited to sit at Merv's desk with the chain-smoking host after wrapping up his six-minute hunk, he was introduced to the celebrity grab-bag of the day's guests idling on the couch, including professional panelist Kitty Carlisle, the pint-sized singer of the British rock 'n' roll act Freddie and the Dreamers, and Griffin's announcer and sidekick, Arthur Treacher. Carlin's regular spot on the show had been a boon to his nightclub career, he told Merv, nervously attempting some unscripted banter. "There's a level you want to get to, a place you want to work, finally some day if you can," he said. "And I made it." With mock pride, he announced that he'd just been booked into Angie's Roman Numeral Restaurant in Batavia, New York. It was a nice joint, he reported after the laughter died down, even if it did sound "like a real knucklebuster."

With his success on the Griffin show, gigs like Angie's soon became a thing of the past. "The Griffin deal became, I remember rather clearly, like every Tuesday for weeks and weeks," says Golden. "They signed him to a massive deal, they loved him so much." But the comic soon encountered a problem: He was running out of new material.

"Every Tuesday morning he'd call me up—'You gotta come over, I got nothing,'" recalls his former manager. "We'd spend the afternoon making each other laugh. It was a panic. He couldn't be doing 'The Indian Sergeant' every week." One sneaky solution was to write spontaneously updated versions of "The Newscast" ("It's the third divorce for the fifteen-year-old film queen"), which he could read on-air from notes.

Despite the TV breakthrough, Carlin still struggled for recognition within his own agency. A small-time stand-up comedian could be on the clients' list at the agency, says one former employee, "and that and twenty cents wouldn't get you on the New York subway." After one Griffin taping, Carlin was approached by a young agent from GAC's television department named Ken Harris. "I went up to say 'Hi' after the show," Harris recalls. "I said, 'Gee, I thought you were terrific. Do you have an agent?' He said, 'Yeah. GAC.' I felt stupid." At the office, Harris approached Peter Paul and expressed his interest in working with Carlin.

Harris was a good match for Carlin, an energetic, easygoing young guy who'd been hired in the agency's mailroom straight out of college. When he was made an agent, he had no idea what he was doing, he says with a laugh, so he flew by the seat of his pants. One thing he knew was that he wanted to work with talent that spoke to his generation. "When I got the job, I asked, 'Who's our biggest star?' When they said Steve and Eydie, I was very depressed." By contrast, the young wiseguy with the arch take on the modern world seemed like someone Harris could sell.

In September the agency booked Carlin on *The Mike Douglas Show*, another talk show hosted by a onetime big-band singer. Originating in Cleveland in 1961, the show's success in syndication precipitated a move to Philadelphia a few years later. The show, produced by future media mogul Roger Ailes, had just converted to tape delay after airing live in Cleveland. The switch came after the Hungarian-born actress Zsa Zsa Gabor called Morey Amsterdam a "son of a bitch" live on the air.

When "The Indian Sergeant" went over well on *The Mike Douglas Show*, Carlin was asked back, and he appeared three more times that autumn and seven times the following year. As the bookings began to mount, the comic was picking up a pool of allies at GAC. Like Harris,

Craig Kellem was a junior agent, a real go-getter. After working on a CBS show called *The Reporter* with another climber named David Geffen, who soon went off to the mailroom at William Morris, Kellem applied for a job as an assistant in the TV variety department at GAC. "You were there to get the guys coffee and type the letters," Kellem recalls, "schlepping, learning the business. Those were extremely colorful days. Stars were born coming into your office, doing their little comedy routine, and two weeks later they'd be on *The Tonight Show*."

Kellem initially worked for an agent named Ed Leffler, who represented the Beatles on their first U.S. television appearances. Leffler let his protégé listen in to his phone conversations on an earphone so he could learn the business. Within six months Leffler quit the agency (eventually managing the careers of the Carpenters and Van Halen), leaving Kellem to be promoted into his spot. "All of a sudden, I was an agent. I probably looked fourteen years old," jokes Kellem. But he had chutzpah. He took over the job of placing the agency's most reliable clients—Tony Bennett, the Supremes, "meat-and-potatoes comics like Pat Cooper," an Italian joke slinger born Pasquale Caputo—on *Today*, *The Tonight Show*, and Ed Sullivan, where GAC "probably booked a third of the talent." Sullivan, notorious for pulling the plug on guest acts after dress rehearsal, kept the young agent on his toes. "I always had a couple of guys like Cooper in the wings," Kellem recalls. "I'd call and say, 'Is your tuxedo pressed, and do you have six minutes?' That went on all the time."

Though he had inherited a plum gig, Kellem was eager to make his own mark. "You need to find talent you can develop that you think has a future," he says. For him, as for Harris, George Carlin was that talent. "He just cracked me up. He reminded me of a horny used-car salesman, or a cute game-show host. He had all these contemporary media references, with a silly little grin on his face. I was crazed about this guy. I took the sledgehammer approach—you just do everything. Your energy is greater than the resistance that comes your way." Kellem, Harris, and Golden, Carlin's manager, fed off their mutual enthusiasm for their client. "More than just about any other agent, Craig got it," says Golden. "He immediately saw that this was something special, and he became a very intense part of the team. He was lobbying like crazy within the agency to get George jobs."

With both Griffin and Douglas squarely on his side, Carlin was beginning to feel that he'd been discovered. His first full-fledged prime-time exposure came in February 1966, when he was invited to audition for *The Jimmy Dean Show*. The country star best known for "Big Bad John," a story-song about a heroic miner that was a number one pop hit in 1961, was an Air Force veteran, a television personality, and a future sausage mogul who'd occasionally served as a *Tonight Show* guest host. Golden says that Carlin auditioned right in Dean's own high-rise office, with producers and staff in the room. Dean, he says, "was a terrific performer, kind of forbidding. Early morning, Dean walks in, doesn't say a word, motions for George to start. He did 'The Indian Sergeant.' All of a sudden Jimmy Dean falls off his chair. George was instantly booked on the show." In his first of two appearances, Carlin performed "The Newscast."

"I guess the rest of the world knew an entirely different George Carlin than the one who did our show," says Dean. "He had a good haircut, he wore a fine-looking business suit and tie. He was impeccably attired, and not a foul word from his mouth." Yet Dean laughed hardest at the slow-witted Al Sleet, the Hippie-Dippy Weatherman, who was, to the emerging counterculture, unmistakably a heavy dope smoker. For the moment, Carlin could smuggle his drug humor onto television undetected by the Jimmy Deans and the Ed Sullivans of an earlier generation. In another year or two, no one in America could claim to be so naïve.

4

VALUES (HOW MUCH IS THAT DOG CRAP IN THE WINDOW?)

◇　◇　◇　◇　◇　◇　◇

Southern California was a scrubland before the movies arrived in the early twentieth century. By 1966, however, Hollywood sat at the core of a metropolis, and the television industry was drifting westward, too. Since the 1950s, when CBS built its Television City at the corner of Beverly and Fairfax on the site of a former sports stadium (which in turn sat on the site of a former oil field), network programs had been steadily migrating toward the wide-open West Coast, away from the suffocating congestion of midtown Manhattan. In March the Carlin family moved from the comedian's native city to an apartment in the Beverly Glen section of Los Angeles. He brought along a recording of New York City street sounds.

In the long view, Carlin would probably soon be reading for parts in motion pictures. In the shorter term, he had found steady work, at least for the summer. GAC had placed Carlin as a regular performer and comic writer for the thirteen-week summer replacement show *The Kraft Summer Music Hall*. Sponsored by the food company Kraft, the long-running series had originated on radio in the 1930s and was first brought to television in 1958, with Milton Berle hosting. The dazzling smile of the rookie host hired for the summer of 1966 belonged to

John Davidson, a singing, banjo-picking son of two Baptist ministers from Pittsburgh. Like Carlin, he was a future *Tonight Show* guest host.

Ken Harris worked the deal with NBC. Realizing he wasn't especially fond of being an agent, Harris had a proposition for Bob Golden, Carlin's manager: He would move to the West Coast and become the comic's comanager, with Golden handling the business back in New York. At GAC, Craig Kellem would become Carlin's responsible agent. "We all agreed on that," says Harris, now living in the Pacific Northwest. "I still have the telegrams."

Kraft Summer Music Hall—produced by television veteran Bob Banner, who was executive producer of *The Jimmy Dean Show* and had helped launch the career of Carol Burnett—was unabashedly cornball stuff. The supporting cast included a folksy singing duo called Jackie & Gale—Gale was Gale Garnett, who had a 1964 hit, "We'll Sing in the Sunshine"—and a squeaky-clean singing act called the Lively Set. A musical comedian named Biff Rose played Davidson's sidekick—Don Knotts to the host's Andy Griffith, as Rose put it. "It was straw hats and striped jackets, real hokey Middle America," says Harris. "It was real strange when you put George in that context, but he did fine." Among other duties, Carlin joined other cast members in singing "Winchester Cathedral." Neither the client nor his new comanager were complaining as they drove to work at the NBC studios each morning in blazing sunshine. "It was exciting," says Harris. "Hollywood in the sixties."

In fact, something was in the air, and it had a pungent smell. Even the most benign television productions were beginning to acknowledge the creeping influence of the emerging counterculture. The certifiably kooky Rose, for example, would soon move on to a short-lived recording career with arch Tom Lehrer-style saloon songs such as "American Waltz" ("We all love to dance our American waltz/It's our dream come false"). The Kraft series would feature guest appearances by a few old Carlin associates—Richard Pryor, whose rapid ascent was running neck-and-neck with Carlin's, and a new comic duo featuring a chunky, curly-haired Chicagoan named Avery Schreiber and his fellow Second City alumnus, Carlin's former partner, Jack Burns.

Davidson says he recognized instantly that Carlin was having a hard time getting comfortable, despite the familiar faces. "I walked into the first production meeting, and they said, 'This is our writer,'" says Davidson. "Very thin guy, usually standing very erect, but sort of hunched over when he did jokes. Clean-cut. Probably wearing a sweater and slacks. Very business-like, was the impression he gave." Davidson, who was then just twenty-four, soon found his costar to be "the most liberal guy I knew," but somewhat bottled up in terms of the stage. "We had Richie Pryor, Biff Rose, this crazy, off-the-wall musical comedian, and Flip Wilson. All of these people were crazier and more fun than George Carlin. He was very contained back then. He seemed to be always festering. You could tell there was much, much more behind what he was saying."

Early in the run, Carlin and Ken Harris were called into Bob Banner's office, where the producer laid a sizable offer on the table to handle Carlin's career. Harris remembers a proposed annual guarantee of $125,000, similar to the deal Banner had arranged with Davidson. Carlin and his West Coast manager politely declined. "It made no sense for George," says Harris, "but it was nice to be asked."

On the show Carlin did whatever he thought was expected. In one recurring bit, he worked up a variation on his Al Sleet character—Al Pouch, the Hippie-Dippy Postman, in which he brought phony fan mail for Davidson. "There were a couple of monologues they cut. They just didn't work," Carlin later admitted. "I was an undeveloped writer. I was writing superficially from the front of my head." Yet he felt he deserved some respect. During one taping, Davidson introduced the comic with a bit of levity, calling him "Little Georgie Carlin." "I was always trying to make him lovable," Davidson says. "I never thought he was lovable or huggable enough. Later, he asked the producer to ask me not to call him Georgie again. He didn't want to be like Ricky Nelson. He wanted to be taken seriously."

Offstage, Carlin was settling easily into the California lifestyle. He'd always been able to down more than his share of beers ("I was amazed he was so thin," says Davidson), but he was also smoking plenty of pot, a fact that was apparent even to the self-described "goody-goody" Davidson. "I assumed he was smoking grass back then pretty liberally, but he was never stoned at work at all. He was so business-like." On a visit to the Carlins' apartment to drop off a script, the host was slightly embarrassed to find the couple's young daughter running around the house with no clothes on. "They were a free-spirit, liberal kind of family," says Davidson, who credits Carlin with inspiring him to "loosen up." "I wished I could be free like that," he says. "He was very 'street,' and I was very WASP-y. I was jealous of what he was. I wished I could be closer to him."

The two men worked together for some time, including a one-off TV showcase the following year called *John Davidson at Notre Dame*, which featured Judy Collins, the pop group Spanky and Our Gang, and the Notre Dame Glee Club, as well as an extended tour with the starlet Joey Heatherton in 1968. Yet Davidson was well aware that he represented a kind of show business convention that the comic was growing allergic to. "I have a feeling he thought I was too white-bread, that the whole show was just too saccharine," he says. "I know he wanted to be more cutting-edge than that show was. He took the writing job to make money, for the TV exposure, and he was glad to get it. But I would definitely say he was holding back. He had much more to give inside of him, and he didn't know how."

For the moment, however, Carlin wasn't letting on. "He was loving being on major television and being invited back," claims Golden. "The jobs were coming in. He was enjoying having the career he always dreamed about." In July the comic had another breakthrough, of sorts. After a handful of years ironing out his material in basement grottoes and cramped, chintzy backrooms fit for a tarot card reader, Hollywood's newest comic was set to take the stage amid the potted palms at the Cocoanut Grove, the lavish and legendary nightclub on the property of the Ambassador Hotel on Wilshire Boulevard. Kellem had managed to land a double billing for his two pet clients, Carlin and a brassy Australian newcomer, a potential next-Streisand named Lana Cantrell, who'd been making repeat appearances on the Sullivan show and had just recorded her debut album for RCA.

"The question was, who should open for who[m]?" recalls Cantrell, who later became an entertainment lawyer. "Our careers were perfectly parallel at the time. It snowballed very quickly for both of us, but it was very premature to put either one of us at the Cocoanut Grove," which was accustomed to booking marquee names such as Frank Sinatra and Judy Garland.

Mere days before the engagement was to start, not a single reservation had been taken, so the nightclub's jittery management held over Eddie Fisher, the veteran pop singer recently divorced from Elizabeth Taylor, as the headliner. "I opened, George did his thing, and Eddie did his thing," says Cantrell. "It was the longest show in show business history. George wouldn't cut, and I wouldn't cut. It was such a strange week. Eddie didn't want to have anything to do with us." The next week, Kellem's odd couple held down the booking together, without Fisher. "We dragged in a few people and got some decent reviews," says Cantrell.

Though her interaction with Carlin was brief, Cantrell still recalls it fondly. She had experienced outrageous humor up close before. In Sydney, she once opened for Lenny Bruce, who brought a stool onstage and climbed on top of it without a word, prompting an audience member to ask what he was doing.

"It's a good position to be able to pee all over you," said Lenny.

Bruce died in August 1966, a victim of his addictions and persecution. His naked body was discovered in the bathroom of his Hollywood Hills home. The graphic police photo seemed one last slap at the comedian who had no reverence whatsoever for the traditional institutions of American life. Dick Schaap wrote a memorable appreciation: "One last four-letter word for Lenny. Dead. At forty. That's obscene." At a memorial service at a progressive Greenwich Village church, Allen Ginsberg and Peter Orlovsky led a Buddhist chant for the dead; they were followed by a performance by the Fugs, the ragtag Village folk-rock group named for Norman Mailer's euphemistic expletive used throughout his debut novel, *The Naked and the Dead*. Bruce's friend Paul Krassner, founder of the black-humor magazine *The Realist*, hosted.

From Carlin's days in Shreveport, when his roommate first introduced him to Bruce's lethal observations on the *Interviews of Our Time*
album, the younger comic had found much to admire in his predecessor's value judgments and utter disregard for conventional morality.
"Lenny's perception was magnificent," he told the *New York Times* in a
1967 feature story, the first in-depth profile of the younger comic. "He
could focus on the real emotions behind what we say and what we do
in our society. He was the immortal [*sic*] enemy of cant and hypocrisy
and pseudo-liberalism, which is just another form of hypocrisy. What
Lenny was saying should continue to be said until we begin to hear
some of it." On the eve of Carlin's debut in his next prime-time showcase, a summer replacement series for *The Jackie Gleason Show* called
Away We Go, the article revealed that he was considering a role on
Broadway as Bruce, in a script written by the playwright Julian Barry.
Nothing came of it for Carlin, though Barry's script was eventually
produced as the 1974 Dustin Hoffman biopic *Lenny*.

For Carlin, Bruce's comedy "let me know there was a place to go,
to reach for, in terms of honesty in self-expression." Carlin and
Brenda had a cordial relationship with Bruce, who had played the
Racquet Club in Dayton and gotten to know Brenda when she was
assigned to give him rides to the airport. After Bruce's death Carlin
and his wife remained friendly with his inimitable mother, Sally
Marr, who had taught her son everything he knew about speaking his
mind. The combination of Bruce's social surgery and Mort Sahl's dis-
section of power were critical to Carlin's development. Now, with
Bruce gone and Sahl off wandering, undermining his own career as he
conducted a personal, years-long investigation into the JFK assassination, the floor was suddenly open to a new, intrepid comic who
would be fearless enough to address the fraudulence of the American
dream.

NOT THAT CARLIN was ready to be that comic. In early September he appeared on *The Tonight Show* for the first time in the Johnny Carson era,
putting a little extra effort into the Hippie-Dippy Weatherman bit,
which he'd been performing on autopilot for some time. As the

beatifically spacey Al Sleet, he delivered the forecast without breaking character, while Carson cackled off-camera. Although he didn't return to Carson's set at the NBC Studios for two years, it was the start of a long association, with Carlin making more than a hundred appearances.

Less memorable were his spots on *The Roger Miller Show* and *The Hollywood Palace*, an old-fashioned ABC variety hour taped at the former Hollywood Playhouse with a rotating pool of guest hosts. The show, notable for introducing the Rolling Stones to an American audience, was a hodgepodge of celebrity sketches, monologues, and performances. In April, appearing alongside the vapid British folk duo Chad & Jeremy, Carlin was introduced by host Martha Raye. In thick-framed glasses and tightly pegged pants, he sat behind a stock-issue desk on an otherwise empty stage and read "The Newscast" from notes. The segment let him roam from mildly Sahl-like wisecracks about current events ("Tonight the world breathes a little easier, as five more nations have signed the Nuclear Test Ban Treaty. Today's signers were Chad, Sierra Leone, Upper Volta, Monaco, and Iceland") to surreal nonsense. "Quickly now, the basketball scores. We are running late. 110–102, 125–113 . . . and an overtime duel, 99–98. Oh, here's a partial score: Cincinnati, four."

Safely disguised as the cartoonish Al Sleet, he also dropped a sly reference to his own daily habit as he delivered the weather forecast: "Tonight's low, twenty-five. Tomorrow's high, whenever I get up, heh heh heh."

"George was always a little subversive that way," says Ken Harris. "When I met George, he was a pot smoker. Being with him on the road, he'd wake up in the morning, and before brushing his teeth, he'd smoke a joint. And throughout the whole day. It didn't seem to affect him much, except to make him happier." After the Carlins moved into a rented Spanish villa–style house on Beverwil Drive, Carlin finally convinced his reluctant West Coast manager to try smoking with him. "He was my guide," says Harris. "I think it was a Peter, Paul and Mary record we were playing—we had just bought new stereo equipment together. And he said, 'Now just pick out one instrument and focus on it.' It was the first time I ever got stoned."

The show business veterans with whom Carlin was rubbing elbows had little idea they had a budding hippie in their midst. "Folks, it's great to see new comedians come along. If there's one thing the world can always use, it's a smile," said Jimmy Durante, introducing the twenty-nine-year-old Carlin as "one of the best" on another *Hollywood Palace* episode, taped in late 1966. That particular show must have felt like a real carnival to the clean-cut young stoner, featuring as it did a group of trained elephants and the momentary singing sensation known as Mrs. Miller, a matronly housewife from Claremont, California, who ignored the raucous laughter that accompanied her truly horrendous singing. Carlin did a version of his "Wonderful WINO" routine, poking lighthearted fun at the youthful generation that he was beginning to realize he had more in common with than his own.

"I'm sure you're aware of the fact that teenagers today are the most powerful group in the country," he began, explaining the premise of his Top 40 parody. "First of all, there are more of them than ever before, and teenagers are so much better organized today than they ever have been before. . . . Many of them are armed." This was the sort of surefire, cheap-shot joke that was beginning to strike him as disingenuous. At a time when American culture was being increasingly influenced by dissatisfied, idealistic twenty-year-olds, he was still toiling to think of ways to make their middle-aged elders laugh. His next birthday would be his thirtieth, situating him squarely in the middle of the yawning generation gap. Carlin was starting to realize he should be appealing to his juniors, not his seniors.

Yet the "Wonderful WINO" routine underscored the debt he owed his predecessors. The bit had a pronounced resemblance to a 1958 spoof called "Chaos, Parts 1 and 2," a 45 rpm. single recorded by Bob Arbogast, a radio personality and comedy writer, and his partner, Stan Ross. A quick-selling novelty record that was reportedly suppressed by radio stations when they realized they were the butt of the joke, "Chaos" (set at KOS—"Chaos Radio") featured Arbogast's rapid-fire patter, snippets of song parodies, a mock commercial for a product for teens who feel left out by their lack of acne ("Pimple On"), and an update of late baseball scores—"five to one, fourteen to three, and four to nothing." The similarities of Carlin's own radio routine are too apparent to ignore. "He had to have heard it," says Arbogast's son, Peter, a sports announcer for the University of Southern California. Arbogast was accustomed to finding his material recycled elsewhere. He also came up with a comic segment called "Question Man," which was adopted (with credit) by Steve Allen and (without) by Johnny Carson, as the long-running *Tonight Show* bit Carnac the Magnificent. Although Bob Arbogast sometimes joked about Carlin owing him a phone call, says his son, he shrugged it off. "You can't put any copyright on comedy," says Peter. "People take each other's bits and use them all the time."

With Carlin's television exposure adding up, the nightclub gigs were improving. He played the Drake Hotel in Chicago twice in 1966; moved up in Dayton from the Racquet Club to a much bigger stage, Suttmillers; and did Las Vegas for the first time, opening for the singer Jack Jones ("The Impossible Dream") at the historic Flamingo. Along with the prestige and increasing income came a distinct feeling that his act was being monitored at the more upscale clubs. "I told him to be very careful what he did at Suttmillers," says Dayton promoter Shane Taylor. "But he wanted to work there—the money was good." Over Thanksgiving weekend Carlin was booked into the Roostertail in Detroit, a swanky, split-level function complex along the city's riverfront. Opened in 1958 as a fiftieth birthday gift for the wife of owner Joe Schoenith, the club was operated by Schoenith's son Tom from his twenty-first birthday. The club had a tradition of attracting top talent, in part by giving the entertainers lavish gifts—a car for Wayne Newton, diamond watches for the Supremes. "We gave Tony Bennett his first acrylic paint set," says Schoenith. "They were wined and dined when they came here."

Although they didn't roll out quite that sort of red carpet for the lesser-known Carlin, the venue was the setting for the taping of his first solo comedy album. Comedy hadn't been a real priority for RCA Records since the label had enjoyed some success with the pseudo-evangelical put-on artistry of Brother Dave Gardner, a drumming, scat-singing, deep-South Lord Buckley who was a Jack Paar favorite before he was busted for marijuana in 1962. The record company assigned a young A&R (artist and repertoire) man, Tom Berman, to produce Carlin's *Take-Offs and Put-Ons*, which gathered all of the comic's top-drawer material to date—"The Indian Sergeant," "Wonderful WINO," "The Newscast"—in one place. The album also featured an eight-minute hunk about advertising and a routine called "Daytime Television," which introduced another of Carlin's farcical characters, a cross-eyed, featherbrained game show contestant named Congolia Breckenridge. Though the cover featured a grid of black-and-white photo-booth shots of the comic's seemingly bottomless reserve of puerile facial expressions, he and his producer were on the same wavelength about the deceptive depth of Carlin's material. "It's a risky business to take comedy too seriously," wrote Berman in the album's liner notes, before proceeding to do just that. "What had seemed funny or outrageous or ridiculous becomes much more than that after repeated listening. . . . In the company of Carlin's people"—Biff Burns, Al Sleet, the "tragic heroine" Congolia—"we become very susceptible to laughter and veiled tears."

The feeling in the Carlin camp was that it was only a matter of time before the comic began fielding offers for sitcoms and films. Old friend Jack Burns beat him to it. When Don Knotts left his Emmy-winning role as Andy Griffith's bungling deputy on the beloved *The Andy Griffith Show*, Burns was hired as his replacement for the show's sixth season. His role as Deputy Warren Ferguson introduced the country to Burns's comic trademark, a pompous, all-purpose demand for recognition: "Huh? Huh? Huh?" But Knotts's endearing Barney Fife character proved impossible to replace, and Burns was dropped from the show after eleven episodes.

Meanwhile, Burns's old partner made his first appearance as an actor on the new ABC sitcom *That Girl*, which starred Danny Thomas's daughter, Marlo, as a mod-ish aspiring actress in New York City. In an episode that aired in late 1966, Carlin played the star's agent, George Lester. Working the phone from his client's apartment, he kibbitzed with a booking agent on the other end of the line: "That's the trouble with this business. You can't trust anybody. Trust me, Martin."

In January of the new year he prepared to take his first bow on the big cheese of the variety hours, *The Ed Sullivan Show*. Nearing the end of its second decade on the air, the implacable gossip columnist's program still represented the pinnacle of television success for singers, dancers, novelty acts, and comedians. *Newsweek* noted the rising star's impending appearance with a short feature, commending his "high-fidelity ear for the transistorized pop gabble of the mid-'6os." Carlin's reliance on the fertile source material of electronic entertainment—his slick anchormen and disc jockeys and clueless game show contestants—was noted as a potential dead end. "Eventually, he's going to have to branch out," Johnny Carson told the unnamed reporter. "If you base all your material on one subject, sooner or later you reach a point of diminishing returns."

Though GAC handled the Sullivan show and booked a disproportionate number of its guest spots with in-house talent, Carlin had resisted making his debut there for some time. "I heard they chewed young comedians up," he said. "Just before you go on they come and they say the roller-skating chimpanzees went long, so we need you to cut another minute. This is a live show, you're about to go on in another five or ten minutes. . . . I was afraid of that." Though he'd never had many qualms about performing, to Carlin, Sullivan represented the most unforgiving, least appealing aspect of show business, and he was frankly daunted. The audience inside CBS's Studio 50 on Broadway, the Ed Sullivan Theater (now home of *The Late Show with David Letterman*), "were dead. Just dead people. Yes, they laughed at Myron Cohen, and Jack E. Leonard could mow them down with energy." But the studio audience in Sullivan's theater, he felt, was preoccupied with being seen, overdressed in minks and pearls and waiting for the house lights to go up when the host introduced a special guest in the crowd—"Joe Louis or Babe Ruth's widow or somebody. . . . On those Ed Sullivan shows I began to realize I didn't fit. I was missing who I was."

By this time Kellem, Carlin's responsible agent, had also become Sullivan's agent. "I lived at the Sullivan show," he says. "September to June, or whatever it was, I was there." Television had no more nerve-racking stage. "It was blood and guts, man. You saw the veins in the neck, the eyes. There was something viscerally very pleasing about it, and it was exciting." When he finally felt ready, Carlin appeared in a lineup that included the bandleader Woody Herman, singer Mel Torme, comedian Nipsey Russell, an acrobatic troupe called the Seven Staneks, and the banjo sing-along group Your Father's Mustache.

Despite his reservations, Carlin made three more appearances on *The Ed Sullivan Show* in 1967 and eleven in all, taping his last commitment in the waning days of the show in early 1971. If the Sullivan show was a powerful symbol of television's boxy limitations, Carlin's next gig was especially confining. In May, just as the Summer of Love was blooming—the hit song of the moment was Scott McKenzie's "San Francisco (Be Sure to Wear Flowers in Your Hair)"—Carlin spent an uncomfortable week as the center square on the smug game show *The Hollywood Squares*.

He did a series of dates—Cleveland, Toronto, Phoenix, Warwick, Rhode Island, and Wallingford, Connecticut—as part of the package tour with John Davidson and Joey Heatherton. And for the second summer in a row, he was cast as a writer and featured performer in a summer replacement series. This one was a placeholder for *The Jackie Gleason Show*, whose portly superstar was a critical client for GAC. The variety program was called *Away We Go*, after Gleason's signature catchphrase. "It was manifest destiny for George Carlin at the time to get his own TV show," says Kellem. "We sold the show with Carlin as the star via Jackie Gleason's company." Carlin was paired with Buddy Greco, a Sinatra-style singer from south Philadelphia, with the infamously profane drummer Buddy Rich (who'd once appeared on a Lenny Bruce special on local New York City television) leading the house band.

"Things were going very well for me," says Buddy Greco, who still performs at his own nightclub in Cathedral City, California. "I was doing movies, had hit records. I got a call from CBS. They wanted to do a series, and they said, 'Who would you like?' I said, you gotta give me my best friend, Buddy Rich. And they said, 'We need a comic.'"

Greco, who has worked with virtually all of the Buddy Hackett-Shecky Greene Vegas *tummlers* (Borscht Belt comedians) in his long career, says he could tell that Carlin was a little different, though he was still perfectly presentable. "When he worked with us, you could see his ears," he says. "He had a short haircut, a shirt and tie." The sketches sometimes required the show's frontmen to make fools of themselves, including one number called "Brush Up Your Shakespeare." "I have videos of George and I and Buddy in tutus," Greco says. "Can you believe Buddy Rich in a tutu? I was a tough kid from Philly. We're tough guys. It was such a funny thing to see. We went along with it. It was hilarious." But the best material, he says, was the improvised humor the three stars came up with away from the camera. "We did more stuff on the steps of CBS in the back," Greco recalls. "So off-the-wall. I wish we could have recorded those."

Little more than a year removed from those $5 nights at Café Au Go Go, Carlin suddenly had a steady, very respectable income, earning $1,250 a week for the summer series. "It quickly got to a point where we didn't have to worry about George making a living," says Bob Golden. Their experience on *Away We Go*, he says, was "kind of strange. There were a lot of egos involved. In a sense, CBS and the Gleason production company, they didn't care. They were just happy to have something to fill the time with. But between Buddy Rich and Buddy Greco's wife, there was always insistence that everyone do the same amount of time. It got to be pretty funny at times."

During this period Carlin's friend Bob Altman spent many nights on the couch in the front room of the house on Beverwil Drive, where, he says, the famously meticulous Carlin had already amassed "a whole fuckin' wall full of file cards" containing lists of ideas and premises for new material. He says that Carlin was beginning to express his affinity with the counterculture by wearing the sloganeering buttons that were popular at the time. "He used to wear all the buttons—'Free the whales,' or whatever the fuck—and it would drive Buddy Greco crazy." Lana Cantrell appeared as a guest on the show's second episode. In the fourth week, Pryor had a guest spot. In the fifth, the musical guest was Spanky and Our Gang, another new client of Kellem's at GAC.

Spanky and Our Gang was a folk-rock vocal group from Chicago whose first single for Mercury Records, "Sunday Will Never Be the

Same," was on its way to becoming a million-seller. (The following summer one of the band's singles, the civil rights song "Give a Damn," was banned for profanity in several cities.) Carlin was already good friends with the group's big-voiced singer from Peoria, Elaine "Spanky" McFarlane, whom he'd met several years before on the Playboy Club circuit, when McFarlane was part of a vocal group called the Jamie Lynn Trio. "At the Playboy Clubs, there were several rooms of entertainment—the Library, the Speakeasy," she recalls. "George was with Jack Burns. We met in the entertainer's lounge over the pool table. Not *on* the pool table," she is quick to amend, letting out a hearty chuckle.

Carlin quickly became good friends with McFarlane's new band mates, including the West Virginia–born, Coral Gables–raised bassist Paul "Oz" Bach, an actor by training and an amateur comedian by reputation, who had performed with such folk fixtures as Fred Neil, Tom Paxton, and Bob Gibson. As Spanky and Our Gang's debut single was climbing the charts, they spent an evening with Carlin in New York City, where he was preparing to tape another *Tonight Show* appearance the following day. The band was in the middle of an engagement at a Midtown club called The Scene, says McFarlane. On a night they all had off, Carlin came to the band's hotel to visit. "We didn't have anything to smoke, but we had heard you could smoke bananas—the peel," she says with a laugh. "You scrape the inside of the peel, bake it in the oven, and smoke it. It was hilarious." The next night, on Carson, Carlin joked about trying to get high from banana peels. "I thought, 'Oh, my God, I hope my parents aren't watching,'" says McFarlane.

The year 1968 began with accolades for Carlin, starting with a Grammy nomination for *Take-Offs and Put-Ons*. In the Best Comedy Recording category, the album was up against Flip Wilson's *Cowboys and Colored People*, the posthumously released *Lenny Bruce in Concert*, and a record by former country music radio personality Archie Campbell, who would soon become a star of *Hee Haw*. The fifth nominee, Bill Cosby's *Revenge*, was virtually preordained as the winner, with Cosby in the midst of a six-year streak of winning every comedy Grammy. Carlin took home a consolation prize when he was honored as one of the "Hollywood Stars of Tomorrow," as the outstanding young male performer in the variety format for *Away We Go*. Carlin beat out Pryor (for his work on *The Merv Griffin Show*) and Flip Wilson, a future colleague.

He was reaching a certain level of acceptance in Hollywood. "I became known as a reliable prime-time variety show comedian," said Carlin. In February Gleason grabbed Carlin for his own variety hour. Sullivan wanted him back for more; so did Carson. Anything-goes producer Chuck Barris, angling to capitalize on the recent successes of *The Dating Game* and *The Newlywed Game*, booked Carlin for two weeks on a mercifully short-lived game show called *How's Your Mother-in-Law?* In January Barris's production company made Carlin a guest host for *Operation: Entertainment*, a USO-style grab bag shot at various military bases. One week after celebrity impersonator Rich Little hosted the show's debut episode, Carlin emceed a taping at Lackland Air Force Base in San Antonio, Texas.

For some nagging reason, none of these opportunities felt quite right. One particular letdown was Carlin's first film role. Eyeing the comic acting career of Jack Lemmon, who turned a largely uneventful resume as a television role player into box-office stardom (*Some Like It Hot*, *The Apartment*), he took a supporting role as a goofy carhop in *With Six You Get Eggroll*, a romantic comedy showcase for the perennial American sweetheart, Doris Day. By 1968 Day was old enough to be offered a part as the disillusioned Mrs. Robinson in *The Graduate*. Uncomfortable with the character's seduction of a twenty-one-year-old college boy, she turned down the part in favor of *Eggroll*, an innocuous tale of a widow and widower (Brian Keith) who make halting, mishap-riddled attempts to connect.

As Herbie Fleck, Ye Olde Drive Inn's carside attendant in a white waiter's jacket, a bowtie, and a boat-shaped soda jerk's hat, Carlin clowned shamelessly for the camera, warily monitoring the budding romance between his regular customer, Day's character, and the interloper, played by Keith. "Dame must be a masoquist," he clucks, mangling the word, when Day's character apparently gets stood up.

"He sort of mugged his performance," says Jamie Farr, who had a supporting role in the movie as an exotic hippie. Farr was living with his wife a few blocks from the Radford Studios—CBS Studio Center, on Radford Avenue in Studio City—where the film was shot. "George would stop by with a six-pack of beer," he says. Despite the camaraderie, the experience on the set, Farr says, was "not a milestone moment, probably, for either of us." In fact, Carlin's part was a joke, and he quickly came to regret it. "He felt like furniture," says Golden. "Anybody could've done it. I know that had a bit of an effect on him. Plus, Doris Day was going through a horrible time in her life and marriage at the time. It permeated the entire experience for everyone."

Overnight, Carlin dashed his own dreams to build a Danny Kaye–type acting career for himself. He wouldn't appear again in a feature film until 1976. "I found out . . . that I couldn't act in movies," Carlin said. "I found out I can't do this shit. Man, they want you to change a little bit here, get out of Doris Day's light, don't lean in too far, lean back, you're off-mike, you're out of the light, you can't do this, stand there, keep your legs crossed, remember this, say it with a little bit of sadness. . . . Fuck all that!" He might have remembered Evan Esar's definition of *actor* in his *Comic Dictionary*: "A man who tries to be everything but himself."

In May Carlin opened a three-week engagement at the Frontier Hotel on the Las Vegas Strip, the first lengthy residency of a high-paying, three-year commitment. The first venue to book Elvis Presley in Vegas, the Frontier was then owned by the billionaire Howard Hughes, who'd bought the complex for $14 million in late 1967. Carlin's live gigs were growing tonier, which meant his audiences were increasingly removed from the cultural transformation then taking place on the streets, not just in San Francisco but in every major city and college town across the country. For years Carlin's running partners had been the folk and rock musicians he befriended on the nightclub circuit, many of whom were fellow pot smokers, and most of whom were jumping into the hippie pool with both feet. They certainly weren't the targeted ticket buyers for Jack Jones or Joey Heatherton. Harris, who was traveling regularly with Carlin at the time, remembers that his client was growing conflicted. "He'd often come offstage angry—'Those assholes.' He was playing for these audiences he didn't have much respect for, and he was trapped by his own success. He was struggling inside."

The folkies had laid the groundwork; now pop and rock were socially motivated, too. Meanwhile, Carlin was catering to the middle class—the same people his musician friends were rebelling against. "The music was protest, and I was hearing people who were using their artistic talent to further their ideas and their philosophies," he recalled. "It was starting to dawn on me that I'm not using my abilities to further these thoughts and ideas that I agree with. . . . I'm entertaining these businessmen and shit in these nightclubs, doing people-pleaser shit."

Something had to change, and it soon did. At the beginning of the Frontier gig, Carlin called Golden, then Harris, and told them both he needed to let them go. "At a time when he really should've been happy, he obviously was not at all pleased with how things were going," says Golden. "I understood totally why he was unhappy, yet as a manager, you know—if it wasn't broke, don't fix it. Finally it got to a point where it was like, 'Hey, let's part friends.' I knew I was not capable of selling what it was he now wanted to do." Golden went on to manage a few musicians and entertainers—guitarist Kenny Burrell, flutist Hubert Laws—before becoming the talent and marketing director for the Blue Note Jazz Club.

Harris tried to take the split in stride, too. "The first thing you learn is that everybody leaves," he says. "At some point, they get unhappy, and they shoot the people around them. You're kind of conditioned to that." Still, he couldn't help but think he'd failed his client. "I felt very bad. I maybe felt I didn't do a good enough job."

Carlin's new manager was Bill Brennan, the Racquet Club owner from Dayton, Ohio, whose wife was a close friend of Brenda's. In June Carlin did a week at Bimbo's near San Francisco's Fisherman's Wharf, a plush cocktail room just up the avenue from the hungry i and the Beat bookstore City Lights. A month later he appeared on *The Joey Bishop Show*, ABC's short-lived answer to Carson, featuring Carlin's fellow Cardinal Hayes alumnus Regis Philbin in the sidekick role. It was just weeks after Bishop had conducted an uncharacteristically solemn show, on the night after presidential candidate Robert F. Kennedy was shot to death at the Ambassador Hotel. His guest that night was a Los Angeles radio reporter who had an audiotape of the immediate aftermath of the shooting.

In August Carlin returned to the Frontier for three more weeks. Another Sullivan, another Gleason, and another week at Paul's Mall in Boston rounded out a relatively quiet last few months of the year, which closed with rehearsals for an upcoming role on an episode of *The Smothers Brothers Comedy Hour*.

In their third (and what would prove to be final) season for CBS, the folk-singing comedy team of Tom and Dick Smothers was becoming a flashpoint for the counterculture, grappling with the network's Standards and Practices Department over their program's socially and politically charged content. The brothers and their writers, including Rob Reiner (soon to be known as Mike Stivic, aka "Meathead," on *All in the Family*), part-time composer Mason Williams ("Classical Gas"), and a then-unknown Steve Martin, were testing the public's capacity to confront the polarizing issues of the day—the civil rights movement, the war in Vietnam, the emergence of the pill—with humor.

Though guests during the show's inaugural season in 1967 were hardly controversial—Jack Benny, the Turtles, Nancy Sinatra, and Frank Sinatra Jr.—by the time Carlin appeared, the Smothers Brothers were feeling besieged. In Pete Seeger's first network television appearance since the days of the Hollywood blacklist, the veteran folk agitator savaged the war effort with his song "Waist Deep in the Big Muddy," which was cut from the broadcast. CBS then demanded that the producers submit completed episodes several days before airtime, so the network would have time to review the content. At the beginning of the third season, Harry Belafonte sang "Don't Stop the Carnival" accompanied by a montage of clips from the recent Democratic National Convention in Chicago, where police in riot gear had clashed violently with protesters. That segment was removed, too, as was a biblical satire by stand-up newcomer David Steinberg.

Carlin was familiar to the Smothers Brothers. He'd been a guest in July on the awkwardly titled *The Summer Brothers Smothers Show*, a replacement series hosted by Glen Campbell. "We met him in the early sixties, when it was still Burns and Carlin," says Tom Smothers. "We kept bumping into them in Chicago." While Carlin was showing faint signs of letting his hair grow out during the December rehearsals—he had sideburns and the makings of a ducktail—other performers on the show were fully committed to the youth movement. The musical guest was the Doors, with their lion's-mane singer Jim Morrison wearing leather pants. The San Francisco comedy troupe called The Committee featured future sitcom players Peter Bonerz (*The Bob Newhart Show*) and Howard Hesseman (*WKRP in Cincinnati*), whose facial hair was full muttonchop. Even Dick Smothers, who had taken the summer off while his brother worked behind the scenes on the Glen Campbell replacement series, came back for the third *Smothers Brothers* season with shaggier hair and a mustache. "I was so goddamn envious," says Tom Smothers. "The following summer I let my hair grow—I thought maybe I'd have curly hair too. It was long and stringy, and I grew a mustache, and it was long and stringy, too."

On the Smothers' set at Television City, Carlin was introduced to Lenny Bruce's old friend Paul Krassner. *The Realist*, Krassner's magazine of hardcore sociopolitical satire, was a key voice in the development of the American counterculture. It was launched in the late 1950s as a moonlighting project out of the New York office of *Mad* magazine, where Krassner was a contributor. Krassner's sense of outrage was acute, and he had an uncanny ability to drum it up in others. In response to reports that Jackie Kennedy had demanded deletions from William Manchester's 1967 book *The Death of a President*, Krassner wrote a notorious, black-comic essay called "The Parts That Were Left Out of the Kennedy Book," imagining graphic sexual congress between Kennedy's successor, Lyndon Baines Johnson, and the corpse of the assassinated president.

Kurt Vonnegut once lauded the "miracle of compressed intelligence" of a *Realist* bumper sticker that read "Fuck Communism." Forcing jingoists into a conundrum—either confront the taboo over four-letter words, or give the Reds a pass—was "nearly as admirable for potent simplicity," Vonnegut wrote, "as Einstein's $E = mc^2$. [Krassner] was demonstrating how preposterous it was for so many people to be responding to both words with such cockamamie Pavlovian fear and alarm."

The Realist, Carlin wrote years later, was critical to the conversion he was about to undergo. A "rule-bender and law-breaker since first grade," he'd been leading a double life throughout the 1960s, straining to please "straight" audiences even as his "sense of being on the outside intensified. . . . All through this period I was sustained and motivated by *The Realist*, Paul Krassner's incredible magazine of satire, revolution, and just plain disrespect," Carlin wrote in an introduction to one of Krassner's books. "I can't overstate how important it was to me at the time. It allowed me to see that others who disagreed with the American consensus were busy expressing those feelings and using risky humor to do so."

The Smothers Brothers Comedy Hour was equal parts consensus-bucking and primetime inanity, with singers and dancers in straw hats and mod fashions straight from the department store rack. Following the hosts' topical opening gag (Tommy in a gas mask and riot helmet) and the Doors' pantomimed version of "Wild Child," Carlin dusted off "The Indian Sergeant," introduced by Tom Smothers as a routine that had "already become a classic." In a suit and tie, Carlin gamely donned a headband with a single feather sticking out.

Later in the program he joined the hosts—all three dressed in matching red turtlenecks and black slacks—in a peppy rewrite of folk songwriter Tom Paxton's "Daily News," interspersed with comic vignettes drawn from newspaper headlines. One, "Church Split on Birth Control," gave Carlin a chance to appear onstage in a priest's collar. Dick Smothers, playing a reporter, noted that the priest was liberal, having just gotten married. How did the Father feel about the Pope's denunciation of birth control? Oh, Carlin replied, he could never contradict the Pope on birth control. But what if he should find out that his wife has been taking the Pill? "Well, I think I'd have to file for divorce," he joked. Corny, but like Krassner's "Fuck Communism" sticker, it was also a succinct jab at institutional hypocrisy. Although he was still going through the whole song and dance just to get the opportunity, little by little he was slipping social commentary into his comedy.

In the strange brew of 1960s culture, at the intersection of thread-bare vaudevillian showmanship and staged *Laugh-In*–style anarchy, there might have been no other way for him to advance his craft. "The art's gotta be out there before you can put the content in," says Tom Smothers. "If you're singing protest songs, you better be a fuckin' good singer. And you better be funny if you're gonna do social commentary." Hollywood had accepted the thirty-one-year-old Carlin as a funny guy. Now he was ready to let his hair down.

5

THE CONFESSIONAL

It was simple, solipsistic advice, useful nevertheless: "The more you know about yourself, the more you stand to learn." As Carlin strained to balance his fast-moving career with his growing impulse to be true to his comedy, he heard this axiom on, of all places, a game show. On a short-lived Chuck Barris creation called *The Game Game*, ordinary people matched wits with a celebrity panel, answering a series of questions designed to illuminate their personal psychologies. How do you vote: by party, issues, candidates, or the advice of friends? What traits, if any, do the people you've dated share? How do you choose your toothpaste?

Sitting alongside actor Andrew Prine and *Valley of the Dolls* author Jacqueline Susann, his slicked hair curling at the edges, Carlin strained for geniality as he endured the excruciating twenty-three-minute taping. Answering a weird question about how the contestants would handle a potential housemate accused of "unruly behavior," he replied that it wouldn't bother him. "I'm not very ruly," he explained.

His unruly urges were beginning to show. Making his second appearance on the Gleason show in January 1969, Carlin managed to attract the attention of the FBI. Introduced by the host as "a real oddball," Carlin wondered why incidental television programming—the test pattern, or the sign-off hour "Star-Spangled Banner"—was never nominated for Emmy Awards. Having laid out the premise, Carlin imagined that the

97

FBI's late-night "Most Wanted" report had a production budget like *The Tonight Show*'s. His mock host, "J. Edgar Moover," then performed a monologue of aggressively bad jokes: "Did you hear the one about the two guys planning to rob a bank? So did we. We put 'em in jail."

Several days after the broadcast, Gleason's office received two letters of complaint. "The crime wave is not a subject for levity or humor," wrote the first aggrieved viewer, from Dallas, "and the Department of Justice is not a subject to be made fun of, any more than it would be proper to make light of the U.S. Constitution. The hippies and the yippies might be taking serious things lightly but the majority of the people in the United States are law abiding citizens and do not appreciate anyone making fun of crime." The second letter, sent from Connecticut, referenced the appearance by "an individual named George Carlin. I believe he was supposed to be a comedian." Carlin's spoof, wrote the viewer, "was shoddy, in shockingly bad taste, and certainly not the sort of thing one would expect on your show." The correspondent then noted that he was a former special agent of the FBI.

> In the field of law enforcement there are no more respected names than the Federal Bureau of Investigation and J. Edgar Hoover. In the field of entertainment there is no greater personality than Jackie Gleason. It's a shame that a third-rate hanger-on would use the generosity of one to belittle the reputation of the other.

An internal FBI memorandum ultimately determined that the appearance of this "third-rate hanger-on" "was in very poor taste," and that "it was obvious that he was using the prestige of the Bureau and Mr. Hoover to enhance his performance." The author of the memo proceeded to (clumsily) document part of Carlin's routine, bringing to mind Lenny Bruce's exasperation when he had to listen to the detective in his New York obscenity trial fumble his own material in court. Bureau files, the deputy noted, "contain no information identifiable with Carlin." The Miami FBI office, which acknowledged prior contact with Gleason and his PR man, Hank Meyers, helped settle the matter by filing the helpful addendum that Gleason himself "thinks that the Director is one of the greatest men who has ever lived."

The FBI was too big a target for Carlin to ignore. A year later the Bureau added several pages to his file when the comic reprised his bit about the "Ten Most Wanted" list on *The Carol Burnett Show*. A viewer from Cocoa Beach, Florida, wrote to Burnett, explaining that although she and her husband considered themselves fans of the show, "tonight our mouths fell open and almost to the floor in utter dismay and shock." "Malcontents" such as Carlin, she wrote, owed it to their country to offer solutions to, not just snide comments about, its problems: "To destroy rather than build, in my opinion, is not the way our country achieved 'a walk on the moon.'"

Forwarded a copy of the letter, Hoover scribbled a note at the bottom before passing it down the Bureau's need-to-know chain: "What do we know of Carlin?" The answer, surprisingly, never came. At the time, the FBI was devoting countless man-hours to the systematic evaluation of certain celebrities the bureau considered a threat to American security, including Jane Fonda, the Smothers Brothers, the poet and activist Allen Ginsberg, and John Lennon, whose nude portrait with wife Yoko One on the cover of the 1969 album *Two Virgins* prompted an inquiry from Hoover to the attorney general wondering whether a pornography charge was in order. But Carlin's own file apparently never grew beyond the twelve annotated pages about his prime-time FBI jokes, as the comedian eventually learned when he filed a Freedom of Information Act request years later. Hoover's death in May 1972 left the FBI without its longstanding public spokesman. Carlin, however, continued to joke about the director after his death, imagining a Washington, D.C., operative who knew his phone was wiretapped and answered it with a cheery "Fuck Hoover!"

A milder cussword got the rebellious comedian in trouble next. In October 1969 Carlin checked into Las Vegas for another residency at the Frontier, which had become a key component of his livelihood. After debuting there the previous year, he'd already played two three-week stints in 1969. From $10,000 a week to start, he'd been bumped up to a whopping $12,500, at a time when sitcom actors were lucky to be making $1,500 a week. The money was almost embarrassing. Lenny Bruce had commented on the ridiculous discrepancy between the extravagant sums paid to entertainers and the paltry salaries of schoolteachers: While a teacher in Oklahoma might be making $3,000 a year, he said, Zsa Zsa Gabor was getting $50,000 a week in Vegas. "*That's* the kind of sick material that I wish *Time* would've written about," he said.

If the money was guilt-making, the marquee lineups Carlin was sharing in Vegas were downright discouraging for a guy who longed to be as hip as Lenny. "I was opening for—try not to smile—Robert Goulet, Barbara Eden, and Al Martino," he recalled. "I was terribly out of place." During his October engagement, opening for Goulet, Carlin did an early show for a private group of businessmen in town for the Howard Hughes Invitational golf tournament. The men stumbled in late, drinking heavily. The incident set off the comedian's long-held antagonism toward golfers. (One joke, years later: "O.J. Simpson has already received the ultimate punishment. For the rest of his life he has to associate with golfers.")

For some time Carlin had been referring in his act to his skinny body type, the fact that he had "no ass." "I'm one of these white guys who, if you look at me sideways, I go from the shoulder blades right to the feet. Straight line. No ass. When I was in the Air Force, black guys used to look at me in the shower and say, 'Hey, man, you ain't got no ass. Where your ass at?'" He did the bit for the golf crowd, thought nothing of it, then moved on to another topic. After leaving the stage, Carlin was informed that Robert Maheu, Howard Hughes's right-hand man, had been in the audience with his wife, and she'd been offended by the joke.

Maheu, longtime spokesman for the world's richest man (whom he claimed to have actually glimpsed only twice), was nearly as much of a puzzle as his exceedingly strange employer. During World War II Maheu went undercover for the FBI as a Nazi sympathizer. After setting up his own investigations outfit, he took clandestine assignments from the CIA, including, famously, a plot to assassinate the Cuban dictator Fidel Castro, for which he recruited Mafia *capo* Sam Giancana. As the self-appointed chief executive officer of Hughes Nevada Operations, which oversaw the management of the reclusive investor's holdings in the state, Maheu saw it as his duty to police the Frontier's entertainment on the night of the golf tournament. Carlin was abruptly dismissed from the remainder of his engagement—paid and sent home. "I was more or less flabbergasted," he said.

He'd just done a week without a hitch at the Holiday House outside Pittsburgh, a ritzy, art deco–style dinner theater with hotel rooms and a pool. *Variety* reviewed him favorably there, calling the show "a sock." "We probably paid him $7,500—very good money," says Bert Sokol, who, as the son-in-law of the club's owner, was booking the entertainment in those days. The main showroom was big, seating a thousand. Rumored to have mob ties, the Holiday House expected clean material from its comedians, which included plenty of veteran names—Milton Berle, Jack E. Leonard, Totie Fields ("a little risqué for a woman," Sokol recalls)—as well as up-and-comers like Carlin, David Brenner, and Joan Rivers. "The comedians were restricted with the language they could use on our stage," says Sokol, who had no problem with Carlin, picking up the club's two options on him for the following year.

Provocative content was becoming a hot topic in the entertainment industry. The introduction of the Motion Picture Association of America's self-imposed film rating system in 1968 served as an acknowledgment that some subject matter, such as that of 1969 Best Picture winner *Midnight Cowboy*, was inappropriate for young audiences. For comedians, the fact that they were still held to the "clean" standard in clubs and on television, while movies and so-called legitimate theaters were increasingly exploring mature themes and language, seemed unfair. *Variety* reported on the complaints of stand-up acts in England: Some British comics were being fined for cursing, while their stage-acting counterparts were immune to censure. The article also cited the double standard of what the writer termed "boondock situations," in which comedians working lower-class barrooms could get away with using profanity, whereas those in finer establishments could not. "Presumably the local constables wink at the hardcore prose," the *Variety* correspondent concluded. "Some who've played the sticks say it's tough following a four-letter act."

Like so many in his business, Sokol considered Jules Podell's Copacabana in New York the epitome of classy American supper-club entertainment. "All the stars wanted to work at the Copa," Sokol says. The club advertised itself as "New York's heart-quarters for great stars. . . . The Copa is the showcase of show business." Carlin, however, was not feeling quite so peppy about the place. Booked over the December holidays into the red-leather-upholstered hotel basement on East Sixtieth Street by Irvin Arthur, GAC's well-connected nightclub agent, from the start of his two-week engagement the comic sensed that he was in for a confrontation.

The Copa's connection to the powerful underworld figure Frank Costello was a poorly kept secret. "The Copa was a tough room," veteran comic Jack Carter once said. "The Murderers Row would come in every show." And Podell had a longstanding reputation for tyrannical behavior. When singing sensation Johnnie Ray rushed off to an acting gig near the end of a wildly successful run at the club, Podell had staff members toss one of Ray's record-company handlers into the freezer. In another incident, a hungry busboy grabbed a half-eaten roll off a plate he was clearing. Podell, who saw him do it, sweetly asked the young man if he'd like to take a moment to eat. The busboy was treated to a full meal—steak, dessert. When he was finished, Podell smiled at him. "Glad you liked it. You're fired!"

Podell was notorious for a particularly obnoxious habit. "If Jules wanted attention," remembered Peggy Lee, "he would knock his big ring on the table and everyone would come running." Podell's table took a pounding during Carlin's engagement. The comic was opening for William Oliver Swofford, a fresh young pop star who took his middle name as his stage name. Oliver had smash hits that year: "Good Morning Starshine" from the Broadway musical *Hair*, and "Jean," a ballad written by the poet Rod McKuen, heard as the theme to the film *The Prime of Miss Jean Brodie*. But the audience's enthusiasm for the theatrical song stylist from North Carolina did not extend to his opening act. Whether or not they recognized Carlin from *The Holly-*

wood Palace or *The Ed Sullivan Show*, he got nothing but indifference from the paying customers, as the silverware clinked and the chatter continued unabated.

After a few nights trapped in his penguin suit—Podell insisted that his entertainers wear tuxes—Carlin was desperate to get out of the suffocating atmosphere. "I hated that fuckin' place," he said. "It was everything I didn't want. I died every night." He started castigating the audience, telling them that places like the Copa had gone out of style twenty years before. Then he began to express his displeasure by killing time in absurd ways—lying on the dance floor and describing the ceiling, for instance, or crawling under the piano and reading from its manufacturing label. Like the performers at Zurich's Cabaret Voltaire a half-century earlier, where nonsensical performance was inspired by the horrors of World War II, Carlin was subverting the social contract by knocking it on its ear. He began announcing that he was a Dada comedian. "I'd say, 'I don't know if you're familiar with the Dada school of philosophy; it concerned itself in part with the rejection of a performer by his audience. The point is that it's as difficult to gain your complete rejection for thirty minutes as it is to gain your acceptance, and I can go either way.'"

Directly addressing a table of GAC executives one night, Carlin implored them to book him into more appropriate venues, with crowds that would understand him. Podell was enraged—who did this kid think he was, giving lip to his loyal customers? Still, he refused to give the comedian what he wanted. Instead, he let him suffer. "He would never fire me, that fuck," Carlin remembered. Obligated to pay him whether or not he completed the run, the Copa's kingpin let him dangle. On the last night of the stint, the sound and light guys effectively ran Carlin out of the building. Before he was finished with his set, they slowly began to dim the lights and fade out the sound. "It was very artistic, very cinematic," he said. "Very dramatic. It was almost sweet in a way. And I knew I was free."

Carlin certainly wasn't the first to earn Podell's ire. Shecky Greene was opening for Nat King Cole at the Copa when he tried a joke in a voice that sounded like Popeye. Unbeknownst to him, Podell's guttural rasp was often compared with Popeye's. Almost immediately the lights went down and the microphone went dead. The stubborn comic kept doing the joke; the stubborn club bully kept shutting him down. "Three weeks I had of that," said Greene.

Craig Kellem was with the GAC gang on the night of their client's meltdown at the Copa. He'd already sensed Carlin was getting restless, but the agent wasn't sure how to handle it. Besides, his own star was rising at the agency. "I had made my bones," he says, "and I wasn't staying up at night worrying about the fact that the guy was changing." Like Golden, Kellem struggled to understand why this talented performer would sabotage his own career: "The brand was working, and he was changing the brand. I would love to tell you I was prophetic—that there was greater comedy to come, and in order to do that, he's gotta become a social spokesman. But that's not what happened."

GAC had already seen another of its young comedy stars suffer a very public identity crisis. Soon after his debut on network television and in the high-rollers' nightclubs, Richard Pryor began to crack. Opening for Trini Lopez at Basin Street East, he performed while lying on the floor. The manager of the Sands called Pryor's agent, Sandy Gallin, to complain that the wiry kid was "swinging from the chandeliers" during his week there on a bill with Steve Lawrence and Eydie Gorme. But the real freak-out occurred in September 1967, when Pryor froze onstage at the Aladdin Hotel in Vegas. He'd been trying to fit in as a junior version of Cosby, spinning amusing yarns with little acknowledgment of the problem of race in America, which was then coming to a head.

"My days of pretending to be as slick and colorless as Cosby were numbered," Pryor later wrote. "There was a world of junkies and winos, pool hustlers and prostitutes, women and family screaming inside my head, trying to be heard. The longer I kept them bottled up, the harder they tried to escape. The pressure built til I went nuts." Seeing Dean Martin looking at him expectantly from the audience at the Aladdin, the comedian stood mute for a painfully long time. Who are they looking at? he asked himself. "I couldn't say, 'They're looking at you, Richard,' because I didn't know who Richard Pryor was," he claimed. Finally, he mustered the courage to open his mouth. "What the fuck am I doing here?" he asked, and walked off.

It was a question Carlin was trying to answer for himself. After appearing as a "Mystery Guest" on *What's My Line*, he glumly told the studio audience that he was appearing at the Royal Box in midtown Manhattan, where Frank Sinatra had sat a few years earlier with Gleason and Toots Shor, watching Frank Jr. make his singing debut. Host Wally Bruner tried to get his guest to open up; more than most of his fellow comedians, he noted, Carlin considered himself a writer as well as an entertainer. "It's the only way," Carlin replied. "I like to make things from my own head."

By his own admission, it was around this time that Carlin began experimenting with LSD and peyote. Hallucinogenic highs were no longer the well-kept secret of the intellectually intrepid underground. Psychedelic music, art, and fashion had been an undeniable part of American life to all but the most naïve Americans since the massive media coverage of the Summer of Love. Users reported "dazzling states of heightened awareness or mystical experiences worthy of St. Teresa of Avila," noted *Time* magazine as early as 1966; "others claim insights that have changed their lives."

Timothy Leary and Richard Alpert, the two former Harvard psychologists whose experiments with mind-altering drugs helped usher in the new age of expanding consciousness, had already been celebrity figures for several years—Leary with his ubiquitous motto, "Turn on, tune in, drop out," and Alpert, by this time known as Ram Dass, leading the counterculture's spiritual quest to India and beyond. Paul Krassner accompanied Groucho Marx on the aging vaudevillian's maiden voyage on the drug; Cary Grant was another film star who admitted he'd taken dozens of trips, as therapeutic treatment, before LSD was banned. "It opened my eyes," Paul McCartney of the Beatles told *Life* magazine. "It made me a better, more honest, more tolerant member of society." World leaders, he suggested, would be ready to "banish war, poverty, and famine" if they would only try it.

Carlin's own experimentation with acid didn't last long, but it helped him to see that he was out of his element with the "straight" crowd. "Those drugs served their purpose," he recalled. "They helped open me up." Though he would have future problems with other drugs, he looked back on his LSD period as a positive experience. "If a drug has anything going for it at all, it should be self-limiting," he said. "It should tell you when you've had enough. Acid and peyote were that way for me."

Still, he had obligations. He did the Sullivan show, on a night that also featured Bob Newhart, just after wrapping up the disaster at the Copa. He appeared twice more on Sullivan's stage in a matter of months—the first time alongside singer Bobby Goldsboro, impressionist David Frye, and Pryor (who remained a favorite of the taciturn host); the second with Don Rickles and the Jackson 5.

His changing perception was beginning to show in his physical appearance. He no longer looked like the dutiful middle-manager type. When he checked into a hospital for a hernia operation, he stopped shaving and quickly decided to keep the beard. Returning to Mister Kelly's in Chicago for a summertime engagement, Carlin drew a rave from *Variety*'s reviewer. With other Chicago clubs coasting through the quiet summer season, owner George Marienthal could have followed suit, the unnamed writer pointed out. Instead, Mister Kelly's had put together a fine lineup, including an "attractive thrush" named Taro Delphi, that would have been a nice draw in a busier season.

Carlin, "no stranger hereabouts," unveiled new material "that reaffirms early impressions that he is one of the most creative and engaging laugh producers playing the café circuit." Though prone to "offbeat routines," the reviewer continued, "he has the ability to couch them in jargon and imagery that is palatable to a wide range of tastes." He mixed topics well, alternating "typical grogshop stuff," like his advertising spoofs, with social commentary, "per his assessment of the country's burgeoning drug orientation." Little did the critic know how deeply invested the comic was in his new material; during Carlin's last visit to Mister Kelly's the previous year, he'd been in the midst of an acid binge.

In September 1970, Carlin dragged himself back to the Frontier, which still held options on him through the end of the year. The headline act was the Supremes, who were returning to the hotel after performing their last show with Diana Ross there in January. Carlin was scheduled for three weeks with the group, followed by one more week with Al Martino, the former construction worker from Philadelphia whose singing career would lead to a role in *The Godfather*.

Opening night with the Supremes went off without a hitch. In fact, *Variety*'s reviewer was more impressed with Carlin than with the headliners, who, performing with the house's Al Alvarez Orchestra, were "gradually becoming bleached in musical content and direction." Carlin, the writer suggested, had "come up a modish contemporary fellow complete with a well-trimmed beard." The "brand-new whimsies" in his repertoire reportedly caused "plethoras of sidesplits," and, after a momentary lull, his finale about drugs and druggists inspired the audience to show its appreciation with "vigorous palming."

But Carlin was still stung by the previous year's episode at the Frontier. He was feeling devilish; during the engagement he came up with a way to test the management's tolerance while seemingly keeping his own innocence intact. He'd been thinking about how certain comedians got away with working "blue." For years Buddy Hackett, who was so firmly entrenched at the Sahara Hotel that owner Del Webb made him a vice president, had been doing raunchy jokes about sex and ethnicity. Redd Foxx, an old friend of Malcolm X who became one of the first black performers to work for white audiences in Las Vegas, was an underground celebrity for his risqué "party" records long before the launch of his television show *Sanford and Son*. Both of those Vegas regulars said the word "shit," Carlin noted onstage. "I don't say 'shit' in my act," he said. "I may smoke a little, but I don't say it."

Carlin had been smoking "shit" habitually since he was thirteen years old. "I'd wake up in the morning and if I couldn't decide whether I wanted to smoke a joint or not, I'd smoke a joint to figure it out," he once admitted. "And I stayed high all day long. When people asked me, 'Do you get high to go onstage?' I could never understand the question. I mean, I'd been high since eight that morning. Going onstage had nothing to do with it." Now he was outwardly identifying with the real-life Al Sleets of the world, acknowledging his predilection for getting high right there in his act. In a guest appearance on the syndicated *Virginia Graham Show*, Carlin confessed his "secret" dependency on national television. The hostess was delighted to hear it. The composer Henry Mancini had only recently told her the same thing, she said. "Virginia Graham was a real shit-stirrer," Carlin remembered.

It may have been the admission; it may simply have been his sneaky way of slipping the word "shit" into his act. It may have been the fact, according to the comic, that this particular crowd was largely composed of salesmen from Chrysler and Lipton Tea, some of whom took exception to the comedian's observations about God and country. In any case, when he strode offstage at the Frontier, Carlin was summarily dismissed from the remainder of the engagement. This time he felt a strange sense of elation. "They did the job for me," he told Brenda. "They broke it off. This is good."

Though he'd been renting Phyllis Diller's Vegas house, he'd never felt a part of the fraternity of Vegas comics. Now he didn't have to pretend he did. "I never went over to Don Adams's house for dinner," Carlin soon told *Rolling Stone*. "I never bought an alpaca sweater, and I never learned how to play golf."

His clash with the Vegas audience was mirrored a few weeks later when another comic innovator, Robert Klein, had his own showdown in the desert. With his newfangled style, like a dry-witted social studies teacher, the mildly shaggy Klein was embarking on a career path similar to Carlin's. He did his first *Tonight Show* in 1968 and had just completed his own summer replacement TV hosting gig. Opening at the Las Vegas Hilton at year's end for Barbra Streisand—then Vegas's biggest attraction, alongside Elvis, both making $125,000 a week—the comic left the stage in a pique one night when a customer threw a pencil at him. Streisand's manager, Marty Erlichman, was irate. Now his singer would have to go on early. After the show, Streisand consoled her opening act. "She was so sweet," says Klein. "She completely sided with me, and she made her manager go out and get Chinese food for us."

On another night Rodney Dangerfield, who had taken Klein under his wing, brought the legendary Jack Benny to see the up-and-comer.

When Klein said the word *shit* in his act, Benny laid down a verdict. "The kid works dirty," he said.

"That was a heartbreaker," says Klein. "I had a few rough nights there." Increasingly the old guard of funnymen, and the slot machines and scantily clad cocktail waitresses that marked their natural habitat, were proving a fatal combination for comic insurgents like Klein, Pryor, and Carlin.

Trusting his intuition, Carlin soon took matters into his own hands. Again ready for new management, he took a meeting with Ron De Blasio and Jeff Wald. The two talent managers had recently left Campbell-Silver-Cosby, a production and management agency owned in part by Bill Cosby. Among other enterprises, Campbell-Silver-Cosby operated a record label called Tetragrammaton, distributed by Warner Bros. The imprint had released albums by the rock band Deep Purple, Carlin's fellow *John Davidson Show* alumnus Biff Rose, and an unusual comedian, a Lenny Bruce soundalike named Murray Roman, whose twisted wit included a record with an all-black cover called *Blind Man's Movie*. Tetragrammaton also became the U.S. distributor for John Lennon and Yoko Ono's *Two Virgins*, with its full-frontal-nudity cover photograph, when Capitol Records refused to sell it. Carlin, avid record collector that he was, knew the label well.

Wald was a piece of work. A streetwise product of the Bronx, he got into the entertainment business as a gofer for the songwriter and civil rights activist Oscar Brown Jr., who introduced his pugnacious young assistant to Malcolm X and Martin Luther King Jr. After managing Brown's career for a time, Wald took a job in the William Morris mailroom, comparing notes with his friend David Geffen. "I sold grass in the mailroom on the side," Wald told one writer. He was a ruthless businessman in the making and a wicked practical joker, pissing in the plants of an interoffice rival after hours.

He married an aspiring singer from Australia named Helen Reddy, and they moved to Chicago, where Wald spent a few years booking the rooms at Mister Kelly's and the London House. There he befriended performers including Pryor, Miles Davis, and Flip Wilson. On the night that King was assassinated, Pryor was opening a run at Mister Kelly's. "By the second show, the National Guard had surrounded the club and closed us down," recalls Wald. He and Pryor drove through the city, smoking a joint and lamenting the destruction that was already underway: "There were troops and people shooting, rioting, and he was crying. He was supposed to do *The Ed Sullivan Show* the following week, and he didn't do it."

Feeling restless in Chicago, Wald had told Cosby that he wanted to be in Hollywood, and the star put him in touch with his manager and business partner, Roy Silver. Wald's first experience at Campbell-Silver-Cosby was working with the agency's newest signee at the time, Tiny Tim. Though the money came rolling in, he soon took the advice of Norman Brokaw, the chairman of William Morris, to go into business for himself. With a $30,000 loan from his old employer, Wald put out his shingle, taking De Blasio with him.

By the time Carlin and Brenda walked into the office, Wald was working hard to get his wife's career off the ground. De Blasio took the meeting. "I gave the pitch to Carlin," says De Blasio. "He was pretty much my responsibility." The comedian made it clear: He was hungry to find an audience that would understand where he was coming from. De Blasio, who would soon be working with Pryor and David Steinberg, assured Carlin that he and Wald could help. "I'd worked with Cosby, so I knew the comedy area very well. If you're working with Cosby, you certainly know what comedy is about, especially in those years. I saw what he wanted. I knew the area he was playing was at that time a graveyard."

Wald had vague memories of Carlin from his days at Café Au Go Go, where Oscar Brown Jr., was a regular. "Howie Solomon chased me around the club once with an axe," says Wald. "Those were fun days. You could walk in a two-block radius and see Dylan, Joni Mitchell, Richie Havens, Carlin, and Pryor."

Before his new managers could create a plan to put Carlin in front of hipper audiences, he had some outstanding contracts to fulfill. In November he traveled to Wisconsin to appear at the Lake Geneva Playboy Club, the jewel of the franchise, with its ski resort and a hotel lodge architecturally influenced by Frank Lloyd Wright.

Carlin had been on a Hefner television show, *Playboy After Dark*, earlier in the year, just after starting his beard. Between performances by the Modern Jazz Quartet and Johnny Mathis, he appeared on a couch on the bachelor-pad set, gazing glassy-eyed at a blonde named Connie, who cooed that she loved Taurus men: "They're so lovable. They grow great beards, and they're *sooo* funny."

On Carlin's other side was Hefner, wearing a tuxedo, gripping his pipe in his front teeth. After some awkward banter with the host, Carlin got up to deliver his routine to the roomful of swingers. Standing in front of the fireplace, he dusted off a hunk he'd been using for years, a satire of cough-and-cold-remedy commercials. Funny how your pharmacist knows more about you than anyone, he said: "He knows what you're hooked on. He knows what you take too much of. He knows"—nudge, nudge—"where you put the ointment." Then he segued into some newer material, beginning with a nimble romp through a grocery list of snappy product names—No-Doz, Dentu-Grip, Ora-Fix. He imagined the day when birth control would be marketed over the counter: Preg-Not, Embry-No, Mom Bomb. It was the sort of clever wordplay for which the emerging George Carlin, the word-junkie and list-maker, would become justly noted, broaching volatile topics through the disarming use of playful language.

His sense of mischief did not go over so well in Lake Geneva. Carlin was beginning to lampoon the Vietnam conflict in his act. "Of course, we're leaving Vietnam," he said, referring to the Nixon administration's claims. After a pregnant pause, he let out a suppressed snort. "We're leaving through Laos, Cambodia, and Thailand. It's the overland route!" Gotta remember why we're over there in the first place, he said. Then he stopped short, adopting the blank expression of someone who has suddenly forgotten how to spell his own name.

The audience in the Penthouse Room included several military veterans, and they began to heckle him and question his patriotism. What he said in reply has been lost to posterity, though the club's entertainment director, Sam Distefano, reported, "George made a gesture with his finger and a remark. In so many words, he told the audience they were jerking themselves off." According to Jerry Pawlak, then the Playboy Club's maitre d', he'd been preoccupied with business until someone notified him that customers were arguing with the entertainer. He looked up just in time to see Carlin stalk offstage. "I've only had three people walk offstage on me," Pawlak recalled. "Joan Rivers, Buddy Rich, and Carlin." Some in the audience, he said, were incensed. He had to convince one Marine not to follow the comedian backstage. "It was terrible. We had to comp everyone for the show."

The whole episode brought to mind another Lenny Bruce joke: that he didn't mind when people walked out on him, except in Milwaukee, "where they walk *toward* you." In his hotel room Carlin grew nervous when he heard voices calling outside his door. He called De Blasio, who had yet to start earning commission on Carlin's dates. "He said, 'Listen, I think I got myself in trouble,'" says De Blasio. Carlin had already been notified that he was fired from the engagement, and that he should check out in the morning. "He said, 'Right now, I got people outside my door.' I said, 'Oh, my God. Stay there and don't confront them. Call the manager and ask for security.'"

De Blasio hung up and called the Playboy Mansion in Chicago. He knew Hefner well; Cosby was a good friend of the magazine mogul. He got Bobbie Arnstein, Hefner's assistant and chief of staff, on the phone and demanded to speak with Hefner, blustering about how Hefner professed to be an advocate of free speech. "This is something Hef can't get into right now," Arnstein told him.

Meanwhile, Carlin drove down to Chicago, where he got in to see Hefner. "Hefner is saying to me that he has to wear two hats in this situation," he recalled. On the one hand, he was a great fan and champion of subversive comedy. On the other, "Well, you see, I have to do business with these assholes."

De Blasio figured that someone in the press would pick up the story and run with it, so he tipped off *Variety*, hoping to head off bad publicity by shaping the news from his client's side. "I got a guy named Murphy," he says. "I thought, boy, this is great. I've got all the

Irishmen on my side." The story appeared on the front page of *Variety* the following Wednesday. According to the report, the early show had gone smoothly, but Carlin's "routine about materialism in American society, press censorship, poverty, Nixon-Agnew, and the Vietnam War apparently incensed the late-night crowd." A club manager named L. W. Pullen was quoted as saying the performer had "insulted the audience directly and used 'offensive language and material.'" The story noted that Carlin had been canceled in Vegas a few months prior for using "vulgar" language.

The front-page exposure made Carlin's new approach common knowledge around the industry. "We got phone calls from everyone," says De Blasio. "Mostly people who wanted to know if George was OK. A couple people said, 'What the fuck are you doing? Are you crazy? This is going to ruin him!' I said, I don't think so." Kellem, who was nearing the end of his tenure as Carlin's agent, saw the article and panicked. "Not only did they not like him, but he kind of got chased off the stage," he says. "It's one thing getting a bad review. It's another when they run you off the plantation."

Among those who contacted Wald and De Blasio was Monte Kay, Flip Wilson's manager. Kay and Wilson could see what Carlin was trying to do, and they thought they could help.

A hip Brooklynite who had his own apartment in the Village by the age of fifteen, Kay's youthful enthusiasm for swing and bebop led to a close friendship with disc jockey Symphony Sid Torin, with whom he produced concerts, including a notable appearance at New York's Town Hall by Dizzy Gillespie and Charlie Parker. As a manager, he handled Sonny Rollins, Stan Getz, and the Modern Jazz Quartet, among others. Like many of the artists he represented, he tended to favor dashikis, and he wore his hair in a Jewish 'fro. When Kay began dating his first wife, the black singer and actress Diahann Carroll, "it never occurred to me that he was white," she wrote in her autobiography.

Kay "felt the music pushed the races together when nothing else did," says his daughter with Carroll, Suzanne Kay Bamford. "I wouldn't say he was an idealist—he just believed this was something that could bond people, could help dissolve these silly separations." When Kay got into comedy with Wilson, the transition was natural. "Comedy did the same thing," says his daughter. "It could poke fun at institutions. It dissolved some of those divisions when everybody was in the room together, laughing. He was drawn to it at a deep level because it did good in the world."

By 1970 Wald already had what he considered a "long-term relationship" with Kay and Wilson, from the comedian's performances at Mister Kelly's. "Basically, we smoked a lot of grass together," he says. Kay and Wilson had just established a boutique record label together, Little David, a subsidiary of Atlantic Records. Kay had briefly been an executive with the parent company, befriending the influential brothers Ahmet and Nesuhi Ertegun. But he was ill-suited for a corner office with a nameplate on the desk, so they agreed to let him run an imprint instead. Little David launched in 1970 with Wilson's fourth album, *The Devil Made Me Buy This Dress*, which won the good-natured comedian a Grammy award.

Though their friendship was relatively brief, Wilson's support of Carlin came at just the right time. Born into an enormous New Jersey family, Clerow Wilson Jr. got his nickname in the Air Force, when fellow airmen told the hyperactive cut-up he was "flipped out." As a comedian he became a fixture at the Apollo Theater and other black stages, such as the Regal in Chicago, before breaking into television on *The Ed Sullivan Show* and *The Tonight Show*. By the late 1960s Wilson was well-known to the American audience for his signature catch phrases, "What you see is what you get!" and "The devil made me do it!" He had a wacky repertoire of characters, including the Reverend Leroy, pastor of the Church of What's Happening Now, and Geraldine Jones, a sassy, finger-wagging woman for whom Wilson dressed shamelessly, like Uncle Miltie, in drag. Following a highly rated special on NBC in 1969, Wilson's own variety series kicked off in the fall of 1970 with the British interviewer David Frost and Big Bird, the huge feathered puppet from the new *Sesame Street* children's series, as the guests.

The first thing Wilson and his manager could do for Carlin was give him a record deal. Three years after the release of *Take-Offs and Put-Ons*, RCA still held an option on Carlin's next album, though nothing was imminent. De Blasio felt no allegiance. It was safe to assume, he felt, that RCA would have little interest in helping Carlin reach out to the college crowd. "They were busy chasing Perry Como's next hit," he says. Atlantic, on the other hand, was an R&B and jazz label, home to giants such as Ray Charles and John Coltrane. The company had been making inroads with young rock fans, having recently muscled its way into the new arena by signing the British bands Led Zeppelin and Yes. It seemed like a natural fit. Monte Kay "loved to help people who he thought were outside the mainstream," says his daughter. "That's why he named the company Little David. It was always the little guys' rights he wanted to fight for." The label's logo was an illustration of the young David, who slew the Philistine giant Goliath, dressed in a tunic and carrying a slingshot.

Carlin's new managers began booking him into the old folk clubs and underground showrooms he'd effectively left behind after the Village years. Wald got him started with a meager $250 for a one-night booking at the Troubadour in West Hollywood, where Lenny Bruce was once arrested for obscenity and Richard Pryor recorded his debut album in 1968. Carlin had no complaint about the money, says Wald, "because he was doing material he wanted to do, and the audience was responding." Before the switch, he'd been earning a few hundred thousand dollars a year, much of it in Vegas. "I always brag that I took him from two hundred fifty grand to twelve grand," says Wald. "He was smart enough to know that if you do the work, the money comes."

In New York Carlin played the Bitter End and the Focus. At the latter, on the Upper West Side, owner Larry Brezner saw a nervous wreck who was unrecognizable to his own fans, who had filled the place to see him. "Everyone had come there to see George Carlin, but they had no idea it was him," Brezner said. "People walked right by him. I mean, nobody recognized him. He looked like any freak hanging out in the place."

In Pasadena he played the Ice House, then a decade-old folk den that was starting to handle more comedy bookings. He'd just bought a new Trans Am, which he parked on a side street near the club. During his set someone sideswiped the car, caving in the door. Carlin took that as a sign, a test of his decision to change direction. He'd splurged on "a nice, new, mainstream car, an old-fashioned toy," and now it was badly damaged. How much would he be willing to sacrifice for his comic peace of mind?

Significantly, Kay and Wilson helped their new colleague by inviting him to write for *The Flip Wilson Show*. Working alongside comedy-writing veterans such as Mike Marmer, an old television hand who'd written gags for Milton Berle, Ernie Kovacs, and Steve Allen, Carlin also made several appearances on the program. His first spot, in February 1971, featured skits with fellow guest Joe Namath and a two-man version of "The Newscast" with Wilson, rechristened the "What's Happening Now News," with the comics sitting at a pair of desks in loud plaid jackets. Carlin did Al Sleet and sports reporter "Biff Barf," who provided some new scores ("Cal Tech 14.5, MIT, 12 to the third power") and plugged an upcoming appearance at which he would be "presenting the National Two-Man Pallbearing Championships."

Also that month, he returned to the Ed Sullivan Theater for an episode that would turn out to be one of the last for the host, then approaching twenty-five years on television. The comic's new look was especially startling on the old, familiar Sullivan set. Young comedian David Brenner, also booked on the show, was a big Carlin fan. He made his manager promise not to let him leave without an introduction. After running through his own rehearsal, Brenner sat down in the theater to watch the other acts, which included the Everly Brothers, singers Shirley Bassey and Jerry Butler, and a unicycling team called the Brockways. "A stage hand comes along and he sits next to me," Brenner recalled. "He's got a beard, he's wearing a cap, and he's got on old jeans. . . . We sat there about a half hour watching the show." During a break, Brenner rousted his manager to remind him about introducing him to Carlin. "You were just talking to him for a half hour," his manager replied.

At the rehearsal Carlin told two topical jokes that came to the attention of producer Bob Precht, Sullivan's son-in-law, who had the unenviable job of informing rock 'n' roll acts such as the Rolling Stones and the Doors that they were expected to alter their potentially offensive lyrics. "Ed had a big tent," says veteran director John Moffitt, who got started in television as a production assistant on the show before moving up to the director's chair. At a time when households only had one TV set, Sullivan's show drew in the whole family. "The kids would watch for a musical group. The mom would watch for an opera star or a matinee idol, and the husband would watch for sports figures, like the Mets singing 'Take Me Out to the Ball Game.' So Ed was very protective—you don't go too far, one way or the other."

Yet Moffitt maintains that Sullivan is sometimes unfairly characterized as a prig. "Ed was, in his own way, very liberal. He gave black performers opportunities before it was fashionable." When Bob Dylan wanted to perform his "Talkin' John Birch Society Blues" on the show, Sullivan told him he could do it, but he was overruled by CBS censors. Dylan walked. Sullivan, says Moffitt, had no problem with Elvis Presley's gyrations; it was Standards and Practices that made the show shoot him from the waist up.

The first of Carlin's jokes involved the confrontational Alabama politician George Wallace, whose campaign to regain the governor's office was marked by racially charged rhetoric. Wallace, who would soon join the Democratic field as a presidential candidate for 1972, routinely referred to Northern elites as "pointy-headed intellectuals." Noting this, Carlin asked, "Have you ever seen the sheets they wear down there?"

The second joke concerned Muhammad Ali's ongoing struggle to be reinstated in boxing after his conviction for refusing, as a conscientious objector, to be drafted. Stripped of his title in 1967, the former heavyweight champ had finally been permitted to box again in the fall of 1970. Within months the U.S. Supreme Court would overturn his conviction by unanimous vote. Although his stance was unpopular in the mid-1960s, by the turn of the decade the American public was increasingly turning against the war, and a majority felt that the boxer was being unfairly punished. Ali's job, Carlin joked, was to beat people up. The government wanted him to kill people. "He said, 'No, that's where I draw the line. I'll beat 'em up, but I won't kill 'em.'" And the government replied, "Well, if you won't kill 'em, then we won't let you beat 'em up."

After rehearsal, Bob Precht told the comic that he could do either the Wallace joke or the Ali joke—but not both. "Oddest censorship I ever experienced," Carlin recalled. He chose the Ali joke.

Bringing that joke, and his new hair, onto the Sullivan stage was daring enough. But Carlin reserved his real television coming-out for a springtime appearance on *The Mike Douglas Show*, during a week of special episodes broadcast live from a seaside amphitheater at the United States International University in San Diego. Without preamble, he jumped into new material that he had tried out on the Sullivan show, a bit of poetic doggerel called "The Hair Piece":

I'm aware some stare at my hair. . . . But they're not aware, nor are they debonair. In fact, they're real square. They see hair down to there, say beware, and go off on a tear. I say, no fair.

Hair, and not just Carlin's, was demanding an inordinate amount of attention at the time. After an appearance as a morning show guest host on ABC, fellow comic Robert Klein had received a copy of a letter protesting the network's hiring of such a "sloppy and hippy character. . . . He is actually dirty-looking with that despicable hair and untidy appearance." Carlin would get a lot of mileage over the next year or so out of his "Hair Piece." It may have been a silly little poem, but it was also, like Krassner's "Fuck Communism" slogan, a masterful bit of cerebral jujitsu. He turned the audience's potential discomfort with his appearance back on themselves, by pointing out the absurdity of the cultural bickering about men with long hair. "I've had my extra hair for about a year now," Carlin noted. "Actually, it's the same hair I've always had. It just used to be on the inside."

He segued from the Vietnam jokes he'd done in Wisconsin into a parody of "America the Beautiful," satirizing our national urge to modernize the world by "whipping a little industry on them": "O beautiful for smoggy skies, insecticided grain/For strip-mined mountains' majesty, above the asphalt plain." (Fellow wordplay fanatic Biff Rose had printed a similar verse, "America the Ugliful," on the back sleeve of his 1968 album *The Thorn in Mrs. Rose's Side*: "Oh! Ugliful for racial skies—And ample chance for pain." Flip Wilson, too, had a signature bit that spoofed the song.)

But it was in conversation with Douglas, the host, that the comedian really made his case for his countercultural shift. Sitting in a director's chair under a sunny sky, Carlin said that he was working on a book-length collection of humor, *The Secret Papers of George Carlin.* He also explained that he was involved with a new nonprofit group, a public policy organization called Committee to Bridge the Gap, which he described as a growing network of college students reaching out to political moderates, "just trying to make it less fearsome for people resistant to change. . . . The planet and the species and the country are in a kind of emergency," he said. Two decades later he would amend himself. "The Planet Is Fine," he called one of his favorite routines, but "the people are fucked."

For now, though, he was happily enjoying his newfound popularity with the college crowd. Douglas told his guest that he could tell this was his type of audience. "I spent a lot of time in nightclubs banging my head against the wall," replied Carlin. "I started as a coffeehouse rapper about seven or eight years ago, and I'm really just coming home. That's all it is." Though old show-biz types were lamenting that the younger generation had no sense of humor, Douglas noted, "They're really just laughing at different things." The young America had changed everything, Carlin agreed. Music, clothing, morality. Why not comedy?

"The Myron Cohens, the Jack E. Leonards were becoming passé," says Jeff Wald. "People realize when you're false. The sensibility George had didn't fit the material he was doing. He was not being true to who he was. As soon as he became who he really was, which was a pot-smoking, hip guy, then the success started—the real success. I guess making a quarter-million was pretty successful, but he wasn't happy. He was getting into trouble. He was being a phony, in a way."

That spring Carlin stumbled onto another opportunity that gave him an added boost of confidence. Mort Sahl had been scheduled as the opening act for the rock band Spirit at the outdoor amphitheater of what was then known as Santa Monica City College, but he had to cancel due to illness. Asked to fill in, Carlin was nervous. Though he was doing the clubs again, a rock 'n' roll audience was another story. "I'd never done a real college-audience-in-the-Sixties kind of thing," he remembered.

With about 400 students in attendance, the show took place at midday. "These are rowdy rockers," recalls Uncle Miltie's nephew, Marshall Berle, who was managing Spirit at the time. As a young agent, Berle had signed the Beach Boys, Ike and Tina Turner, and others to the William Morris Agency before moving into personal management. At the college gig with Spirit, he was amazed that the promoter would book a comedian to open a rock 'n' roll show. "This was the psychedelic era, at a time when everyone was getting high," he says. "Carlin comes out, and he's getting laughs. I remember saying, This guy's got a lot of balls."

To Carlin's great relief and elation, the audience gave him a standing ovation. "I killed. I thought, 'This is it, man.'"

To make a great leap forward in his art—and in fact Carlin was beginning to let himself think of his craft in terms of artistry—he'd taken several giant steps back. How he got where he went next, he could never have predicted.

6

SPECIAL DISPENSATION

Habitually, Carlin came down on the side of the outlaws. That was rarely more clear than the night Specs O'Keefe came to dinner.

Joseph "Specs" O'Keefe was one of the masterminds of the infamous Brinks job in Boston in 1950. For nearly two years, eleven coconspirators planned an armed break-in at a downtown Brinks office, staging dry runs and removing various locks to have duplicate keys made. When it was time to carry out the crime, the thieves dressed in pea coats and Halloween masks, overwhelming surprised security guards inside. The immaculate heist netted O'Keefe and his cohorts nearly $3 million in cash and money orders, making the robbery the biggest in U.S. history to that point.

After a hit on his life failed, O'Keefe finally agreed to cooperate with law enforcement officials, only days before the statute of limitations would have expired. O'Keefe served four years in prison. Eight of his partners were sentenced to life behind bars.

Years later O'Keefe was in Los Angeles, working odd jobs under an assumed name. He met Carlin while making a package delivery—booze—and the comedian, always fascinated by the underworld, invited the ex-con to his house for dinner. Jeff Wald and his wife, Helen Reddy, were also invited. It was, says Wald, one of the most unusual evenings he ever spent. Both men were deeply intrigued by his background and perversely delighted to be in his company. (When O'Keefe died a few years later, says Wald, one newspaper claimed the thief had a circle of friends in show business: Wald, Reddy, Carlin. "It was hilarious.") Carlin, of course, was looking forward to getting away with a transgression or two of his own.

THE CELLAR DOOR was a lively folk and jazz room at the bottom of 34th Street in the brownstone neighborhood of Georgetown in Washington, D.C. Richie Havens and Miles Davis had both cut live sessions at the club in 1970. Over two nights in late July 1971, Carlin made the recordings that would become his first album for Little David. He called it *FM & AM*.

On the radio, rule-benders were finding they had a place to experiment on the new FM band. Whereas AM stations were often rigidly formatted, playing popular hits expected to help sell commercial airtime, many stations broadcasting on the upstart FM dial were providing a safe haven where the mind was free to wander. Carlin, the onetime disc jockey and lifelong free thinker, was intrigued.

FM disc jockeys played a haphazard mix of blues, jazz, soul, and fifteen-minute acid rock tracks. Rather than stick to the logbook, they often expounded at length on whatever topic came to mind. On KPFA in Berkeley, the first listener-supported station in the country, future literary critic John Leonard debuted his free-form *Nightsounds* program: poetry, jazz, and satire. In New York acting hopeful Bob Fass created WBAI's *Radio Unnameable*, an overnight forum in which the host featured regular phone-ins from Yippie agitator Abbie Hoffman and debuted Arlo Guthrie's eighteen-minute sing-along "Alice's Restaurant." At WBCN in Boston, a classical format was gradually phased out in favor of something called "The American Revolution," a mix of progressive rock 'n' roll and radical investigative reporting.

FM grew so quickly that its idiosyncrasies became an instant source of parody. In a ludicrously relaxed voice, Robert Klein lampooned the aggressively nonaggressive style of the "FM Disc Jockey" in a bit by that name on his first album: "We'll be bringing you the best in musical sounds these next thirty-eight hours." If FM was hash pipes, macramé belts, and mellow testimonials for macrobiotic foods, AM radio was pop-top beer, white leather, and strident used car ads.

Carlin saw an apt metaphor for his own career in the two radio bands. He had come of age in the entertainment world, first as an AM disc jockey, playing Paul Anka and "Theme from *A Summer Place*." As a comedian he developed an agreeable parody of his old career, mocking the canned, overheated delivery of his fellow DJs—"The *boss* jock with the *boss* sounds from the *boss* list of the *boss* thirty that my *boss* told me to play!"—and the disposable culture that bred them. His early work in comedy had been the equivalent of a hit parade for middle-class couples; now he was offering heady amusement for the communards and the war protesters.

With a recording truck parked outside the Cellar Door, Carlin spent two nights opening for the Dillards, the traditional bluegrass band that had portrayed a fictional act called the Darlings on *The Andy Griffith Show*. The Dillards had earned themselves some rock 'n' roll credibility by adopting electric instruments, a move that inspired the Byrds, the Flying Burrito Brothers, and many of the other groups of the Southern California country-rock movement of the late 1960s.

Carlin was back in familiar company, among the banjo players, collegiate juicers, and bohemian night owls. Still, he was unsure of himself. He worried that the audience he sought, many a decade or more younger than he, might think of him as "a counterfeit," a calculating entertainer "trying to cash in on the hippie craze." As eager as he was to turn the page, he could not quite bring himself to bury some of his old standbys just yet. The routines he cut for *FM & AM* included an update on "Wonderful WINO" featuring Willie West's successor (a new Carlin character called Scott Lame) and the vapid housewife Congolia Breckenridge, who joined her husband on an imaginary game show called *Divorce Game* ("Welcome to *Divorce Game*, brought to you by National Van Lines!"). There was also a primer on doing an accurate Ed Sullivan impression and, of course, a mock newscast. After Al Sleet bumbled through the weather report for the umpteenth time ("Tonight's forecast—*dark*"), Carlin's high-tenor anchorman remarked with a knowing giggle, "I think we know by now, Al's been into the mushrooms."

Those familiar bits would appear on the record's B side—the "AM" side. Carlin hoped to capture his old persona "in its final form," contrasting it with his new social perspective. If AM radio was "now being thought of as hokey and old-fashioned, full of commercials," he said, FM was hip, underground. The album's "FM" side made Carlin's metamorphosis unmistakable. Right out of the gate, he went autobiographical, recounting his dismissal at the Frontier—"for saying 'shit,'" he noted, "in a town where the big game is called crap."

Buddy Hackett said it; Redd Foxx said it. Now Carlin, too, was saying *shit*, without qualms or apology. It might have been seen as an act of defiance, if the bit weren't so deliberately congenial. *Shit*, he noted, is "a nice word—a friendly, happy kind of word." The middle class, he continued, has never been too comfortable with it, though it does slip out on occasion. Mimicking a homemaker who's just dropped a casserole, he squawked, "Oh, shit! Look at the noodles. . . . Don't say that, Johnny. Just hear it."

It was the debut of the new Carlin, the self-taught stoner linguist who instinctively recognized that the key to culture lies in how people communicate with one another. Observing that *shit* is almost always used in the figurative sense, he rattled off a series of common expressions—*Get that shit out of here, I don't have to take that shit, you're full of shit*. Like Bruce before him, Carlin was demystifying a taboo. Soon he would become notorious for it. The routine was called "Shoot," after the popular euphemism. "They can't fool me," he joked. "*Shoot* is *shit* with two *Os*!"

Other material on the "FM" side covered a broad range of hot-button issues, from the "Hair" poem and "Birth Control" to double standards about drug use and sexual innuendo. If it was easy to identify the subliminal messages of so many television commercials, Carlin joked, sometimes the intimations were bizarre: In his favorite dirty-old-man's voice, he croaked, "I'd walk a mile for a Camel."

After the second night of taping, he walked out of the club while Doug and Rodney Dillard and their band prepared to take the stage. Rodney Dillard had watched Carlin's act closely. The Dillards incorporated plenty of comic banter into their sets, and Cosby and Lily Tomlin were among the comedians who opened for them. Dillard thought Carlin had gone over very well with the group's audience. Carlin, however, felt otherwise. Aimlessly wandering the streets of Georgetown, he rolled his performance over in his mind and began to cry. He hadn't quite nailed it, he thought. "They weren't on my side totally," he recalled. "They *tolerated* me."

Though he may have felt that way about the small gathering at the Cellar Door, the record-buying public responded enthusiastically to *FM & AM*. The album was released in January 1972, quickly selling hundreds of thousands of copies and earning a gold record certification. Although he wasn't sure how his makeover would be received, it was suddenly apparent that the audience he was seeking had been looking for a comedian to call its own. Carlin's new album put him in some good company. Cosby's records, released at an annual pace, had been consistent top sellers for years, and Newhart's *Button-Down Mind* and Vaughn Meader's *The First Family* were bona fide landmarks. But whereas those records appealed to the Ed Sullivan audience, *FM & AM* spoke directly to the next generation. A classic example of an overnight success that was years in the making, the album presented a thoughtful, socially relevant comedian who, with his Christlike hair and beard and his embroidered bell-bottoms, now looked reassuringly like his evolving audience.

When *Rolling Stone* magazine, the countercultural Bible, interviewed Carlin that year, the comic explained that he understood fans needed to warm up to his new image. "It's natural for people to distrust what appears to be a change," he said. "Especially from entertainers. They assume you're trying to trick them somehow. That's because they've been tricked and shucked so many times already."

His record sales were undoubtedly boosted by Carlin's recurring appearances on Carson and *The Flip Wilson Show*. After an involuntary hiatus from *The Tonight Show*, he was welcomed back to the set in Burbank with open arms, making a rash of visits in 1971. According to Carlin, Carson and his staff had been reluctant to book him for some time. The comedian's confrontations were becoming common knowledge, and some in Hollywood knew he'd missed a taping for the game show *Beat the Clock*. "They'd heard about it in show business—'It's the acid,'" he said. At one point he'd gone in to see the mighty Carson to plead his case. He brought a new, tongue-in-cheek press kit that Brenda had prepared for him, which he'd signed with his left hand. Unfortunately for Carlin, as he later admitted, he was high on cocaine at the time, and his manic state didn't help his cause: "I went over to explain to him that it was a rational choice I had made. . . . The trouble was that I was on a coke run when I went over. I was kind of speedy, I had a tie-dyed T-shirt on, and I think it further distanced them from me." But Carlin was undoubtedly an entertaining guest, and he could always get a laugh out of Carson.

Just after the album release, he joined Flip Wilson on the *Tonight Show* panel. Before Carlin was called out, Wilson spoke about Little David's role in his friend's new direction. "It's an opportunity for George to feel freer as an artist, and for me to be a part of maybe, in some way, helping a guy that I admire," he told Carson. Though the host referred to Carlin as "Crazy George," the only thing outrageous about the guest was his appearance. His hair was now long enough to be pulled back in a ponytail, his beard was bushier than a lumberjack's, and he wore a form-fitting pullover over his twiggy frame. After amusing Carson with his advice for Ed Sullivan impressionists and noting that RCA had forbidden him to include the "Birth Control" routine on his first album four years earlier, he thanked his host and his colleague for giving him the television exposure that was easing his transition into the college theaters.

Carlin's generational appeal was confirmed when John Lennon and Yoko Ono chose him as one of several radical guests for their week in February as guest cohosts on *The Mike Douglas Show*. The former Beatle and his wife had recently relocated to New York, where they swiftly came under FBI surveillance. The couple knew something about censorship issues: Lennon's 1972 single "Woman Is the Nigger of the World," so named for a statement Ono once made about woman's subservient role in a male-dominated society, was widely banned from airplay. Lennon and Ono's guests for their week on the Douglas show included Black Panther leader Bobby Seale, consumer advocate Ralph Nader, and antiwar activist and Yippie cofounder Jerry Rubin.

On the program Carlin introduced a concept that he would keep in the act for some time. Calling attention to the absurdity of stand-up comedy itself, he came out and greeted the audience like a man inviting a visitor into his corner office. "Welcome to my job," he joked. It was a quintessential stoner moment—*wow, this is weird.* Midway through an otherwise straightforward set, he announced that it was time for his break. Sitting down on a stool, he stopped talking and stared off into the distance, stealing a glance at his watch. A seemingly small gesture, it was the kind of "meta" comedy that only became commonplace years later, in the disassociated humor of Andy Kaufman or Mitch Hedberg.

When Carlin joined the cohosts on the panel, Douglas held up a copy of *FM & AM* and pointed to a sticker on the cover. "It is recommended that the contents of this album are screened carefully before clearing for airplay," he read. Yoko laughed. Douglas noted that he'd never seen such a warning sticker on a record before: "Are they going to rate albums now, George? Is this an X-rated album?"

Though none of the material was that raunchy, Carlin's compulsion to challenge prudery with language was evident right on the cover. In a hint at the one-line non sequiturs that would eventually become a staple of both his act and his writing, his photo on the back of the album was framed in fine print with a couple dozen zingers, several of them off-color: "Beer nuts is the official disease of Milwaukee. . . . A car-raising contest is a jack-off." Although the longhaired hipster in the photo looked nothing like the product of a parochial school education, in such shameless juvenilia it was easy to hear the voice of the class cut-up doing time in Father Jablonski's detention hall.

The host also wanted to know whether Carlin's change had made him a better person, a better comic. "I don't know about 'better,'" he replied. "It's made me more efficient." His old repertoire of silly characters had effectively crowded out the real George Carlin from his own act, he said. "I was hiding behind these things. Television rewarded that. . . . I was not in my act anymore." This time, it was Lennon who chuckled empathetically.

Carlin may have felt more efficient, but he was again exhibiting some of the erratic behavior the entertainment industry had been leery of a year or so earlier. In the spring he missed a few gigs due to laryngitis. On one visit to *The Tonight Show*, Carson mentioned that Carlin had almost had to cancel. "I've been staying up a little late," Carlin offered lamely. A few months later he told *Rolling Stone* that his "laryngitis" was exacerbated by his new fondness for snorting cocaine. For most of his life, he said, he'd been waking up and getting high. "After twenty years of that, I discovered cocaine and how good that was. And what was scary was that I discovered I could afford it."

When a "German doctor" advised him to lay off the blow, he and Brenda had a heart-to-heart. "We decided to cut it all out," Carlin told the magazine. "We said, 'Well, we've been through the first half of our life stoned, let's try the second half straight.'" Whatever his level of intoxication, Carlin's career was suddenly flying. At the end of May he recorded a performance at the Santa Monica Civic Auditorium. The set became his second album, *Class Clown*. On July 3 he guest-hosted *The Tonight Show* for the first time. Five days later he sold out the main auditorium at Carnegie Hall.

Over the years, guest hosting *The Tonight Show* became a semi-regular occurrence for Carlin. Carson routinely used substitutes, taking most Mondays off and going on frequent vacations. Rat Pack sidekick Joey Bishop was the primary fill-in for much of the 1960s; Jerry Lewis was another regular replacement. Later, John Davidson and Joan Rivers, among others, served stints as Carson's regular guest hosts. Carlin, with his hair pulled back in a ponytail, wearing an airbrushed long-sleeve T-shirt, was an unorthodox-looking guest host, to say the least.

When he was offered the gig, he put in three requests for the guests he wanted to interview: Jane Fonda, Ralph Nader, and Lenny Bruce's mother, Sally Marr. All three were turned down. Fonda was preparing for the release of the documentary *F.T.A.* (alternately identified as "Free the Army" and "Fuck the Army"), an account of her "antiwar road show" with fellow actor Donald Sutherland, a sort of pacifists' version of Bob Hope's USO tours. Fonda would make her infamous trip to Hanoi a little later, in July. Nader, who was briefly considered as a third-party presidential candidate for 1972, was denied because of his relentless criticism of the automotive industry's safety standards; *The Tonight Show* was heavily supported by advertising from U.S. car manufacturers.

The disagreement over Sally Marr, Carlin recalled, was especially disappointing. "That was really the capper," he told *Rolling Stone*. "I had to call Sally and say, 'Sally, you won't believe this. [Lenny's] been dead for six years and they're still scared of him.'" Carson's producers did make a few concessions, booking the Committee, the hippie sketch-comedy troupe that had been on the *Smothers Brothers* show with Carlin; former pro football linebacker Dave Meggyesy, known for his 1970 exposé *Out of Their League*, which blew the lid off the inhumane culture of the NFL; and Dan Hicks and His Hot Licks, led by a psychedelic gypsy-jazzbo born in Little Rock but shaped by San Francisco's Summer of Love. (At the time Hicks and his band were in talks with Monte Kay to become the next Little David act, though it never panned out.)

"I remember thinking, Wow, they got some pretty hip people on the show," says Meggyesy. He had interviewed a year earlier with a *Tonight Show* producer who, he says, was a "flaming right-winger"; only when Carlin agreed to host did the show find time for the radical linebacker. The singer and actress Debbie Reynolds was the sole representative from traditional show business, but even she brought along a bit of political baggage: She had recently been in the news for her quarrel with NBC over its use of Big Tobacco sponsors for her short-lived sitcom, *The Debbie Reynolds Show*.

In his opening monologue, Carlin spoke frankly about his transformation, attributing his newfound self-awareness to his experiences using acid. Not surprisingly, the admission was omitted from the tape of the show.

With *FM & AM* selling like a hit rock album, the comedian was no longer scrambling for gigs. On the eighth of July he headlined a sold-out Carnegie Hall. Stand-up comedy had some select history in the old Italianate auditorium, onetime home of the New York Philharmonic:

Lenny Bruce had played there in February 1961, recording a charged set at midnight during one of the fiercest snowstorms ever to paralyze Manhattan. Brother Theodore, a legend of underground comedy who called his warped stream-of-consciousness "stand-up tragedy," had a standing engagement of midnight performances in the building's Recital Hall during the mid-1950s, billed as a "One Man Show of Sinister Humor." In 1961 the foul-mouthed comedienne Belle Barth, whose recordings included one called *I Don't Mean to Be Vulgar, But It's Profitable*, headlined; legend has it that her show was a failure, because she'd been warned to clean up her act for the billing. Mort Sahl, Bob Newhart, Jackie Mason, and Dick Gregory all appeared at Carnegie Hall during the 1960s, and Bill Cosby made his debut there in 1971.

It was prestigious company for Carlin. After a dozen years of hustling, alternating real achievements such as *The Tonight Show* and Sullivan with the disappointments of the supper clubs and the game shows, Mary Carlin's mischievous younger son was set to command the stage at the symbolic top of the show-business heap. He'd known how to get to Carnegie Hall all his life: He practiced.

In sharp focus, he did an hour and a half, relying heavily on new material about his parochial school upbringing, aversion to big business, and disdain for authority. Backstage at the reception, Mary appeared stricken. Elated that her "sensitive" son had earned a standing ovation at Carnegie Hall—Carnegie Hall!—she was nevertheless deeply conflicted that they were applauding his blasphemy and vulgarity. "She didn't know it had reached this level. She didn't know it had this force," Carlin remembered. "It was dawning on her that this tough, irreverent thing was OK in many people's eyes."

At the heart of the matter was a particular segment Carlin had been working on for months, recording it during the Santa Monica Civic show at the end of May. The piece was an expansion of the ideas about language that had caused him so much trouble in Vegas. Plenty of potentially offensive words, he reasoned, could be safely uttered on television, depending on their context. An *ass* could be a biblical donkey, a *bitch* a female dog, a *bastard* an illegitimate child, and so on. What, then, were the words that had no redeeming meaning whatsoever? The resulting routine, "Seven Words You Can Never Say on Television," was destined to become a landmark not only for stand-up comedy, but for the history of free speech in America.

There are 400,000 words in the English language, he reasoned, "and there are seven of them you can't say on TV. What a ratio that is! Three hundred ninety-nine thousand, nine hundred ninety three . . . to seven." Carlin's "heavy seven"—*shit, piss, fuck, cunt, cocksucker, motherfucker,* and *tits*—were the ones that would "affect your soul, curve your spine, and keep the country from winning the war." (When *Class Clown* came out later in the year, the album arrived with a front-cover "warning" that repeated this line.) Far from being a provocation, "Seven Words" was Carlin's attempt to expose the absurdity of outlawing words. His tone was playful, not confrontational: "*Tits* doesn't even belong on the list, ya know? . . . Sounds like a nickname, right? 'Hey, Tits, meet Toots. Toots, Tits.'"

Even the mainstream media recognized the gentleness in the approach. "He takes seven expletives and analyzes the meaning and use of each of them with the wit and skill of the most compelling professor of linguistics," wrote a *New York Times* contributor. "In the process, the *verboten* is rendered suitably ludicrous. It is an energized, intense, though never strident, and frequently hilarious turn."

Carlin wasn't alone. Adult language was becoming increasingly common in comedy by 1972. Lenny Bruce had left behind a small army of comic imitators who carried on the business of liberating four-letter words, and then wondered why they had difficulty getting booked on talk shows. Pryor, after radicalizing himself to the Black Power movement while living in Berkeley, had released an album the previous year called *Craps (After Hours)*, which not only made ample use of most of the words on Carlin's list, but also featured bits on masturbation, farting, and the mysterious legend of the "Snappin' Pussy."

Carlin found himself ideally suited to have it both ways, with his years of service in the pursuit of innocuous variety-show chuckles counterbalanced by the emergence of his genuinely rebellious nature. He'd once told his friend Bob Altman—the free-associating thinker everyone called Uncle Dirty—that he was going to show him how to perform the kind of subversive, socially incisive comedy they both adored, "and make a million bucks at it." Larry Hankin, an avowed Bruce admirer, suggests that Carlin's breakthrough was a matter of emphasis. While others simply complained that their language kept them from landing television bookings, Carlin drew fresh material from the taboo itself. "He turned the mirror on us, on the comedians who were saying 'fuck,'" says Hankin. "He made a hunk out of it, out of the complaint. . . . He pointed out the holes in the logic. And the best comedians—Mort Sahl, Lenny—they pointed out the holes in the logic."

ON JULY 21, 1972, Carlin was due to headline the main stage at Milwaukee's Summerfest, a multiple-day fairground event then entering its fifth season. Inaugurated in 1968 by longtime Milwaukee mayor Henry W. Maier, who envisioned an Oktoberfest-style celebration for his largely Germanic city, the festival was conceived with a distinct ethnic cast, including polka bands and a tribute to King Gambrinus, patron saint of brewers. The original name of the festival, Juli Spass— "July fun" in German—was quickly abandoned when various groups began lobbying city hall for a more inclusive concept. One protester recommended retitling the event the Fantastic Harlequin Kaleidoscope; organizers finally settled on the rather less fanciful Summerfest.

Adopting a something-for-everyone approach, the festival booked Bob Hope and Led Zeppelin, among many other acts, in its early years in scattered locations around the city. By 1970 the lineup had expanded considerably, including appearances at a new lakefront site by James Brown, Sarah Vaughan, and Chicago. An enormous throng, estimated at well over 100,000, gathered that year to see Sly & the Family Stone, whose late arrival fed the crowd's restlessness, nearly resulting in a riot. The *Milwaukee Sentinel* reported that "marijuana smoke was so thick in the area that if there had been a shift in the wind, a good share of the community of Grand Rapids, Michigan, might have gotten stoned."

Carlin's opening act at Summerfest was a blues group called the Siegel-Schwall Band. The group's cofounders, singer Corky Siegel and guitarist Jim Schwall, had known Carlin for some time. In earlier years, when he was spending a lot of time in Chicago, he'd become a fan of theirs at Big John's, next door to Second City in Old Town, where Siegel-Schwall became the house act after the Butterfield Blues Band hit the road. By 1972 they were already Summerfest regulars.

"The beer flows pretty freely at Summerfest," says Schwall. So Carlin was set to address a huge gathering of boisterous Midwestern hippies. Booked elsewhere on the grounds that day were Arlo Guthrie and Brewer & Shipley, the latter still enjoying the residual success of their 1971 hit "One Toke Over the Line." Despite the like-minded billing, bad omens appeared from the start. Carlin was concerned that the size of the audience might hinder his ability to establish a rapport, and he said so when he hit the stage. At one point during his set his microphone went dead, and the local newspaper reported that a woman climbed onstage twice to holler at the comedian.

As he worked his way through the "Seven Words" material, which had quickly become a signature part of his set, there was a sudden commotion in the wings. A police officer named Elmer Lenz heard the seven words while strolling the fairgrounds, and he was incensed. Hustling over to the main stage, he was about to stride into the spotlight and arrest the speaker on the spot. At the last moment, Lenz was stopped by fellow officers who'd been assigned to the backstage area, who convinced the irate cop to wait until the comedian finished his set.

The backstage patrolmen knew the drill at Summerfest, says Schwall. "They were specifically told, 'You're not here to bust the entertainers. You're here to protect them.' The stage backed up to Lake Michigan, about forty feet behind, and it wasn't at all unusual for members of the bands to go out on the breakwater and twist one up."

But Lenz's wife and young son were on the grounds. He waited until the comedian walked off the stage, then read him his rights. "I couldn't believe my ears," Lenz said. "I couldn't see why nobody was doing anything about it." Behind the many rows of logs and railroad ties laid out as seating for the main stage, there was a carnival midway, where nine-year-old Kelly Carlin was going for rides on the Tilt-a-Whirl and the Ferris wheel, accompanied by a volunteer from the Summerfest staff. The main stage had a powerful amplification system, says Schwall ("If you heard the band Chicago play there, you could pick out the individual horn parts from the back of the crowd"), easily carrying Carlin's voice beyond his immediate audience to the fairground attractions. There'd been no indication that he should curb his language, Carlin recalled: "No one said to me, you know, 'Your voice is going to carry over to the cotton candy dispenser, so we don't want you to do that.'"

As the comedian, wearing faded jeans and open-toed sandals, was being escorted away, Brenda collared Schwall and whispered a few terse words in his ear, something about George's denim shirt in a desk drawer in the dressing room. "I knew what she meant," Schwall says. "She didn't have to spell it out." The guitarist slipped into the dressing room, pulled out the shirt, and quickly pocketed the contents—a small envelope of cocaine. Moments later, the police searched the room. Though Carlin later joked that he'd made lifelong fans of the Siegel-Schwall Band when he left them with his blow, Schwall says he gave it to a Summerfest staffer later that night, after checking to be sure that Carlin would be bailed out. "When he gets out, he may want this," he said to the assistant, pressing the package into his hand.

Clearly Carlin had reverted to using cocaine, after temporarily quitting on his German doctor's recommendation. "Brenda and I laid off of everything for two months and then all of a sudden, we decided to celebrate the Carson thing and the Carnegie thing by getting high," he said that summer. "So now we know we can stop and be off everything and then all of a sudden we might say, 'Hey, let's have another one of those weeks of getting high.'" It was an attitude that would catch up with him soon enough.

When the assistant district attorney refused to file a state criminal charge against Carlin, Lenz and his colleagues turned to the city offices, which charged him with disorderly conduct, then released him on $150 bail. The promoters, meanwhile, tried to cover their own asses. Summerfest executive director Henry Jordan, a former Green Bay Packer, told one local newspaper that he "had no idea he was like that. I have seen him many times on the Johnny Carson show and I had no idea he would use that kind of vulgarity. Summerfest is supposed to be a family show."

Yet Carlin was not in the mood for apologizing. "I wouldn't have changed anything I did if I had known there were children in the audience," he told a local television station. "I think children need to hear those words the most, because as yet they don't have the hang-ups. It's adults who are locked into certain thought patterns." (Schwall maintains that Carlin, having arrived at night by limo and performing in the bright glare of floodlights, in fact may not have realized that there were carnival attractions nearby.) The whole episode was rife with irony: "I find it kind of funny to be hassled for using [the seven words] when my intention is to free us from hassling people for using them," he said.

Variety gave the story little attention, running just three paragraphs in a lower corner on an inside page the following week. Someone on the staff, however, couldn't resist a bit of editorializing. The last paragraph ran as a parenthetical editor's note:

> (Hinterland managers have expressed themselves to *Variety* that they just can't understand why comedians, who feel that "the kids loved it at the Bitter End and at Carnegie Hall," do not understand that provincial family tastes differ from what the hypersophisticated audiences will accept in the metropolitan centers.—Ed.)

Following his arrest Carlin contacted the law offices of Coffey, Murray, and Coffey, who were known in the Milwaukee area for their defense of Father James Groppi. Groppi, a liberal Catholic priest raised in Milwaukee's white, middle-class Bay View neighborhood on the city's South Side, became nationally known during the late 1960s for his vigorous civil rights activism. Campaigning for school desegregation and fair housing practices, he led numerous marches across a viaduct that stood as a symbol of his city's racial segregation. In 1969 Father Groppi led a sit-in at the Wisconsin state legislature in Madison with a group of about a thousand welfare mothers, protesting proposed welfare cuts.

Charged with contempt of the legislature, Groppi retained Coffey, Murray, and Coffey. "Our firm represented him all the way to the U.S. Supreme Court," says former defense attorney John Murray. "We lost in every court we appeared—the state courts, the federal courts, the Federal Court of Appeals. And the U.S. Supreme Court reversed unanimously in our favor. It was big news at the time."

Murray was the firm's attorney on duty the night of Carlin's Summerfest arrest. Around midnight he got a call from his partner, William Coffey. Murray quickly went down to the city jail, where he told Carlin he'd have him out in minutes. In fact, the comedian was held for nearly two hours. "They jacked us around, I recall vividly," Murray says. The police insisted on running a National Crime Information Center check on the comedian, "which was absurd," says Murray, "because he was nationally known." Finally released in the wee hours of the morning, Carlin and Murray regrouped at the posh Pfister Hotel downtown, meeting Brenda and William Coffey and his wife there to discuss how to proceed. The next morning Carlin appeared with his lawyer in the city attorney's office and was formally charged.

Though his defense team recommended he pay the fine, Carlin chose to fight the charges. Because the case involved a city ordinance, Murray advised Carlin that he could waive his right to appear in court.

Carlin's case, after being adjourned several times, finally came up for trial in mid-December. The prosecuting attorney was Theophilus "Ted" Crockett, a longtime member of the city attorney's office. "They threw the chief deputy city attorney at me," says Murray. "The police were very upset, in particular this Lenz. He wanted to bury [Carlin]—he was very, very angry." But Murray was familiar with the judge who drew the case, Raymond E. Gieringer, an out-of-town reserve from Adams County. "I felt very good after I knew Judge Gieringer was going to be the trial judge," says Murray. "Nothing much bothered him. He was pretty world-wise, even though he was from a smaller county in Wisconsin."

The city called one witness, a Catholic schoolteacher named Donald Bernacchi, who had attended Summerfest that night with four boys. Though he testified that he had been offended by the comic's language, when asked whether he had seen any disturbances caused by the performance, he admitted that he had not. One of the defense's two witnesses was a young assistant DA named Tom Schneider, who had been present at Summerfest. He was also the on-duty DA who had declined to charge Carlin criminally the morning after the show. Schneider, says Murray, "was a reasonable DA who saw nothing but trouble with that case." Had Schneider seen any disturbance that would amount to a disorderly conduct charge? No, he had not. What did he see when Carlin uttered the seven words? "I saw people laughing," he replied.

Murray argued that the show had been intended for a late-night audience (Carlin had gone on around ten o'clock), and that it had been clearly promoted as an adult-themed performance. He and his colleagues were well-versed in constitutional law, having handled many free-speech cases (including one concerning the first topless establishment in Milwaukee). Carlin's routine, they felt, was a textbook example of speech protected by the Bill of Rights.

The case was effectively decided when the judge permitted Murray to play the "Seven Words" routine from Carlin's new album, *Class Clown*, which had been released in late September. In Carlin's own voice, the humorous intent of his social commentary was unmistakable. When the defense set up a record player in the courtroom and put the needle down on the last track on side two, even Gieringer had difficulty keeping his composure. "The judge laughed through the entire thing," says Murray.

"Jeepers creepers, you can imagine," Gieringer recalled years later. "I tried to maintain as much dignity as I could under the circumstances."

For Murray, the trial was a bit of a good-luck charm. Several years later, having left the firm to pursue a career in civil law, he auditioned in Milwaukee to become a contestant on the game show *Tic Tac Dough*. Asked to offer a personal detail about himself, he mentioned that he had defended Carlin in the Summerfest case. The producers' eyes lit up. "I went to Hollywood and was on the show for two weeks," he says. "I made thirty-five thousand dollars."

Carlin wasted no time exploiting the notoriety surrounding his arrest. He joked about the incident on *The Tonight Show*, giving the persecuted words a group name, like the Chicago Seven or the Little Rock Nine—the "Milwaukee Seven." On the set of *The Dick Cavett Show*, he walked on to the strains of "On, Wisconsin," the official state song and the fight song of the Wisconsin Badgers. After Gieringer dismissed the case, Carlin told Carson he was indebted to "the swinging judge from up north." Even if the Seven Words themselves remained forbidden on the television airwaves, alluding to them was good for an easy laugh or three.

Despite the objection of vigilantes such as Officer Lenz, the "Seven Words" worked because Carlin made them go down easy. Six years after Bruce's death, the nation was a very different place than it had been in 1966. Carlin was becoming an unofficial ambassador of the counterculture, representing the hippie fringe to the mainstream. Bending the show business forum to his own devices, he was helping to explain the younger generation's changing attitudes to the alarmists from the moral majority. If people behaved badly and treated each other poorly, it wasn't the English language that was responsible. "There are no bad words," he argued, ever so gently. "Bad thoughts. Bad intentions. And *words*."

"It wasn't a rant. It was a shrug," says musician Chandler Travis, who met Carlin in 1971 at the Main Point in Bryn Mawr, Pennsylvania. "He was such a fan of Lenny Bruce. I think he did take some pride in being the guy who picked up that baton. I think he took that responsibility seriously, to the extent that he took much seriously. . . . George's natural proclivities led him to take [what Lenny did] and push it in a much goofier direction, much more benign."

Typical of the stages Carlin was then playing, the Main Point was a folkie coffeehouse serving gingerbread and brownies and, for those who needed a meal, plates of baked beans and bread for eighty cents. The talent the cramped space attracted was considerable—Cat Stevens, Dion, and Curtis Mayfield all played there in 1971. (A couple of years later, young New Jerseyite Bruce Springsteen made several appearances.) Travis and his performing partner, Steve Shook, were a frequent opening act with their musical comedy shtick, Travis Shook and the Club Wow. On one booking, they were scheduled to support a summer weekend for folk-blues guitarist and singer Dave Van Ronk, Greenwich Village's "Mayor of MacDougal Street." When Van Ronk had to cancel, club owner Jeanette Campbell booked Carlin as an emergency replacement; he had just spent a well-received Fourth of July week there opening for Tom Paxton.

En route to the gig, Travis and Shook were stopped by police in Fishkill, New York, where they were detained for possession of marijuana. Searching for more illicit substances, the cops found the musicians' Band-Aid canister, but somehow missed its contents—several tablets of MDA (methylenedioxyamphetamine), the narcotic then enjoying some popularity as "the love drug." When they finally got to the Main Point, Travis and Shook shared their remaining stash with the headliner, who in turn shared his own grass. It was the beginning of a professional relationship that would last nearly ten years. Travis Shook and the Club Wow became a regular opening act for Carlin, warming up the comic's third appearance at Carnegie Hall in October 1974 and enduring Groucho Marx's discouraging assessment—"These guys have been on way too long"—at the Roxy in Los Angeles. Carlin also helped get them booked on *The Tonight Show* a few times.

Like P. D. Q. Bach, the musical comedian Peter Schickele's fictitious son of a better-known Bach, or the concert pianist Victor Borge, who peppered his playing with gags, Travis Shook played a daffy mix of music and slapstick that appealed to Carlin's lighter side. "He liked the nonsensical nature of what we did, the anarchy of what we were doing," says Travis. "By any modern standard, there wasn't any anarchy in it, but it sort of felt that way at the time."

Another colleague who became one of Carlin's longstanding opening acts was the songwriter Kenny Rankin, a soft-rocker whose song "Peaceful" was about to become a Top 20 hit for Jeff Wald's wife, Helen Reddy. The artists on the tiny Little David roster looked out for one another whenever possible. Singer Dan Cassidy had made his lone *Tonight Show* appearance alongside Carlin in June. (After a short career in music, Cassidy went on to found a collegiate Irish studies program in San Francisco, where he wrote a book called *How the Irish Invented Slang*.) And Little David would soon release *Pure B.S.!*, an album of sketches by Carlin's old partner, Jack Burns, and his Second City cohort Avery Schreiber. Following on the heels of the comedy team's summer variety hour on ABC, *Pure B.S.!* featured the same kind of premise-driven humor, heavy on generation-gap satire, that Burns and Carlin had explored on their lone album together years before.

Whereas *FM & AM* was a validation, Carlin's next album was a true cultural event. The cover featured a photo of the bare-chested comic, in jeans and an unbuttoned denim shirt, sitting on a stool in front of a blackboard, pretending to shove a finger up his nose. *Class Clown* came out in late September 1972 and took off immediately. Curiously, given the comedian's prolonged effort to break with his past, the material focused in large part on his Catholic school upbringing. Routines such as "I Used to Be Irish Catholic" and the three-part title track were infused with nostalgia for the knockabout years of Carlin's childhood and adolescence, when he thrived as class clown. "You'd be bored, and you'd figure, Well, why not deprive someone else of their education?" he joked. Instigating inappropriate laughter had been the great joy of his childhood. Now he was making a career of it.

Ron De Blasio, his comanager, had booked the show into the Santa Monica Civic Auditorium, where the legendary concert film *The T.A.M.I. Show*, featuring the Rolling Stones, the Beach Boys, and James Brown, had been filmed in 1964. For a time the facility had also been home of the Academy Awards. Other than that, Santa Monica, where the Carlin family was living at the time, was still a lazy beach town. "I called it the last Midwestern town in southern California," says De Blasio. Though *FM & AM* was doing well at the time of the taping, De Blasio was nervous about his client filling the auditorium's 3,000 or so seats with a supportive crowd: "But I'll be a son of a bitch—we got an audience, and a great audience. They loved him. Absolutely loved him."

Onstage, Carlin reminisced about the endless ways to get laughs out of your classmates—knuckle-cracking, "Hawaiian nose humming," and, of course, making fart sounds in every way imaginable. The most basic—putting your tongue between your lips and blowing—has a scientific term, he informed the audience: "bi-labial fricative." "I was so glad when I found out that had a real, official name to it, man," Carlin said, sounding either genuinely blissful or especially high, or both. "*Bronx cheer* and *raspberry* never made it for me."

He explained why the act of swallowing happens in two distinct actions ("Your throat knows your mouth is crazy"), and he pointed out the sad symbolism of businessmen buying and selling prop gags such as fake dog crap and fake vomit—a topic, he acknowledged, that had once been explored by Lenny Bruce, who received special mention in the liner notes on the album's inner gatefold: "Special thanks to Leonard Schneider for taking all the chances."

The comic also spoke at length, with a surprising amount of fondness, about his Catholic school experience. It could have been any garden-variety parochial school—"Our Lady of Great Agony . . . Saint Rita Moreno . . . Our Lady of Perpetual Motion." Given the progressive ideals at the Corpus Christi School, however, his was not a stereotypical education by cruelty. Like Bruce, who dug deeply into religion as subject matter, Carlin found his schooling a rich vein of material, and he thanked the nuns and priests by name in the album's notes. Then, in an abrupt shift, the album closed with his one-two jab at unthinking patriotism—"Muhammad Ali—America the Beautiful"—and the tour de force "Seven Words."

When the Grammy Award nominees for 1972 were announced, *FM & AM* was on the list, alongside Flip Wilson's *Geraldine*, an *All in the Family* cast recording, and *Big Bambu*, the second album by a pair of bong-addled character comedians named Cheech and Chong. Carlin took home the Grammy for *FM & AM*, but it was *Class Clown* that really put him over the top in 1972. Club dates at places like the Troubadour and the Cellar Door, for a short time the comic's bread and butter, were quickly becoming a thing of the past. In November he finished a run of five dates at the venerable Palace Theater on Broadway, totaling a then-considerable box office take of $40,000.

Class Clown easily earned back the comparatively minuscule outlay of a live comedy recording, virtually carrying Atlantic Records, Little

David's parent company, for a time. One Atlantic salesman told De Blasio that receipts from the Carlin record and from Led Zeppelin's blockbuster fourth album together were covering the company's operating costs. "And the recording costs [for *Class Clown*] were probably what the crafts services bill for Led Zeppelin or the Rolling Stones would have been," says De Blasio. "Very minimal. They saw profits immediately. You didn't have to promote anything—he was just out there."

The acknowledgment of "Leonard Schneider" on the inside cover of *Class Clown* was clear confirmation of what plenty of listeners had been saying for some time: Carlin was the natural successor to "Saint Lenny," the fallen martyr of fearless comedy. As early as 1967, the newcomer had been making the case himself. Lenny's "use of obscene language is very simple for me to understand," Carlin told Judy Stone, "because Lenny was essentially a reporter, and he used the language of the people he was reporting about." There was, however, a caveat: Bruce, for the most part, preached to the converted.

"Seven Words" hammered away at the deepening wedge between the generations. ("The whole revolution is about values," as he said on the album.) But the routine, like almost all of Carlin's self-expressive comedy at the time, also helped explain the counterculture to the mainstream audience. Language, hair, getting high, opposing the war—all could be reduced to trivialities and made more acceptable in the process. For Carlin, the symbolic seven words changed everything. From then on, he would forever be known as the comic who shattered the language barrier, for better and for worse. Lenny, Carlin once observed, "was the first one to make language an issue, and he suffered for it. I was the first one to make language an issue *and succeed with it*."

SEVEN WORDS YOU CAN
NEVER SAY ON TELEVISION

◇　◇　◇　◇　◇　◇　◇

W alking in her Morningside Heights neighborhood one day, Mary Carlin stopped to speak with a couple of nuns from the Corpus Christi School, who were out on their own daily walk. How wonderful George's career was going, said the sisters. Mary put her fingertips to her lips. But what about the dirty language? she asked. She couldn't understand why her son had to talk like that.

The nuns, trained in the progressive policies of the Sinsinawa Dominicans—whose home base, ironically, was in Wisconsin, Carlin's bugaboo state—were quick to explain that they felt the comedian was doing a social service by underscoring the harmlessness of mere words. There was a method to his apparent madness, they said. For the first time, Mary Carlin began to feel that her son's peculiar brand of creativity might be something for her to celebrate, not lament. "She'd gotten the imprimatur from the church," Carlin once said. From then until the end of her life, Mary Carlin exulted in being the mother of the famous comedian, stopping people on the crosstown bus to tell them that George Carlin would be on *The Tonight Show* that week. Joining her son on the *Mike Douglas* set for a taping a few years after his breakthrough, she claimed to have told him from a young age, "Insist on being yourself always, in all ways."

"Mother, eat your words," the boy had replied.

He did insist, and he still had to fight for it. In the summer of 1973 Carlin was in New York filming segments for his first network special, to be called *The Real George Carlin.* Revisiting old neighborhood haunts—Grant's Tomb, the Columbia University campus—and taping some material at the Bitter End, he spoke openly about the conundrum of trying to get exposure without sacrificing integrity. Standing next to a life-sized cardboard cutout of his formerly clean-cut self, the ponytailed comedian told his audience that he'd just begun to let his true self into his act.

The program itself was a compromise, sponsored by Monsanto, the chemical company known as the leading manufacturer of Agent Orange and, until the chemical was banned, a top producer of DDT. The company, looking to improve its public image, was investing heavily in television showcases, producing an ongoing series of variety specials under the title *Monsanto Night Presents.* Henry Mancini, Jose Feliciano, Tony Bennett, Dionne Warwick, and Jack Jones were a few of the performing hosts.

A homecoming of sorts, *The Real George Carlin* featured music by B. B. King and Kris Kristofferson with Rita Coolidge, and several monologues shot on location by the host. It was produced by Jack Sobel, Lenny Bruce's onetime agent. Sitting in a trailer parked at Columbia, waiting for a camera to be repaired, Carlin told a reporter that he didn't expect to get more than 50 percent of his planned material approved for the show, even though he had been promised broad leeway. "Let's face it," he said. "TV is controlled by government and paid for by private industry. Certainly with that combination the result is bound to be mostly junk." He had recently received offers to host his own talk show and variety show, he claimed, but they weren't right for him. "I work best in an auditorium with 2,500 people," he said. "That's really where I belong." Taking the Monsanto offer was a test case: How much freedom would he truly enjoy? If it went well, he thought he might like to do a series of similar specials, maybe one a year.

Carlin felt a compulsion to question every convention. He entered each new business venture with suspicion, fully expecting that the freedoms he was promised were, on some level, contingencies. Smoking pot had unquestionably affected his worldview. "I take a perverse delight in knowing that I never did a television show without being stoned," he said shortly after guest-hosting for Carson the first time. But although marijuana may have heightened his already highly developed sense for detail, cocaine was affecting his performance in other, more insidious ways.

He began to stumble through some performances, occasionally missing them altogether. Scheduled to play the University of Bridgeport, he bailed out at the last moment, claiming that he just wasn't up to it. During a run at the 3,000-seat Capitol Theatre in Passaic, New Jersey, he mumbled distractedly, several times losing his place and asking, "Where was I?" At the Westbury Music Fair, an in-the-round theater on Long Island, Carlin allegedly antagonized the audience, claiming that "its suburban life was a forfeit on legitimacy." *Newsday* reported that a hundred or so patrons stormed out of the theater demanding refunds, "and a number of others just stormed out." The problem wasn't the content of his material, the paper suggested, so much as the fact that the audience simply couldn't understand what he was saying.

One particularly high-profile television gig was nearly disastrous. Dick Clark asked Carlin to host the second annual installment of *New Year's Rockin' Eve*. The first, ringing in 1973, had featured the red hot band Three Dog Night, along with Blood, Sweat & Tears, Al Green, and Helen Reddy. For the second year Clark chose to go with a comedian host. With the event expressly designed to appeal to a generation that had no use for Guy Lombardo's long-running dinner-jacket celebration from the Waldorf-Astoria, the hippie-dippy Carlin seemed the perfect choice. The performers, including musical guests Linda Ronstadt, Billy Preston, Tower of Power, and the Pointer Sisters, were prerecorded from the ballroom of the *Queen Mary*. Only the countdown to midnight was produced live.

Prerecording turned out to be the show's salvation. Though Carlin ran flawlessly through his material during dress rehearsal, he returned from his stateroom for the taping all jacked up—"on air," according to one crew member. In his overloaded frame of mind, the reeling comic attempted to do his act by muscle memory. It was ugly: He lost his place again and again, haphazardly mixing setups from one routine with kickers from another. In a panic, director John Moffitt, who knew Carlin from his days with *The Ed Sullivan Show*, transcribed the routines as they appeared on Carlin's records, then hurried into the editing room. Somehow he managed to splice together a reasonably coherent whole from the puzzle pieces he had to work with. Years later Carlin admitted that his only recollection of the show was a frantic Dick Clark, desperately pleading with him to do an acceptable lead-in to a commercial break.

Once he'd gleaned as much insight as he was going to get from dropping LSD and peyote, Carlin knew he was finished with them. "Cocaine was different. It kept saying, 'You *haven't* had enough.' I became an abuser almost instantly. . . . I started doing coke to feel open, but by that time, the hole had opened so wide that I'd fallen through." By his own admission, he often went four or five days before crashing, then slept nearly all day for a week or more to recuperate. The manic facial expressions and bodily contortions he struck for the cover of his next album, *Operation: Foole*, were the spitting image of a coke fiend, he later admitted. He had made the same faces for the cover of *Take-Offs and Put-Ons*, but those appeared in black and white, with Carlin clean-shaven, short-haired, and in a suit and tie. For *Occupation: Foole* he wore a multicolored tank top, letting down his hair from its now-customary ponytail. He was becoming the unreliable freak the industry had suspected a few years earlier.

Occupation: Foole was recorded over two nights in March 1973 at the Circle Star Theater in San Carlos, south of San Francisco. Opening with several minutes on his occupation—foole ("I'd spell it with a final *e* just to piss 'em off")—he joked about how no one goes right to work: "You might get there on time, but screw the company. Those first twenty minutes belong to you." Much of the material picked up where *Class Clown*'s autobiographical reminiscing left off, with the comedian showcasing his knack for mimicry as he described the ethnic makeup of his childhood neighborhood. He got some of his biggest laughs the easy way, with fart jokes. And he wrapped up with a lengthy (nearly twelve-minute) update on the "Seven Words," beefed up by what was essentially a rerun of the *FM & AM* routine "Shoot." The original seven words you could never say on television should be expanded by at least three more, he suggested on the new track, "Filthy Words"—*fart, turd,* and *twat.* Yet *fart,* as he'd already noted in the earlier bit, was too cute to be harmful. "*Turd* you can't say, but who wants to?" *Twat,* he claimed, is "the only slang word applying to a part of the sexual anatomy that doesn't have another meaning. . . . Even in a Walt Disney movie you can say, 'We're gonna snatch that pussy and put him in a box.'"

Stand-up comedy now belonged to the rock 'n' roll era, and Carlin was suddenly the leader of the band. Still a few years before Steve Martin would become wildly popular for walking onstage with a fake arrow through his head and the cast of *Saturday Night Live* would debut in bee suits, the comedians of the early 1970s were working with their most basic commodity—their words. And they were taking a stand over the words they'd previously been denied. Nearly ten years after Mario Savio's dramatic, impromptu speech at a University of California–Berkeley sit-in galvanized the free speech movement, a raggedy band of clever stooges were staging their own protest, of a sort. In Miami, Cheech and Chong faced four cops positioned at the lip of the stage, waiting to pounce the first time the dopers said the word *fuck* or any of its variations. Three of the officers couldn't help themselves and soon began laughing at the comics' material. During a bit called "The Dogs," with the two comedians crawling around on all fours, Cheech bounded over to the one cop who hadn't broken character and lifted his leg. "I 'peed' a long time on him," the comedian recalled.

Pryor, no stranger to coarse language, named his 1974 comeback album *That Nigger's Crazy.* Newcomer Albert Brooks, younger brother of *Smothers Brothers* writer Bob Einstein, was baptized by fire while opening shows for Sly and the Family Stone. He learned that he could command a restless audience simply by uttering one magic, drawn-out word—*shii-ii-it.* "*Shit* has saved my life," he told author Phil Berger.

"I know it sounds like a *National Inquirer* article, but it's true." Klein, who riffed on his New York boyhood on his debut album *Child of the 50's* much as Carlin did on *Class Clown*, examined the typically unexamined use of words such as *homo* and *whore* (pronounced, in outer-boroughs fashion, as *hoo-er*). And he needled his elders for their embarrassing habit of referring to body parts and functions with ridiculous baby names—tu-tus, boom-booms, poo-poos. "They wouldn't let me say *Jew-boy* on *The Tonight Show*," he said. "NBC, you know. Uptight. Too many letters from Alabama saying, 'Why didn't you say *Jew bastard?*'"

Forceful language was an increasingly newsworthy topic outside of comedy, too. In 1971 the Supreme Court had heard the case of a young war protester convicted of disturbing the peace when he brought a jacket reading "Fuck the Draft" into the Los Angeles Courthouse. By a vote of 6 to 3, the Court reversed the California Court of Appeals's ruling to uphold the conviction. Veteran Justice Hugo Black, a longtime supporter of freedom of expression, nevertheless agreed with the dissenting opinion written by Justice Harry Blackmun, who suggested that defendant Paul Robert Cohen's statement in wearing the coat was "an absurd and immature antic . . . mainly conduct and not speech." With a group of nuns reportedly in attendance at the hearing, Chief Justice Warren E. Burger took pains to ask the lawyers not to "dwell on the facts" of the case. In his majority opinion, Justice John Marshall Harlan made an observation that would become infamous in its own right: "One man's vulgarity is another's lyric."

Just after the release of *Occupation: Foole*, one radio station put that proposition to the test. On October 30, 1973, WBAI disc jockey Paul Gorman hosted a midday show known as *Lunchpail*. His topic that day was an examination of society's attitudes toward language. The volatile political dialogue of the time "was doing great damage to words, in my view," Gorman explained a few years later. On the program, he discussed the fact that the government dropped bombs through its "defense" department; meanwhile, the political Left was playing fast and loose with words such as "revolution." The host read excerpts of George Orwell's writing on language and invited comments from callers, one of whom wondered (as had Carlin) why the four-letter word for the act of love is also used as an insult.

The question was similar to those posed by a mysterious linguist called Quang Phuc Dong, whose satirical paper, "English Sentences Without Overt Grammatical Subjects," had been an underground source of amusement on college campuses for some time. The author's affiliation—the South Hanoi Institute of Technology, or SHIT—gave the parody away. Unlike a simple grammatical construction such as "Close the door," the author wrote, the phrase "Fuck you" cannot be considered an imperative statement. Saying "Fuck Lyndon Johnson," he claimed, was an epithet, not necessarily "an admonition to copulate with Lyndon Johnson." The writer was later revealed to be University of Chicago professor James D. McCawley, who was credited with establishing the fields of "pornolinguistics" and "scatolinguistics." Carlin, despite his ninth-grade education, was carrying out the professor's inquiry.

As part of the *Lunchpail* discussion, Gorman played Carlin's just-released "Filthy Words" routine. He prefaced the broadcast with a warning to listeners that if they were likely to be offended, they might want to change the station and return at the end of the hour. Except for the Carlin routine, the *Lunchpail* discussion was not played for laughs. It was, Gorman recalled, about the power of words—"the moral consequence of words, and the fear we have of words, and the way words arise from the culture and the way the culture redefines itself through its use of words."

Though its origins were benign, WBAI had developed a reputation for probing the issues of tolerance and provocation. A well-to-do New Yorker named Louis Schweitzer purchased the station in the mid-1950s as a pet project—he wanted to hear more classical music on the radio. The station began turning its first profit by the end of the decade, when it attracted new listeners seeking news and information during a newspaper strike. Schweitzer quickly grew discouraged by the amount of advertising required to make a commercial radio station profitable, and he decided to give it away. He contacted Harold Winkler, the president of the Pacifica Foundation, operator of the first listener-supported station in the country, Berkeley's KPFA, and a sister station, KPFK, in Los Angeles. Assuring Winkler he wasn't a crackpot, Schweitzer convinced Pacifica to take over the station.

WBAI began establishing its own identity when the radio novice Bob Fass urged the new owners to let him try out the after-hours show that became *Radio Unnameable*. "He played all kinds of records; he interviewed all kinds of people," writes the author of a history of alternative radio. "He allowed musicians to jam, live, in the studio; he did news reports, took listener calls, and sometimes, his colleague Steve Post recalls, simply rambled, 'free-associating from the innards of his complex mind.' Fass also pioneered the art of sound collage: He was surely the first DJ, and perhaps the last, to play a Hitler speech with a Buddhist chant in the background."

As the sixties progressed, WBAI became a well-known staging ground for liberal thinking in the New York area. The station's Vietnam coverage was groundbreaking, as was its reporting on the civil rights movement. Paul Krassner, a regular participant whose voice was doubtless familiar to listeners of Fass and Post's eccentric shows, once pretended to be a Columbia University student "liberating" Post's time slot during the occupation of the university by students.

About a month after Gorman broadcast the Carlin routine, the Federal Communications Commission (FCC) received a complaint from a Manhattan man named John H. Douglas. The correspondent alleged that he had been driving in his car with his son—some accounts claim the boy was twelve at the time, others, fifteen—when they heard Carlin's "Filthy Words." "Whereas I can perhaps understand an X-rated phonograph record's being sold for private use," Douglas wrote, "I certainly cannot understand the broadcast of same over the air that supposedly you control. Any child could have been turning the dial, and tuned in to that garbage." He had recently read about the FCC fining a radio station for a sexually suggestive call-in discussion program, he wrote. "If you fine for suggestions," Douglas asked, "should not this station lose its license entirely for such blatant disregard for the public ownership of the airwaves?" The complainant was

George Carlin, comedian.

*© Michael Ochs Archives/
Getty Images*

"Bing bong, five minutes past the big hour of five o'clock!"
Courtesy of Photofest NYC

Clowning with Buddy Greco
on *Away We Go*, 1967.

© Everett Collection/Rex Features

*The Smothers Brothers
Comedy Hour*, 1969.

© CBS/Landov

Unveiling "The Hair Piece" on
The Ed Sullivan Show, 1971.
© *CBS/Landov*

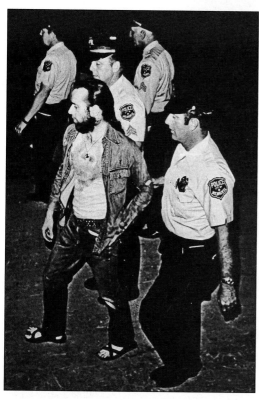

Milwaukee bust, 1972.
© *Associated Press*

Sticking it to the Man.

Manning the *Tonight Show* desk with guest Jimmy Breslin, 1974.

Bridging the generation gap: with Bob Hope and Flip Wilson, 1975.

© *CBS/Landov*

Discussing the Comedian Health Sweepstakes with Richard Pryor on Carson's show, 1981.

© *Associated Press*

In a rare penguin suit at
the Grammy Awards, 1982.

© *Associated Press*

Keeping a few thoughts
to himself, 1994.

© *David Keeler/Getty Images*

With Ned Beatty in the made-for-TV miniseries *Streets of Laredo* (1995). One of Carlin's proudest moments as an actor.

© *CBS/Landov*

Cameo in *Jay and Silent Bob Strike Back* (2001). Less proud.

Miramax/View Askew Productions/ The Kobal Collection

Aspen, 2007.

said to be a minister and a member of the planning board of an organization called Morality in Media, to which he sent a copy of his letter.

From its original incarnation as a neighborhood watchdog group in 1962, Morality in Media had grown to a position of national prominence. When pornographic material began circulating among sixth-grade boys in a parish elementary school, Father Morton A. Hill of St. Ignatius Loyola Roman Catholic Church on New York's Upper East Side quickly responded to parents' complaints. A Jesuit priest with snow-white hair, he spearheaded an effort to found a local antipornography campaign. Then known as Operation Yorkville, Hill's group was created as an interfaith coalition, including a rabbi and a Lutheran minister. By 1967 the neighborhood group had grown into a national organization, renamed Morality in Media. The group's profile was established when Hill, its president, was invited to debate the novelist Gore Vidal, author of the racy best seller *Myra Breckenridge*, on *The David Susskind Show*. When the U.S. Congress announced the formation of President Johnson's Commission on Obscenity and Pornography, Hill was appointed one of the commission's eighteen members.

Father Hill and his supporters believed that the president's commission was weighted heavily in favor of First Amendment "absolutists," and they felt their concern was validated when the commission's report was published in 1970. The report recommended increased emphasis on sex education for children and the decriminalization of all pornography for adults. Members of Congress and the Nixon administration expressed their outrage, adamantly denouncing the commission's suggestions, and the whole episode took on an element of farce when a publisher brought out a notorious illustrated edition of the report. In response, Father Hill and a fellow clergyman on the commission, Dr. Winfrey C. Link, collaborated on a dissenting opinion that came to be known as the *Hill-Link Minority Report*, which was read into the record of the U.S. Senate and the House of Representatives and would soon be cited in Supreme Court obscenity hearings.

When John Douglas filed his complaint about the "Filthy Words" broadcast, the FCC could simply have rejected it, because the petitioner couldn't provide the required transcript or audio recording. Instead, the commission sent WBAI a request for comment and a copy of the broadcast. The FCC was looking for a "test case" that would weigh the First Amendment against the commission's oversight of potentially offensive broadcasting, says Larry Josephson, a longtime WBAI manager and program host. "If we hadn't taken the case, they would've found some other licensee to go after."

Without an archived recording of the program, WBAI directed the FCC to the "Filthy Words" track on *Occupation: Foole*. The station argued that that the routine was protected under the landmark Supreme Court ruling—the "Miller test," devised in the 1973 case *Miller v. California*, in which a distributor of pornographic material was charged for advertising by mass mailing. In *Miller*, the Burger court had decided upon three criteria to establish obscenity: that the work appealed to prurient interest, that it was patently offensive, and that it had no redeeming social value. WBAI emphasized the social value of the comedian's work:

> George Carlin is a significant social satirist of American manners and language in the tradition of Mark Twain and Mort Sahl. Like Twain, Carlin finds his material in our most ordinary habits and language—particularly those "secret" manners and words which, when held before us for the first time, show us new images of ourselves. . . . Carlin is not mouthing obscenities, he is merely using words to satirize as harmless and essentially silly our attitudes towards those words. . . . As with other great satirists—from Jonathan Swift to Mort Sahl—George Carlin often grabs our attention by speaking the unspeakable, by shocking in order to illuminate. Because he is a true artist in his field, we are of the opinion that the inclusion of the material broadcast in a program devoted to an analysis of the use of language in contemporary society was natural and contributed to a further understanding of the subject.

To the FCC, however, playing the Carlin routine over the air seemed like a flagrant affront. Originally known as the Federal Radio

Commission, the FCC was created under the Radio Act of 1927 and charged with defending the "public interest" regarding the new medium, without infringing upon broadcasters' constitutional right to free speech. Legislators nevertheless saw fit to include a provision for punishing licensees who abused the privilege of the airwaves: "No person within the jurisdiction of the United States shall utter any obscene, indecent, or profane language by means of radio communication."

Until the 1960s the provision had little use. Most broadcasters, concerned primarily with attracting and keeping advertisers, voluntarily self-censored; for decades the FCC fielded only rare complaints. But the introduction of listener-supported radio removed the influence of advertisers from those stations. KPFA, WBAI, and their ilk could claim to be serving the cultural and educational needs of their audience alone—the hippies, the peace freaks, the rights activists, and other threats to the status quo.

By the time of the Nixon administration, in an increasingly permissible society the FCC began to see its job as police work. One college radio station was fined a token $100 for broadcasting a 1970 interview with Grateful Dead guitarist Jerry Garcia in which he repeatedly used the words *shit* and *fuck*. Two years later a station in Oak Park, Illinois, was fined $2,000 for the frank sexual nature of the discussion on its call-in "topless radio" show. In the early 1970s attorney David Tillotson, who would work for years on behalf of Pacifica, advised the owners of a Mesa, Arizona, rock station who were being threatened with nonrenewal of their license as a result of their repeated broadcast of Frank Zappa's sexual-escapade song "Dynamo Hum."

Politically the FCC was being pressured to clamp down. A federal study of television violence, cosponsored by the Surgeon General's office and the National Institute of Mental Health, was released in 1972. Its appearance set off a wave of indignant appeals by lawmakers, who demanded the FCC redouble its efforts to expel sex, violence, and crass language from the mass media. Congress's threats led directly to the establishment of television's "family viewing hour," which drew a hasty lawsuit from the Writers, Directors, and Screen Actors guilds.

In the case of Carlin's "Filthy Words" and WBAI, the FCC commissioners maintained that they were most concerned with the timing of the broadcast, in the middle of the day, when minors might conceivably have been listening. Loath to be accused of the dreaded *C* word—censorship—the agency delicately characterized its action as "channeling behavior, rather than actually prohibiting it." In lieu of a fine, the commission added its report to the station's license file, which amounted to fair warning. WBAI "could have been the subject of administrative sanctions," the commissioners noted in their declaratory ruling of February 21, 1975. Whether or not Carlin's work was intentionally "prurient" or could be shown to have redeeming social value was immaterial, the agency claimed: "Obnoxious, gutter language . . . has the effect of debasing and brutalizing human beings by reducing them to their mere bodily functions, and we believe that such words are indecent within the meaning of the statute and have no place on radio when children are in the audience."

Commissioner Glen Robinson acknowledged that he probably would have concluded differently had the monologue been broadcast at night. Despite the soft-pedaling, he could not resist making a withering value judgment: Pacifica's comparison of Carlin with Twain "strikes me personally as being a bit jejune," he wrote. "But no one should suppose that an author must be a giant of letters in order to receive protection for works which have 'serious literary or artistic . . . value.' The Constitution protects lesser literary lights as well as those with the artistic candlepower of Mark Twain."

The FCC's rebuke of WBAI in the Carlin case was hardly an isolated incident. The commission had been eyeing Pacifica for years, going back to the 1950s and KPFA's broadcast of a panel discussion about the *Howl* obscenity case and its impending trial. In March 1957, San Francisco police had arrested bookseller and poet Lawrence Ferlinghetti for selling Allen Ginsberg's allegedly obscene poem at City Lights bookstore in North Beach. For that program, moderated by Pacifica founder Lewis Hill, the station ran a voluntarily expurgated version of Ginsberg's epic poem "simply as a matter of taste," given the early timing of the broadcast. It got the FCC's attention nevertheless.

Well into the 1960s, the commission heard routine complaints about KPFA and its sister stations for controversial or inflammatory content—for a presentation of Edward Albee's *The Zoo Story*, for instance. The scrutiny increased as the stations stepped up their critical coverage of the Vietnam War. War protest being an unequivocal example of protected speech, the FCC acted instead on complaints of "indecency."

In defense, the network became a pro bono client of the Washington, D.C., law firm Arent Fox Kintner Plotkin & Kahn. Arent Fox, originally a tax-law office, had expanded to include several diversified practices, entering the field of communications law with the addition of attorney Harry M. Plotkin, who had previously been assistant general counsel to the FCC. Plotkin, a seasoned trial lawyer who would argue several cases with First Amendment implications before the Supreme Court, headed a team that had been representing Pacifica's stations for years by the time of the "Filthy Words" broadcast.

Thomas Schattenfield, a member of the communications practice who took the lead on Pacifica, says he always felt there were professional moralists keeping tabs on Pacifica's stations. The radical radio group welcomed the challenges, he says: "They were a bunch of bright young people trying to prove themselves to the world." Representing Pacifica in a hearing for new licenses for stations in Houston and Washington, D.C., Schattenfield had a terrible time with the judge. "I was looked upon as a Communist, evil guy—Satan in a suit," recalls the garrulous lawyer, now retired. "I was beat up, just beat up in that trial."

Schattenfield and his colleagues took to calling the predictable letters of outrage about WBAI's conduct "the '*Fuck* Complaint of the Week.'" "A guy would say he'd been listening to the station for three hours and heard the word seventeen times," he says. "Well, why didn't he turn the goddamn thing off?" In fact, the attorney had an unaffiliated client, a station operator in Iowa, who told him he too had played Carlin's "Filthy Words" over the air, without receiving complaints.

David Tillotson was a young lawyer who understood the cultural revolution Pacifica represented. While still in law school in the mid-1960s, he had served in a summer program at Arent Fox. After graduating he took a job in the Latin American bureau of the Agency for International Development, but his post was soon abolished because of what his superiors felt were Tillotson's leftist sympathies. He returned to the law firm in time for the license hearing for the Houston and D.C. stations. The unusual hearing, the attorneys believed, was less an administrative review than a referendum on Pacifica's pattern of behavior and a blatant violation of the network's First Amendment rights. Tillotson had his first taste of playing hardball with the commission when he was asked to draft a petition for extraordinary relief from the hearing. To the lawyers' amazement, the petition was granted. The FCC backed off, and the network got its new licenses.

With Arent Fox on their side, in mid-1975 WBAI and Pacifica appealed the FCC's ruling in the Carlin case to the U.S. Court of Appeals for the District of Columbia Circuit, arguing that the reprimand would have a chilling effect on future broadcasts. The FCC countered that its obligation to protect minors from inappropriate subjects took precedence over the station's First Amendment rights.

At the appellate level, Plotkin and his associates found a sympathetic court. "I don't remember a tremendous amount of sparring over those arguments," recalls Tillotson. The young lawyer was especially proud of an appendix to the brief that he had filed, which featured copious examples of "indecent" words used in respectable newspapers and magazines (including the *Washington Post*, which had recently quoted a White House photographer saying his trip to Vietnam had been "really shitty") and in literary works, including the Bible (featuring a Latinized version of one of Carlin's Seven Words, *pisseth*) and Hemingway ("We had more wire strung than there were cunts in Texas"). The FCC ruling was "overbroad," two of the three appellate justices determined. The decision set the stage for Carlin's historical moment—the Supreme Court hearing of *FCC v. Pacifica*. The comedian's rhetorical question—What, in fact, does it mean to have freedom of speech in this country?—was going to get a hearing. Better yet, he was not required to participate. Unlike Lenny Bruce, who drove himself to the brink by obsessing over his legal problems, Carlin himself was not on trial. He could sit back and watch, knowing that his comic premise—the "Seven Words You Can Never Say on Television"—had forced the judicial system to interpret precisely what sort of jurisdiction the FCC could claim when it came to taboo language.

THE CASE would not be argued before the Supreme Court until April 1978, nearly five years after the WBAI broadcast. In the meantime Carlin had a career to pursue, much of which still required him to watch his language.

He was making regular appearances on *The Midnight Special,* Burt Sugarman's late-night rock 'n' roll showcase, which aired Fridays on NBC, after Carson. The director was Stan Harris, who had worked on *The Smothers Brothers* and a short-lived precursor to *Midnight Special* called *The Music Scene.* Jeff Wald had leverage with the show, which was an ideal forum for Carlin's new direction, with its hip musical guests and raspy radio veteran Wolfman Jack at the announcer's microphone. After the pilot was sold, Helen Reddy hosted the inaugural episode in early 1973, with Carlin and Kenny Rankin making guest appearances. Two years later Reddy took over for a year as the sole regular host in the show's nine-year history. Carlin, the third comic invited to host the show, after Cosby and Pryor, was a frequent master of ceremonies until 1977, sharing the stage with Waylon Jennings, Glen Campbell, Lou Rawls, and many others. At one point he secured a billing for his friends in Travis Shook and Club Wow.

"I wanted to talk a little bit about words," he said during one segment for the show. "Words are—well, they're everything. They're true to you. They betray you. They say too much. They don't say enough." From the particular focus of the "Seven Words," he was unraveling his own clinical fascination with the entire language. For this appearance he stuck to a lighthearted analysis of nonsense words and phrases that we don't often stop to consider—*Kit and caboodle. Odds and ends. This, that and the other.* "I'll take this, and that." "You gotta get the other—it's a set." It was the sort of linguistic deconstruction he would later develop into a comic trademark.

His brief run with Wald and Ron De Blasio was coming to an end. Wald had stepped aside from artist management, concentrating on promoting his wife's blooming singing career. He still saw Carlin, his fellow New Yorker, socially. They took their daughters to horse-riding lessons in Malibu together. Carlin invested in the farm; one time Wald got testy with the rancher. "I was gonna go up and shoot him on behalf of me and George," he claims.

De Blasio stuck with Carlin for another year or so. By this time the manager was handling the career of Freddie Prinze, a fast-rising comic who would soon be starring in the NBC sitcom *Chico and the Man*. (Prinze, who committed suicide in 1977, was once romantically linked to Lenny Bruce's daughter, Kitty.) De Blasio was also on the verge of signing Richard Pryor. With his manager concentrating his efforts elsewhere, Carlin drifted into an arrangement with Monte Kay at Little David. Jack Lewis, Kay's right-hand man, handled the day-to-day obligations. Working with Lewis came naturally, as they were often on the road together. "There were no hard feelings," says De Blasio. "He was very comfortable with Jack Lewis."

But Lewis was a bit of a wild man, not exactly a great influence. Lewis, says Franklin Ajaye, a budding comedian who signed with Little David after cutting two albums for A&M, was "a very eccentric guy. Monte was very quiet, business-oriented. Very mild-mannered. Jack was kind of crazy and loud." Rankin, too, despite his gentle singing style, had a wild streak, says Ajaye, who often opened for Rankin when the guitarist wasn't on the road opening for Carlin.

While a law student at Columbia University, Ajaye had broken into comedy in the early 1970s by studying Carlin, Klein, and Pryor. Booked into the Playboy Club in San Francisco for a week, he had trouble connecting with the clientele. He had quit his job at a clothing store to take the gig. "It wasn't really a progressive place," he says. "I could only make the Bunnies and the band laugh." Told to shave his beard ("Comedians don't wear beards"), he protested. "George Carlin wears a beard," he said. "It was exactly the kind of place in those days that George wouldn't want to play. I got fired."

Little David had a small carpeted office on Sunset Boulevard, on the second floor of a Tudor-style stucco building that once housed an upscale auto dealership. Kay welcomed casual visits from the artists on his roster, who sat around with their feet up on the desks. "Monte was a very good business man. He cut very good deals," Ajaye says.

> His whole thing was creative freedom. Whatever you wanted to do, he gave you that freedom, and he tried to find the places that made it work. Obviously George couldn't play the swanky clubs anymore. It was almost like they created a market, which was the college kids. It was a very passionate time to be a comedian, a thinking time.

Yet the seventies were also clearly a decade of hedonism. Years of high tension over civil rights, Vietnam, and the generation gap were giving way to cultural fatigue, and seemingly relentless bad news such as the 1973 energy crisis and Watergate made many disgusted citizens long for oblivion. And comedy reflected that feeling. *Occupation: Foole* was nominated for a Grammy, alongside Cosby's *Fat Albert*, Klein's debut, and albums from *National Lampoon* and the impressionist David Frye. The award winner, however, was *Los Cochinos*, the third album from the stoner comics Cheech and Chong.

For his fourth album with Little David, Carlin moved away from the boyhood nostalgia that had dominated *Class Clown* and *Occupation: Foole*. *Toledo Window Box*, named for an imaginary strain of homegrown dope, had a cover image of the comic in a T-shirt illustrated with a bushy pot plant. On the back, the picture on the T-shirt was reduced to two barren stems, and Carlin had a bleary-eyed, blissfully vacant expression on his face. (The T-shirt drawings were by Drew Struzan, an album-cover artist who would soon be widely noted for his iconic movie posters for George Lucas and others.)

Recorded in July 1974 at Oakland's art deco-style Paramount Theatre, a lavishly designed former movie house, on *Toledo Window Box* the comedian was idly thinking up "goofy shit," with little design or theme. Other than brief bits on "God" (a primitive draft of the skeptic's rant that would end up as one of Carlin's last notable routines, "He's Smiling Down") and "Gay Lib," social issues were almost entirely absent from the set. With one eye on the new kings of comedy, Cheech Marin and Tommy Chong, Carlin riffed at length on drug use, poking around in nursery rhymes and fairy tales for illicit references. Snow White's Seven Dwarves, he suggested, were all users: Sleepy was "into reds"; Doc was "the connection." Carlin, encyclopedically knowledgeable about comedy, surely knew that Murray Roman had explored the same premise a few years earlier.

Though he spoke often about finding the real George Carlin in his material, on *Toledo Window Box* he relied more than usual on his stock voices, lapsing repeatedly into his seasoned New York accent and throwing in a little Wolfman Jack for good measure. He aired out a category that would become a Carlin staple, the absurdity of oxymorons—*jumbo shrimp, military intelligence.* And he frittered away much of the album on juvenilia such as snot ("The Original Rubber Cement") and, once again, farts. The album went gold, Carlin's fourth in a row to do so. Still, it was uninspired. The rush of his successful transformation was wearing off, and his binges were wearing him down. And Brenda was fighting her own battle, with alcoholism. She was involved in multiple incidents of drunk driving; at one point, before she went through rehab, her weight plummeted below ninety pounds. On a trip to Hawaii the couple were both so out of control that their daughter, not yet a teenager, felt compelled to write up a pact, demanding that they agree to stop using drugs. Putting Kelly in the middle of his and Brenda's addictions was his "biggest regret," Carlin recalled.

Within a few years Carlin would really be struggling to find a new direction for his work. "When I look back on those years," says Chandler Travis, "as much fun as we had—and we did have a good time—I felt like if I'd been smoking a little less pot, I probably would have produced more and the music would've changed quicker. I think that's true for George's stuff as well. He got into the whole hippie thing. There were some years there when he didn't know what was next. He wasn't that anxious about it. I think if we weren't all doping it up so much, he would've changed quicker."

With the exception of a few staples—*The Tonight Show, Mike Douglas*—Carlin's TV gigs were drying up. He did an appearance on Dinah Shore's daytime show, and another on a Gladys Night and the

Pips special that also featured Vegas regulars such as Sammy Davis Jr. and Robert Goulet. Worst of all, he did *Perry Como's Holiday in Hawaii.*

The seasoned host, wearing a huge white lei around his neck, introduced the bearded comic so that he could have a few words. "Yeah, I got a few words for you," Carlin teased, standing in front of the tiki torches. After breezing through a few innocuous words he joked were poorly coined—*hernia* should be "hisnia," *migraine* should be "your-graine"—he addressed the words with which he'd become inextricably linked, even for Como's luau crowd. There are, he marveled, more words to describe dirty words (lewd, naughty, foul, vile, and so on) than there are dirty words themselves: "Imagine all those words *describing* dirty words, and all I could think of were seven of them." He looked considerably less comfortable in a taped bit on the beach, in which he put on a Royal Navy officer's tricornered hat and knee breeches to portray Captain James Cook in a sad adaptation of his long-dormant "Indian Sergeant" routine.

There was one exception to the network mediocrity he was subjecting himself to, which turned out to be a major one, although no one involved could be so sure at the time. NBC was looking for something to fill its late-Saturday time slot. For years network affiliates had been running Carson highlights on the weekends, but now the notoriously work-averse host wanted to reserve his best repeats to fill the additional weeknights he was planning to take off. Impressionist Rich Little was considered for a show, as was the game show panelist and host Bert Convy. Eventually, however, NBC president Herbert Schlosser decided to go with something different. He invited twenty-seven-year-old Dick Ebersol, an ABC executive who assisted Roone Arledge in that network's powerful sports department, out to his home on Fire Island. Ebersol had just turned down Schlosser's offer to run NBC Sports. Determined to get this guy in the fold somehow, the company president made an offer: How would Ebersol like to take a shot at Saturday night?

The young producer quickly decided the show should set itself apart from Carson, the king of late-night comedy, by appealing to the generation under thirty. To line up credibility for the project, he convinced Pryor to come aboard. Pryor's commitment led to verbal agreements with Lily Tomlin and Carlin. But Pryor, who was growing increasingly distrustful of television and its restrictions, soon reneged.

Back to square one, Ebersol began discussing ideas with thirty-ish comedy writer and producer Lorne Michaels, who had written for Phyllis Diller, *Rowan & Martin's Laugh-In*, and the Burns and Schreiber show. Michaels had also produced a pair of specials for Tomlin. He was enthusiastic, and told Ebersol that he wanted to create "the first show in the history of television to talk—absent expletives—the same language being talked on college campuses and streets." The idea, he said, was to cross *Monty Python's Flying Circus* with *60 Minutes*. Ebersol told Schlosser he wanted Michaels to produce the show.

Before potential cast members were auditioned, the charismatic Michaels began identifying possible hosts. Albert Brooks was asked, but declined; according to Brooks, Ebersol and Michaels got the idea of using a different guest host each week from him. Robert Klein was approached. Eventually, with only months to spare, the repertory company began to take shape: Chevy Chase, Gilda Radner, John Belushi from the original Second City in Chicago, and Dan Aykroyd from its offshoot in Toronto.

Needing a known quantity to anchor the inaugural episode, Michaels turned to one of the show's talent consultants, Craig Kellem, Carlin's agent in the 1960s. Kellem recommended they go back to Carlin, who had experience filling in for Carson but was by now an icon to the rowdy young audience the producer hoped to attract. "Trying to get talent for the show was not easy," Kellem recalls. "Lorne wasn't that high on using George, but we needed somebody. George Carlin was still George Carlin." Kellem was a bit puzzled by Michaels's lukewarm response to having Carlin host. It wasn't as though the producer, who was becoming fast friends with pop stars such as Paul Simon and Mick Jagger, had no use for performers who'd been around a few years. "Lorne had his own vision of the who's who of the talent pool out there" in Hollywood, Kellem says. "Some of the people out there fascinated him. Pryor fascinated Lorne, and we did a full-court press. We flew to Florida, met him at a jai alai arena, kissed his ass every which way. For some reason, George Carlin did not have the same fascination."

Nevertheless, once the decision was made, Michaels was glad to have a name on which he could hinge the launch. Carlin, he joked to the press, was "punctual, and he fills out forms well." Still needing a director, he met with Dave Wilson, a television veteran who had recently worked with Jim Henson on the second of two pilots for *The Muppet Show*. Michaels, wearing a "Dracula Sucks" T-shirt and with his hair in a ponytail, was skeptical about Wilson, who was already in his forties. Looking for a way to dismiss the interviewee, the producer asked if Wilson thought he could relate to Carlin (who was, of course, himself nearing forty). In fact, he could. Dave Wilson was "Wacky" Wilson, the New Hampshire camper whom the boyhood Carlin had unseated as Camp Notre Dame's drama award winner. They were old friends, Wilson said. Michaels offered to say hello when he met with Carlin on his next trip to California. "I kept praying, 'I hope George Carlin remembers me,'" Wilson recalled. "Turns out he did, and Lorne, I guess, was sort of impressed by that." Wilson got the job, and he went on to direct more than 300 episodes of *Saturday Night Live* over the next two decades.

As the show came together, the NBC brass at Rockefeller Center grew suspicious. "What was this weird little show with these dirty people riding up and down the elevator?" Kellem puts it. During the week of rehearsals prior to broadcast, Dave Tebet, the network's head of talent, heard that Carlin was planning to step onstage with a soiled T-shirt visible under his suit. Tebet, worried that some undecided affiliates might choose to drop the show if it didn't appear professional, laid down an edict. Carlin would wear a clean T-shirt, and he should probably consider a haircut, too.

How Carlin would appear became "the major focus of the night, weirdly enough," recalled Michaels. "That was a much greater distraction than can possibly be understood." Ultimately the comic bounded through the audience onto the stage of historic Studio 8-H, where Toscanini had conducted the NBC Symphony, in a blue T-shirt covered by a jacket and vest.

Because of Carlin, the ninety-minute show almost didn't go out as advertised—live. NBC had debated using a six-second delay, so the producers would have a window in which to bleep any offending words. In the end, however, the delay was forgotten. Carlin had agreed to do *NBC's Saturday Night*, as the show was originally called, in part because he had a new album to promote. (Though Michaels had asked for fresh material, Carlin essentially did cuts from the new record.) After a "cold opening," a sketch about an immigrant learning English, featuring Belushi and *National Lampoon* alum Michael O'Donoghue, Carlin strolled onstage to the band's energetic theme and Don Pardo's excited introduction. "Talk about a live show! Wow," he said to the boisterous studio audience. Without further comment on the concept for the new show, he jumped into a routine from the new album called "Baseball—Football." It gave him a chance to make a drug joke almost immediately. The rules of football, he noted, had been changed recently: "They moved the hash marks in. Guys found 'em and smoked 'em anyway." The hunk, later expanded into one of Carlin's most beloved routines, pointed out the contrast between football's militarism and baseball's pastoral sensibility. Alternating between the steely voice of a combat officer and a little boy's innocent singsong, he joked, "In football you get a penalty. In baseball, you make an error—whoops!" The premise was surely influenced by his first guest-hosting of *The Tonight Show*, when he and Dave Meggyesy, the former pro football player, got into a discussion of the game's warlike lingo, its "bombs" and its "blitzes."

By his own later admission, Carlin had been on a cocaine bender all week. Getting only a smattering of chuckles out of one line, he asked someone in the front row, "Have I done these jokes before tonight?" Given the near-debacle of *New Year's Rockin' Eve*, it was quite possible he really wasn't sure. Still, he managed. He introduced musical guests Billy Preston and Janis Ian (Michaels had originally wanted Stevie Wonder and Carole King) and a short film by Albert Brooks. He did two more short monologues of absurd tidbits ("Have you ever tried to throw away an old wastebasket?") and one final set, well after midnight, questioning God and religion.

Although Carlin's presence undeniably lent the show some legitimacy, he also caused his share of problems on a very tense and nervous set. All week he had been unenthusiastic about participating in a sketch. Written by O'Donoghue, the sketch imagined Alexander the Great at his high school reunion. After dress rehearsal, with an hour to go until air time, Carlin told Michaels he wouldn't do the sketch. The producer had no choice but to cut it.

Carlin's allotted monologue segments also contributed to the show's first big internal controversy. Billy Crystal, whom Michaels had recently spotted at Catch a Rising Star, had turned down a showcase on a new Cosby special to appear on *Saturday Night*. At the last minute his six-minute segment was bumped from the show. Michaels was committed to keeping newcomer Andy Kaufman's "Mighty Mouse" lip-synching routine, a small masterpiece of modern Dada, and his only other option was to take air time from his host. "I probably didn't have the nerve to cut Carlin," the producer recalled. Crystal's devastation at being left out clouded his relationship with *SNL* for some time.

Then there was the matter of Carlin's last bit. Called "Religious Lift," it was a piece he'd been working on for several months. He had performed a version of it, with a blatant use of cheat sheets and the hoarse throat and grinding jaw of a man in the throes of a binge, on *Mike Douglas* a few months earlier. We're so egotistical about God, he joked on both shows, that we face our dashboard Jesuses toward us, rather than on the road ahead watching out for traffic, as they should be. The routine was incisively Lenny-esque.

As soon as *Saturday Night* ended, with cast and crew breathing a collective sigh of relief, Dave Tebet called from his hotel suite to complain to Ebersol about Carlin's antireligion soapboxing. The NBC switchboard was lighting up with complaints, he claimed. One caller said he was phoning on behalf of Cardinal Cooke, archbishop of New York. Heading home from the wrap party, a dejected Ebersol walked past St. Patrick's Cathedral, checking to see whether the office lights were on. On Monday morning he heard that the call had been a hoax. Try as he might, Carlin couldn't draw the ire of every archbishop in the country.

There had been talk of Carlin agreeing to host several episodes of the new show, but after the first one, neither side brought it up again. (He returned once, hosting in November 1984, during Michaels' several-season hiatus from the show he had created.) Despite a nationally televised plug for his new album—he had held up a copy of the LP, *An Evening with Wally Londo Featuring Bill Slaszo*, as the closing credits began to roll—the record was his first on Little David that failed to go gold. It did earn the comic another Grammy nomination, but Carlin was about to be knocked off his three-year perch atop the comedy world. Ironically, his appearance on the first *Saturday Night Live* seemed to underscore the notion that a new kind of funny was about to sweep the culture.

8

WASTED TIME

R obert Klein looked like a grad student still hanging out with the underclassmen. The thirty-three-year-old stood on the stage of the theater at Haverford College, a prestigious liberal arts school founded by Quakers in suburban Pennsylvania, on New Year's Eve 1975, wearing a preppy red-, gold-, and green-striped pullover, his wavy hair touching the back of his fashionably wide collar. The occasion was a television special called *An Evening with Robert Klein*, the inaugural episode of a groundbreaking comedy series, *On Location*, produced by an upstart cable television network called Home Box Office.

The idea was that comedians would no longer be confined by the time limits and arbitrary standards set by network broadcasters. Working for a privately owned, subscription-based company, they could do a full, uncensored set, just as they would in a nightclub. "This is mature," marveled Klein. "We're grown up. We can say anything. . . . *Shit*! How do you like that?"

Three years after Carlin debuted "Seven Words You Can Never Say on Television," Klein still hadn't listened closely to Carlin's records, not wanting to absorb his material or be daunted by his success. ("I remember I was scared, almost, to listen to *FM & AM*," he says.) The FCC's jurisdiction over the new cable network, HBO, was unresolved, and Klein, not an especially dirty comic—a few years later he recorded a routine called "Six Clean Words You Can Say Anywhere"—gladly took advantage of the opportunity. In a bit about an NFL broadcast on Thanksgiving, he joked about the inadvertent dialogue picked up by engineers and their "soundcatchers" at field level: After a tackle, he said, he distinctly heard a player holler, "I'll get you, Taylor, you cocksucker!"

"My mother dropped the turkey," Klein said with an impish grin.

Television was about to undergo a radical transformation. Cable programming would bring explicit content into homes across the country for the first time, and HBO was leading the way. Originally known as the Green Channel, the newly renamed Home Box Office went into operation in the test town of Wilkes-Barre, Pennsylvania, in early November 1972. In rough weather, a technician held the microwave receiving dish in place as the network transmitted its first offering to subscribers, the Paul Newman and Henry Fonda film *Sometimes a Great Notion*. "It is said that every successful business needs a dreamer, a businessman, and a son of a bitch," wrote one early chronicler of the network. Company founder Chuck Dolan, ousted just months into HBO's first year of service, was the dreamer; Jerry Levin, a former divinity school student and antitrust lawyer, was the businessman; and Michael Fuchs, who rose from director of special programming to president and then chairman of the HBO board, was considered by some to be the SOB.

Though the three major broadcast networks and American institutions such as movie theater owners and Major League Baseball all fought hard to block the incoming cable providers—abetted by the FCC, which envisioned itself protecting the Big Three from the interlopers—HBO got a major break when the networks declined to oppose its request to transmit via satellite. Meanwhile, the cable network challenged the FCC's claim to regulation by filing a lawsuit, scoring a significant victory when the District of Columbia Court of Appeals ruled in its favor. During calendar year 1976 HBO presented a potluck of programming, including an exclusive Bette Midler concert, quirky sporting events such as roller derbies and a rodeo held in New Jersey, and fourteen repeats of *Gone With the Wind,* in addition to its monthly *On Location* series.

Although the comedy show was new, the same wasn't necessarily true of all its talent. Fresh young comedians Steve Martin and Freddie Prinze followed Klein with *On Location* specials of their own, but so did known quantities Pat Cooper, Phyllis Diller, and language mangler Norm Crosby, as well as old revolutionaries such as Sahl and Berman. The series had already been on about a year and a half by the time Carlin taped his own HBO debut in the summer of 1977 at the University of Southern California.

The front office at HBO was well aware that Carlin could be counted on to make the most of this chance to speak his mind. As the comic himself said years later, the new cable giant came into being to solve a technical problem—"crappy reception"—but it was bundled with a big bonus for comedy: freedom. Three freedoms, to be exact: the freedom for stand-up comics to choose their own topics, freedom from commercial interruption, and freedom to use the entire language. The "Comedians' Bill of Rights," Carlin called it.

Stand-up comedy epitomized the kind of "event" programming HBO envisioned for itself, says Levin, the company president, who later went on to run Time Warner. "We were looking for something that would dramatize the nature of the medium itself—that is, subscription, free-flowing, and I don't mean just language. Comedy in a nightclub setting was a hard-ticket value item." Like boxing, the other signature presentation of the network's early years—HBO launched its new satellite feed system with a showcase event, the heavily hyped "Thrilla in Manila" title fight between Muhammad Ali and Joe Frazier—comedy had a rawness that suited the new venture well. Both featured lone gladiators in the spotlight. "Both, in a not-so-subtle way, reinforced to the consumer that they were getting box-office value from something even though it was coming through their TV set," Levin says.

Carlin's ninety-minute set, taped at USC in early March 1977, debuted just as the D.C. Court of Appeals's reversal of the FCC order on WBAI was being handed down. Determined not to self-censor, HBO nevertheless went to considerable lengths to cover its heinie. It summoned former *Life* magazine columnist Shana Alexander, known to television audiences as the liberal half of the weekly "Point/ Counterpoint" segment on *60 Minutes*. "A portion of Mr. Carlin's performance needs special introduction," Alexander said in a taped disclaimer that ran at the top of the program.

> His target is language—how we use it and abuse it. Some would simply say that tonight's language is very strong. Others would say it goes beyond this, and would find it vulgar. Aristophanes, Chaucer, and Shakespeare were vulgar too at times. Anyway, the segment is controversial.

Mentioning the court's ruling, she called the comic an important performer: "one of this generation's philosophers of comedy, defining, reflecting, and refining the way we see our own time." His act "contains language you hear every day on the streets, though rarely on TV." It was up to viewers to make up their own minds about the content.

"It was an adult medium, and people were paying for it," says Levin. Another of HBO's core concepts was to make R-rated movies available to subscribers. "I remember the first time I played an R-rated movie for some people at Time Inc. They were appalled that we were running that on TV. I said, well, that's the concept. If you can see it in a theater, why can't you see it at home?" Landing Carlin, the radical reformer of harsh language, was "a kind of capstone symbolism of what we were trying to do," says Levin. "If some people thought it was exploitative, well, then they thought George Carlin was exploitative. I personally thought he was one of the most brilliant, not just comedians, but commentators we had."

Another disclaimer toward the end of his HBO debut read "THE FINAL SEGMENT OF MR. CARLIN'S PERFORMANCE INCLUDES ESPECIALLY CONTROVERSIAL LANGUAGE. PLEASE CONSIDER WHETHER YOU WISH TO CONTINUE VIEWING." Not that he hadn't already cursed during the set. Doing a bit about cats, he'd noted how they make every clumsy mishap seem like it was intentional. After smashing into a door, he joked, a cat will go behind the couch to hide its pain. Only when it's out of sight will it react: "Fuckin' *meow!*"

HBO was happy to have him, but the broadcast networks were as wary as ever. Pop singer Tony Orlando, a close friend of Freddie Prinze, wanted Carlin for his variety show, which had a new name, *The Tony Orlando and Dawn Rainbow Hour,* for the 1976 season. After a couple of years on CBS, the show was being revamped as a sketch-and-performance show, mimicking *SNL* to a degree. "I was never quite sure of it. It seemed like a bit of a rip-off to me," Orlando recalled. "We weren't about being hip. But, if we were going for *Saturday Night Live,* who better than George Carlin?"

When his producer told Orlando that Carlin's drawing power was slipping and he might be available, the "Tie a Yellow Ribbon" singer implored the CBS brass to bring him in. As Orlando recalls, it was his duty to hand down the network's conditions: Carlin would have to trim his hair (he agreed), and he'd have to promise not to goad the Standards and Practices Department. "You couldn't even use the word 'pregnant' on our show, let alone anything stronger," according to Orlando. For his part, Carlin asked that his six-minute segments be followed by commercial breaks, so the pieces would stand alone.

In several episodes in the 1976 season, which turned out to be the show's last, Carlin worked hard on his contribution. After several years of packed schedules, he could sense that opportunities were dwindling. "You can't be the hot new guy in town forever," he reasoned. Each week he strode onto Orlando's stage with an old brown briefcase under his arm, pulling out a torn sheet of paper that read "Time for George" and pinning it to a bulletin board.

The segments were conceptual, covering such themes as "Time," "Age," and "Rules." They suited Carlin's clinical approach to comedy. In the first, he examined the various ways we describe time: "What's the difference between a jiffy and a flash?" We can never truly live in the present, he said. Just as we identify it, it's moved on to the next moment. "There's no present. Everything is the near future, or the recent past." The "Rules" segment explored the universal language of parental reprimands ("Because I said so!" "You'll break your neck!"). It was the kind of observational humor—a grown-up looking back at childhood—for which a young Jerry Seinfeld soon became well known.

Though the show was good exposure, Carlin was once again exploring a starring vehicle for himself. As a warm-up, he took a cameo part in the film *Car Wash*. Based on a screenplay written by future director Joel Schumacher, it was a slapdash, low-budget production calculated to bring comedy to the same audiences that had made sleeper hits of black dramas such as *Shaft* and *Super Fly*. Carlin's Little David label mate Franklin Ajaye, wearing his hair in an enormous Afro, had the starring role. Guests included Richard Pryor, playing a highfalutin preacher, and Professor Irwin Corey, whose surreptitious activity around the car wash makes him a suspect in a bombing threat. Carlin, who cut a deal to write his own lines, didn't have to stretch much to play a transplanted New York cabbie. In a striped T-shirt and a flat leather cap, he tells a customer, a drag queen played by Antonio Fargas, "I ain't got nothin' against you people. I ain't got nothin' against any people. That's what I think we need—more love in the world." Stuck in bumper-to-bumper traffic, he hollers out the window: "Ya bastards!"

"I probably talked to George on *Car Wash* more than I did at Little David," says Ajaye. "I was a young actor, making hardly any money. He was in and out in a couple of days." To Ajaye, acting was much easier than stand-up: "almost like a vacation. . . . Everyone from Don Rickles to Milton Berle, Jonathan Winters—every comedian can act on some level. You're already doing an act on the nights you don't want to be there [onstage]."

Carlin was at the Roxy when Ajaye recorded his lone album for Monte Kay, *Don't Smoke Dope, Fry Your Hair!* (1976), on which the younger comic made Carlin's language pale in comparison. Getting into college was easy for a black man in the wake of the race riots, Ajaye joked. All he had to do was write on his application, "I'll burn that motherfucker down!"

Motherfucker was still in its infancy. "It would seem to be an American Negro invention," wrote a British anthropologist in 1967, who marveled at how the word was "curse, expletive, epithet, and intensive all at once." The word was not noted in print until the 1960s, the writer claimed, and was probably "not much older" than that in common usage. Ajaye, for one, got plenty of use out of it: In one of his routines he used it to embellish a stoned trip with a friend to Disneyworld, in which a disgruntled Mickey Mouse calls Goofy a "bucktoothed motherfucker."

Now *motherfucker* and the rest of the Milwaukee Seven were about to have their day in the highest court in the land. The prospect of that kind of language rattling off the Spanish marble friezes high above the justices' heads was thrilling for some, and a looming nightmare for others. "As we used to say," says Thomas Schattenfield, "you don't want to get up in front of nine old men and say, 'Please pass the fucking salt.'"

Though Schattenfield had been the Arent Fox attorney working most closely with Pacifica, he had argued against appealing the FCC's declaratory order. The FCC's action on the "Filthy Words" complaint—putting a notice in WBAI's license-renewal file—had been, he felt, a "fairly decent" outcome. The Court of Appeals's decision in favor of Pacifica made the FCC's petition for certiorari to the Supreme Court inevitable. "My feeling was that by going to the Supreme Court, it would be nothing but disaster," says Schattenfield.

With Schattenfield absenting himself, that left the young Tillotson preparing the brief with a colleague, Harry F. Cole. The aging Plotkin, whose lengthy lapse during his argument at appeal had been a source of concern around the office, would argue the case. Tillotson was disappointed. "It was the one opportunity in my lifetime to argue a case before the Supreme Court," he says, "and I think I would've done a better job." Plotkin was known to be tough on the hard-charging junior partner: "He wasn't good at giving Tillotson a chance," says Schattenfield. Still, when the senior partner read the brief, he was impressed. "He told me, 'David, this thing sings,'" recalls Tillotson.

When the Court of Appeals ruled on the FCC order in March 1977, Justice Edward Tamm determined that the commission was in essence censoring Carlin's "Filthy Words." It was "a classic case of burning the house to roast the pig," he said, invoking an old line from Justice Felix Frankfurter. Chief Judge David Bazelon, who joined Tamm in the decision to reverse the FCC's order, made his own case. The critical point, he felt, was that the commission itself had characterized Carlin's words as "indecent" speech, which, unlike obscenity, is constitutionally protected. But the dissenting judge, Harold Leventhal, agreed with the FCC's contention that it was merely "time-channeling" such language, not censoring. His opinion gave the FCC's lawyers, led by Joseph A. Marino, a clear guideline for their Supreme Court challenge. (Leventhal, however, took it upon himself to comb through the complaint, questioning the indecency, for instance, of the word *tits*, "because it is neither a sexual nor excretory organ.") With the FCC petitioning for a writ of certiorari, the Supreme Court agreed to hear the case in January 1978.

Filing amicus briefs on behalf of Pacifica were ABC, the Authors League of America, the Motion Picture Association of America, and the American Civil Liberties Union (ACLU). Representatives of Morality in Media and the United States Catholic Conference filed on behalf of the FCC. The biggest surprise came from the Solicitor General's office, which had sided with the FCC at the Court of Appeals. At the Supreme Court, Solicitor General Wade McCree filed an amicus brief on behalf of Pacifica, and not simply because his office believed the appeals decision was not subject to review. "They took our view that it [the FCC order] had a broad chilling effect on First Amendment rights," says Tillotson, who had only recently convinced the FCC to back down from an attempt to sanction stations playing songs with lyrics that could be construed as promoting illegal drug use. "I can remember meeting at the Justice Department to discuss strategy. They were one hundred percent with us."

As both sides prepared their arguments, WBAI held a legal fundraiser in New York, headlined by Carlin himself. The event was hosted by Josephson, who would later correspond with Carlin about Bob and Ray, the old radio comedians, whose work Josephson produced for years.

The station also prepared an hour-long, news magazine–style recap called *The Carlin Case*, which aired on March 30. Solemnly issuing a disclaimer at the top of the hour, the station led with a reading of Douglas's letter of complaint, complete with its unexpurgated report of his hearing the words "*cocksucker, cunt, fuck, shit*, and a whole list of others." To provide some context, the producers conducted interviews with the writers Allen Ginsberg, William Burroughs, and James T. Farrell about their own obscenity cases. Communications lawyer Jeff Cowan noted the absurdity that few Americans knew exactly why Earl Butz, the former secretary of agriculture, had been forced to resign for comments he had made during President Gerald Ford's reelection campaign in 1976. Asked about the Republicans' loss of black voters, the cabinet member, notorious within the Beltway for telling off-color jokes, had said, "The only thing the coloreds are looking for in life are tight pussy, loose shoes, and a warm place to shit." Under the FCC's Carlin ruling, Cowan said, a radio station "would risk fine or lose its license" if it simply reported the news.

Given the *Miller* test, Tillotson felt certain that the Court would have to agree with Pacifica—that Carlin's routine, though potentially offensive, did not appeal to the prurient interest, and that it did possess serious literary, artistic, political, or scientific value. "I think our immediate feeling was that we had a clean First Amendment case," he says.

The Court heard the case on April 18. Josephson, for one, was "deeply moved" by Plotkin's argument. "The Supreme Court is a very magisterial, august, impressive institution, and it's designed to be that way," says the man who once joked that WBAI listeners were so loyal, the station could have scheduled several hours a week "of nothing but farting, [and] the program would soon have a large and dedicated following." But Plotkin wasn't as sharp as he had once been. During his oral argument, he was asked a hypothetical question. Suppose a radio station played an hour-long recording of someone simply repeating a four-letter word. "Under your definition," asked one of the justices, "would the FCC be powerless because of the censorship statute to affect that?" Plotkin replied that yes, he thought the commission "would be powerless to tell them to stop doing it." The attorney's answer, writes free speech activist Marjorie Hein, was "constitutionally sound but not very politically prudent."

Plotkin's misstep didn't help, but it wasn't the deciding factor. Rumor had it that Chief Justice Warren Burger, having lunch on the day before the ruling was announced with Frank Mankiewicz, then the president of National Public Radio, vowed that his court would never allow such language on the airwaves. Schattenfield had been right: Getting nine old men to agree to "pass the fucking salt" was a losing proposition.

By a 5–4 vote handed down on July 3, 1978, the justices reversed the Circuit Court's finding and sided with the FCC. The Court's newest member at the time, Justice John Paul Stevens, who had been appointed by Gerald Ford and unanimously confirmed by the Senate in late 1975, wrote the majority opinion. He emphasized the uniquely pervasive nature of broadcasting and the Court's belief that children were due full government protection from "indecent" speech delivered over the airwaves. By hewing closely to the facts of the case and acknowledging that the FCC was reserving the formation of broader guidelines in such matters for the unspecified future, the Court passed on an opportunity to clarify which speech, if any, would be subjected to FCC reprimand moving forward, says Tillotson: "They ducked."

The veteran liberal Justice William J. Brennan wrote a sharply worded dissenting opinion, joined by Justice Thurgood Marshall. "Surprising as it may seem to some individual Members of this Court," Brennan wrote, "some parents may actually find Mr. Carlin's unabashed attitude toward the seven 'dirty words' healthy, and deem it desirable to expose their children to the manner in which Mr. Carlin defuses the taboo surrounding the words." That there might not be huge numbers of such parents "does not alter that right's nature or its existence," he wrote. "Only the Court's regrettable decision does that." The adult individual's right to receive information, Brennan submitted, far outweighed the "minimal discomfort" of an offended listener "during the brief interval before he can simply extend his arm and switch stations or flick the 'off' button." Aiming the judicial equivalent of more than a few epithets at his fellow jurors, he lamented their "depressing inability" to appreciate viewpoints outside their own, calling it "an acute ethnocentric myopia that enables the Court to approve the censorship of communications solely because of the words they contain."

The decision was big news in Hollywood. "Court Bans '7 Dirty Words,'" ran a banner headline across page 1 of the *Los Angeles Times*'s final edition that day. A few months later, Norman Lear invited Carlin to join the ACLU's Southern California affiliate at a dinner called "The Politics of Humor." Fellow honorees included Lily Tomlin, *Doonesbury* creator Garry Trudeau, and Lear's onetime partner Bud Yorkin, with whom he'd produced *All in the Family* and *Sanford and Son*. Though Carlin did wear a dark suit—"that's as far as I go, even for the First Amendment," he joked—he couldn't take the event seriously, making faces across the table at his friend Tomlin all night long. "What the hell have two comics and a cartoonist really contributed to the cause of freedom in America?" he wondered.

Legal scholars were keenly interested, too. Commentator George Will applauded the Court's action in an opinion piece published in the *Washington Post* ("Is There a 'Periphery' on the First Amendment?"). In response, Nicholas von Hoffman, the *Post* columnist and onetime *60 Minutes* contributor, wrote a mocking piece headlined "Seven Dirty Words: A Cute Form of Censorship." Von Hoffman, who had been dumped from his television gig by *60 Minutes* producer Don Hewitt for calling Richard Nixon "a dead mouse on the country's kitchen floor," wondered why the Pacifica ruling hinged on the possible presence of children in the WBAI audience at two o'clock on a weekday afternoon. Surely, he reasoned, kids at that hour were "locked up in school taking sex education courses, where presumably Carlin's Anglo-Saxon terminology is replaced with Latin cognates on whose acceptability for broadcasting neither the commission nor our nine most exalted jurisprudes have yet to rule."

Just after Independence Day, the *New York Times* ran its own analysis of the case. The writer led by noting ABC's recent broadcast of a news special called *Youth Terror: The View from Behind the Gun*, which had featured "a good deal of street talk, including words never before spoken on national television." The fact that twenty-one network affiliates had declined to run the program, which the parent company refused to sanitize, was seen in the broadcasting industry as proof that the airwaves were not in imminent danger of being overrun by foul language, no matter how the Supreme Court decided. "Our network operates by its own set of standards that aren't affected by the decision," said the president of ABC-TV. Philosophically, however, the court's ruling set a bad precedent, he said, "with long-range implications on our freedom of expression."

In fact, the FCC stumped everyone by dropping the matter entirely. Incoming chairman Charles D. Ferris, who had succeeded Richard E. Wiley in October 1977, told the *Times* that he didn't consider the Supreme Court ruling a mandate to go after broadcasters. When the commission received complaints about *Monty Python's Flying Circus* from viewers of WGBH, Boston's public television station, who were offended by the show's "scatology, immodesty, vulgarity, nudity, profanity, and sacrilege," the FCC dismissed them. Incredibly, from the Supreme Court's "dirty words" decision until well into the Reagan administration, the FCC did not pursue any complaints at all about broadcast indecency. Mark Fowler, the chairman who took over following Ferris's departure in 1981, even seemed to agree with Justice Brennan's advice about the merits of using the "off" button: "If you don't like it," he said, "just don't let your kids watch it." Controversy over the FCC's jurisdiction in the wake of *FCC v. Pacifica* did not come to a head until many years after the decision.

For Carlin, although the outcome was disappointing, his indirect involvement in a landmark case of American jurisprudence felt like a validation. After all those years of being called in front of the principal, the priest, the barracks sergeant, and the boss, "those transgressions suddenly seemed like small potatoes." "That these nine men had summoned me into their presence to question my conduct absolutely thrilled the perverse and rebellious side of my nature," he said. "I thought, Even if I just become a little footnote in the law books, I'll be a happy footnote forever."

True to form, while the lawyers and commissioners were busy parsing the differences between obscenity and indecency and debating the true intentions of the Radio Act of 1927, Carlin cut to the heart of the matter. "All I want is a list," he said. "When I was a kid, nobody would tell me which words not to say. I had to go home and say them and get hit. As a result of the WBAI case, the Supreme Court has put the FCC in the same position as the parent. It can punish you after the fact, but it can't tell you beforehand exactly what the restricted areas are."

So he took it upon himself to collect them all, like a kid filling a binder of buffalo nickels. By the time his HBO special *Carlin on Campus* aired in 1984, the comic featured in his act "An Incomplete List of Impolite Words" that numbered 350. Two decades later, he was selling posters and T-shirts at his concert appearances featuring small-print lists of "2,443 Dirty Words." By then, he said, he was just the repository for this extended exercise in creative language. The credit was due to the hundreds of fans who'd sent him their suggestions, and to the anonymous coiners of words and phrases, from "butterbags" to "buzzing the Brillo"—"folk poets, all."

Timothy Jay, a professor in the psychology department at the Massachusetts College of Liberal Arts, has the unusual distinction of being a scholar of swearing. He befriended Carlin several years after *FCC v. Pacifica*, often providing the comic with his own lengthy lists of debatable words and their offensiveness ratings. The author of *Cursing in America*, Jay saw how Carlin grew quite serious about his role as the custodian of potty talk.

In Jay's opinion, the Supreme Court decision was simply "bad law." "One of the real weaknesses is that the government offers no evidence that there's anything harmful about this speech," he says. "We presume harm to children, when in fact they know all this shit before they get into school. It's not realistic. Anybody with a good sense of parenting knows that kids know all this stuff."

Shortly before the Supreme Court heard the Pacifica case, Carlin made a sly reference to the juvenile nature of his comic mind. Making a brief appearance on a celebrity-stocked salute to "Mr. Television," Milton Berle, he brought out his prized copy of Berle's joke book, *Out of My Trunk*, which an uncle had given him when he was a boy. Carlin had been a fan, he said, since the origins of *Texaco Star Theater*, when he was ten. "Thanks to your influence, there are still people who think of me as ten years old," he joked.

The attention given the case didn't quite carry over into his career. *On the Road*, Carlin's seventh album—the sixth in five years—had come out in 1977. It was the second in a row that didn't go gold. The album came with an eight-page insert, a "Libretto," which combined transcriptions of the album's routines with cartoon illustrations. The cover was stamped with an R rating—"Recommended for Adult Listening." There were some pedestrian bits on dogs and supermarkets, but Carlin was strangely preoccupied with death, from the cover image—the comic caught in the act of drawing a smiley face on a chalk outline at an accident scene—to a prolonged bit on "Death and Dying."

The exposition on dying ("It's one of the few fair things in life. Everybody catches it once") featured an observation that would become almost as much a staple of the comedy club explosion of the 1980s as the two-drink minimum: the prevalence of dying metaphors in comedy. Comics die. They bomb. An unreceptive room is like a morgue. On the other hand, when their jokes hit the mark, they kill. "Laugh? I thought I'd die."

Despite having done versions of this bit, with segments on funerals, suicide, and the afterlife, on the road for a year or more, Carlin was unprepared for the crisis he faced on St. Patrick's Day in 1978. Driving his daughter to school, he was bothered by an ache in his jaw and the feeling that the pain reliever he'd taken had gotten stuck in his throat. When the pain didn't subside, he drove to his doctor's office, where blood tests confirmed he was suffering a heart attack.

Besides the obvious abuses of his drug habits, Carlin hadn't exactly been diligent about his diet. "He'd come home after a gig and cook up half a pound of stove-top macaroni with a brick of butter," says one friend. "That was his midnight snack." Even after disciplining himself in the kitchen, the comedian lived with the prospect of further heart trouble for another thirty years. His father's first symptom of heart disease, as he sometimes pointed out, had been "a trip to the cemetery."

Within a few months of the first heart incident Carlin was back on-stage in Phoenix, reworking much of the material from *On the Road* for his second HBO special. Taped in the round at the Celebrity Star Theater, the performance took place a few weeks after the Supreme Court decision. When it aired, *George Carlin Again!* opened with a scrapbook-style slide show of the comic as a schoolboy and teenager, posing with various neighborhood friends and his dog, Spotty.

The ninety-minute taping was transferred to film for a proposed feature he had been working on for some time, to be called *The Illustrated George Carlin*. The story would follow his life from birth to death, using a variety of media. "There'll be a lot of concert footage with some cartooning and little vignettes," he explained. "As far as I know, no comedian has made a film with his own concert footage."

He opened the phone book and found a listing for an animator, Bob Kurtz. "I don't think anybody had ever found us through the Yellow Pages before," says Kurtz, laughing. Carlin and Brenda went over to see the artist, who listened to the comic's ideas for the film, then got up and drew a few frames off the top of his head. "Two minutes [after Carlin and Brenda left], I got a call," Kurtz recalls. It was Carlin, telling the animator he had the job. In the pre-cell phone era, Kurtz was dumbstruck by how quickly it happened. Where are you? he asked. "I'm across the street in a phone booth," Carlin responded.

The Illustrated George Carlin preoccupied Carlin for months. "In his very soul, it was the story of George," says Jim Wiggins, a comic friend of Carlin's who worked with him as a writer on the project. "Of course, there were so many layers, it was not really autobiographical." It was, however, "really silly."

Wiggins was the owner of a heating and air conditioning company in the Chicago area when he decided to sell the business and give comedy a try in the early 1970s. Like Carlin, he was a chronic stoner; also like Carlin, he could do a mean radio announcer's voice. Inspired by *FM & AM*, he started writing letters to Carlin. To his surprise, the comedian wrote back. When Wiggins took his first phone call from his pen pal, it was a request: Carlin would be flying in to play the Mill

Run Theater in Niles. Could Wiggins come by with a bag of grass? Wiggins caught every show that weekend, and a friendship was born.

For a few years Wiggins operated a Monday night comedy show in the back room of a gay restaurant known as Le Pub, in Chicago's Old Town neighborhood. Tim & Tom, the biracial act of Tim Reid and Tom Dreesen, were fellow regulars. One winter night Wiggins and his wife, Joan, who was pregnant with their fourth son, drove up to Milwaukee in an unheated Pontiac to bring Carlin another stash. Sitting on the edge of the stage together long after the show had ended, Joan spontaneously asked Carlin to be the baby's godfather.

Shortly thereafter Wiggins packed up his family and moved to Hollywood, where they put $8,000 down on a big old dilapidated house with an extension that had housed a doctor's examining rooms. Wiggins converted the place, a few blocks northwest of Hollywood and Vine, into a rooming house for aspiring comics trying to break in at Mitzi Shore's Comedy Store and Budd Friedman's Improv. Several months into the project, strapped for cash, Wiggins asked Carlin for a $1,500 loan to buy drywall. He'd repay it when he got his check for writing gags for Chuck Barris on *The Gong Show*, he said. Carlin sent a messenger with three grand and told Wiggins not to bother paying him back. Set the money aside, he said, as an emergency fund for the comedians staying in the rooming house. "Then tell them they don't owe it to you. Tell them to pass it on to somebody else."

Working to establish his own comedy career, Wiggins (who now calls himself "The Last Hippie") had the nagging suspicion that people would think he was deliberately emulating Carlin. "We could do wordplay like ping pong," he says. "We had the same kind of laugh, the same kind of attitude. It was always in the back of my mind." Working on a screenplay for *The Illustrated George Carlin*, they began spending afternoons in an old office Carlin kept in a Santa Monica building right out of a film noir: "Like an old detective's building, down a corridor with glass-paneled doors," Wiggins recalls. There they spent countless hours writing gags for the proposed movie. One day Carlin told Wiggins that their shared sensibility was likely to stand in the way of Wiggins ever becoming a well-known act. The death of Lenny Bruce had left a void for him to step into, he said. "You're not that lucky. I'm not gonna die." When Carlin was hospitalized, Wiggins sent him a telegram:

Dear George,
Try again.

As Wiggins remembers it, Carlin finally abandoned the film project after a lengthy series of negotiations with the Canadian Film Board. He called his writing partner into the office to deliver the bad news. He couldn't get an agreement on the level of control he wanted. "Wigs," he said, "remember—if you ain't got control, you ain't got shit."

At the end of 1978 Little David put out what would prove to be its last Carlin album, a compilation intended to capitalize on the notoriety of the Pacifica case. Smartly titled *Indecent Exposure*, it was a best-of collection specifically focused on the comic's taboo topics and forbidden language, with routines including "Sex in Commercials," "Bodily Functions," and "Teenage Masturbation," bookended, of course, by "Seven Words" and "Filthy Words." The cover pictured Carlin in another pose connecting his comedy to crime—wearing a pair of running shoes and a flasher's overcoat. As much as the dirty words had made him a household name, he was ready to move on. "Frankly, I feel dated, because I've continued to do that material for so long that I feel a bit of a prisoner," he said.

For Carlin, the next couple of years were wilderness years, a time for regrouping. "It was like a breathing-in period," he reflected. "Everything can't be constantly on an upswing. Nature shows you there's inhale and exhale. . . . Other people would call it 'His career was going in the shithouse.'"

Gradually weaning himself off his cocaine habit, he was emotionally drained. His continued use strained his relationship with Brenda, who was working hard to stay sober. Their relationship was not always a happy one. Carlin admitted on occasion to physical altercations with his wife during his drug years. Even so, their love for each other was apparent. "They had this wonderful rapport," says Bob Kurtz, who watched the couple hug like honeymooners during the recording sessions he conducted for Carlin's voiceover.

Carlin also learned that he had major problems with the IRS. He had seriously neglected his taxes, which he blamed on bad advice and his own cocaine habit. "By the time 1980 arrived," he recalled, "I believe I was about two million dollars upside down with the IRS, and it got to be another million before the saga was finished." He had a new manager, a regional promoter named Jerry Hamza, a native of Rochester, New York, who had booked some of Carlin's shows before agreeing to handle the comic's career. Before handling Carlin, Hamza had specialized in country music, organizing appearances by iconic artists such as Johnny Cash, George Jones, Merle Haggard, and Loretta Lynn. With Hamza's help, the comedian began the long, grueling task of paying off his enormous debt.

His personal problems were affecting his ability to see where his career was headed. He knew it, but he was philosophical about it. "My album career had faded, and I didn't have a personal vision of myself anymore," he said. "I'd gone through my autobiographical stage. Then I started to get into what they call 'observational' comedy—these things that have no importance at all, but they're universal. . . . It was a casting about, a wallowing in the backwater of this career success I'd had."

He agreed to a guest appearance on *Welcome Back, Kotter*, the ABC sitcom starring the former Village comic Gabe Kaplan as a high school teacher returning to his old Brooklyn neighborhood. Carlin played Wally "The Wow" Wechsel, a popular disc jockey who was once one of the Sweathogs, the remedial students who were the stars of the show. Somewhat more intriguing was the gig he took narrating *Americathon*, a weirdly prescient futuristic scenario written by the Firesign Theatre's Phil Proctor and Peter Bergman, who had established their loony brand of sketch comedy on Pacifica's KPFK. With an ensemble cast including John Ritter, Fred Willard, a young Jay Leno, and the new wave rock 'n' roller Elvis Costello, the movie imagined the United States two decades down the road, in the year 1998. Having run out of oil and on the verge of bankruptcy, the government sponsors a telethon. Not only did this now out-of-print film predict a rash of eventualities (such as China's compromise with capitalism) that seemed ludicrous at the end of the 1970s, it also neatly predicted the gleeful doomsday prophesies of the latter years of Carlin's own career.

He continued to make a handful of *Tonight Show* appearances each year, working out his new material on the national stage. (Carlin would claim to have done the show 105 times by the time Carson retired in 1992.) He and Muhammad Ali were two of the guests on an episode guest-hosted by Diana Ross; he appeared with Richard Pryor not long after Pryor's infamous freebasing accident. During one guest-hosting spot in early 1981, he sat at a desk during the monologue and trotted out the latest version of his old standby, the mock newscast. One item involved the "Gay Liberation Front, who along with the Tall People's Association have announced they will oppose the Army Corps of Engineers next week when it attempts to destroy a fifty-foot dike." With Debbie Reynolds once again a guest, as she had been on his first guest-hosting night in 1972, Carlin rounded out the episode by discussing sexual fantasies and men's beards with Dr. Joyce Brothers.

At the end of the 1970s, comedy in America was on the verge of its own kind of gold rush, with thousands of prospectors and a fortunate few who would cash in. The folk clubs of the sixties, with their regular showcase opportunities for comedians, were almost a thing of the past. The momentary heat of the disco scene was also fading fast. The vast disillusionments of the 1970s—war, political corruption, garbage strikes, hostage situations—left a gaping opportunity for comic relief, and nightclubs devoted to comedy soon began popping up in cities across the country. In LA, the Improv and the Comedy Store faced fresh competition with the opening of the Laugh Factory in 1979. Two years later Caroline Hirsch opened the original Caroline's in New York, where the Improv, Catch a Rising Star, and Comic Strip were already fixtures. Boston, another fertile breeding ground that would produce Leno, Steven Wright, and Paula Poundstone, among many others, had the Ding Ho, Nick's Comedy Stop, and the Comedy Connection.

In San Francisco's financial district, the entrepreneur behind a rock venue called the Old Waldorf converted the room's former backstage area into an English pub for the lunch crowd, then asked a local promoter to turn the space into a comedy club at night. That place became the Punch Line. With Cobb's Comedy Club just up Columbus in Fisherman's Wharf and a hovel called the Holy City Zoo out in the Richmond district, San Francisco soon renewed its reputation as a comedy mecca. Homegrown talent such as Robin Williams, Dana Carvey, and Bobby Slayton crossed paths nightly with carpetbaggers like Poundstone and Ellen DeGeneres.

The rise of *Saturday Night Live* was often credited as one reason for the resurgence of interest in comedy. Another was HBO, which was reminding home viewers of the pleasure of seeing a comic craftsman work in long form, as opposed to the six-minute allotments of talk show appearances. "If you were in Birmingham, Alabama, and said 'stand-up comedy,' people would think Bob Hope," said one veteran standup. "It took cable to expose America to comedy as an art form."

Carlin, of course, was well beyond the nightclub stage by this time. Having established that the rock 'n' roll crowd would pay to see a comedy star in a concert setting, he had helped clear the path for major concert draws such as Cheech and Chong, Steve Martin, and Eddie Murphy. Ironically, the new emphasis on club comics had the effect of pushing Carlin off into his own realm.

He was a hero to many of the new generation of comics, who loved the twisted recesses of his mind and his insistence on concise language. "There are so many comedians that wanted to be a comedian because of him," says Steven Wright. "What a brain he had." But Carlin was also considerably older than the new breed, turning forty-four in 1981. He'd been too young for Lenny's generation and too old for *SNL*, and now he was too successful to join the fraternity of the clubs. He had become an island—a creature of show business who would just as soon have nothing to do with show business. His record sales had dropped off, his movie had fallen through, and he didn't know where the HBO affiliation would lead. It would be some time before he realized that his unique voice had only begun to develop.

9

AMERICA THE BEAUTIFUL

◇　◇　◇　.◇　◇　◇　◇

Carlin's resurrection began, funnily enough, just after his second heart attack in the summer of 1982. Scheduled to tape his third HBO special, this time at Carnegie Hall, Carlin suffered a much more serious heart attack than the first, while watching a baseball game at Dodger Stadium. After checking into the hospital, he was flown to Atlanta, where an Emory University Hospital surgeon named Andreas Gruentzig was experimenting with balloon angioplasty, at that time an innovative method of opening obstructed arteries. Carlin was an early recipient of the treatment.

A year before the heart attack, he'd had an accident behind the wheel. Driving from Toronto to Dayton, where Brenda was visiting family, he hit a utility pole in the early morning hours in downtown Dayton, breaking his nose and suffering cuts on his face. Taxes, heart scares, car crashes: Still, he muddled through. In January 1981 Carlin stepped up as the first guest host of a year-old sketch comedy show on ABC called *Fridays*. An unabashed attempt to elbow in on some of the audience NBC had amassed for its wildly popular *Saturday Night Live*, *Fridays* enjoyed a honeymoon season with its ensemble cast before reformatting to accommodate a weekly guest host. As he had been on *SNL*, Carlin was the guinea pig. This time, though, the connection was stronger: The show's writing staff was headed by old friend Jack Burns, who also served as the on-air announcer.

Fridays was a curious blend of old school and new, with a cast and crew of TV neophytes, several of whom would later reconvene on *Seinfeld* (co-creator Larry David, writer Larry Charles, actor Michael Richards), and a hip selection of musical guests including the Pretenders and the Jim Carroll Band. (Carlin's episode featured meat-and-potatoes rockers George Thorogood and the Destroyers.) The week after Carlin was on, Shelley Winters was the guest host; the Methuselan Henny Youngman followed her.

The show, which was soon doomed by ABC's decision to expand its popular *Nightline* news program to include Friday nights, had a short-lived reputation for especially risqué political and drug-related humor. One memorable recurring sketch featured the Three Stooges as heavy pot smokers. A month after Carlin hosted, Andy Kaufman made a notorious appearance in which his refusal to act in a live sketch precipitated a skirmish with Burns, who charged onto the set from offstage. Only a few cast members knew about the ploy in advance, and for years many viewers believed they'd witnessed an actual brawl on TV.

The Carlin episode featured a mockumentary-style short film purporting to be a behind-the-scenes look at the real source of the comedian's observational humor—a writing team of ordinary folks, including a retired drill-press operator and a part-time beautician, plucked from the street. The bit had Bob and Ray written all over it. "I figured out early on that if I was going to stay in tune with the public, well, I'd better have a writing staff that was representative of the public," Carlin tells the camera.

His style was so familiar to fellow comics that Carlin became a target of parody on another *SNL* knockoff, *SCTV*, the sketch show of Toronto's Second City. New cast member Rick Moranis began doing a wicked impression of him. In absurd scenarios—Carlin playing Biff in *Death of a Salesman*, for instance—Moranis portrayed the comedy veteran as an incessant one-track mind, taking notes for bits during ordinary conversations, prefacing every comment with "Didja ever notice? . . ." and exhaling "Weeeeird!" after every inane observation. When someone gets knocked out and then comes to, Moranis wondered, why don't we say he's knocked *in*?

If Carlin's observational phase constituted a bridge between the self-expression of his boom years and the social criticism he would soon undertake, it hit a sudden high point with the title hunk of his next album, *A Place for My Stuff*. His first in four years, it was released on Atlantic, the parent company of Little David. (By the time of his next recording, *Carlin on Campus*, Carlin and Jerry Hamza had a deal in place with Atlantic for distribution of their new boutique label, Eardrum Records, which bore the motto "Stick it in your ear." Eventually the partners purchased the Little David catalog and reissued Carlin's early albums, individually and in the boxed set *The Little David Years*.) *Stuff* was an anomaly in the Carlin catalog, featuring live tracks alternating with studio-recorded commercial and game show parodies. The seven "Announcements" tracks were the same kind of fast-moving, jack-of-all-trades radio parodies—book club promotions ("How to Turn Unbearable Pain into Extra Income"), an ad for a television movie about a guy who wants to be an Olympic swimmer ("Wet Dream")—that he'd created as a schoolboy with his Webcor tape recorder.

The "Stuff" routine, a lighthearted take on the human pack rat—"That's what your house is—a place to keep your stuff while you go out and get . . . more stuff"—didn't appear on an HBO special until his fourth, but it was an instant favorite among fans and fellow comedians. When Carlin did the bit on the first American *Comic Relief*, the HBO fund-raiser hosted by Robin Williams, Whoopi Goldberg, and Billy Crystal, he stole the show. "We all talked about that again and again," says director John Moffitt. "That was such a big hit. Perfect delivery. Everyone who worked on the show, and I kept in touch with most of them, always talked about George's 'Stuff.'"

Three months after his heart attack, Carlin was at Carnegie Hall for the third HBO special. In a taped opening, he visited the old neighborhood, asking average New Yorkers the old joke, "How do you get to Carnegie Hall?" One guy gives him directions by bus. How about the subway? Carlin asks. "Got a gun permit?" the guy replies.

At the hall, he strolled across a huge oriental rug covering the venerable stage and led with the kind of deliberately outrageous icebreaker that marked all his HBO specials to come: "Have you noticed that most of the women who are against abortion are women you wouldn't want to fuck in the first place?" It was a calculated rejoinder to Ronald Reagan's quip about pro-choice activists: "I notice that everyone in favor of abortion has already been born."

He'd recently taken six months off, the comic said, only three of them voluntary. Just as Richard Pryor had turned his self-immolating freebasing incident into inspired material for his own act, Carlin joked that it was time to update the "Comedians' Health Sweepstakes." He now led Pryor two to one in heart attacks, he said, but Pryor was beating him one to nothing in "burning yourself up." Though the performance flew by the seat of its pants—there was no opportunity to tape a backup set, as was customary with the *On Location* series, and they couldn't even get in to set up until late in the day because of an afternoon recital—the show went a long way toward ensuring that Carlin would remain an HBO fixture for years to come.

"The orchestra chairs are piled behind Carlin on the stage of the great hall, giving the impression that he and a full house of laughing fans sneaked into the building while none of the authorities were looking," wrote Tom Shales in a *Washington Post* review. Though the comedian might have "spent a bit too much of his recuperation staring into his refrigerator or contemplating bowls of Rice Krispies," overall, the critic found that the performer had not lost his touch, "and his touch is frequently cherishable."

"HBO didn't kick in for me until 1982," Carlin later suggested. "That's when I learned who I was in that period." His first two specials for the network were directed by Marty Callner, who was doing all of the *On Location* shows at the time, but *Carlin at Carnegie* was directed by first-timer Steven J. Santos. He'd worked on a crew the previous year for *The Pee-Wee Herman Show*, which was directed by Callner. Santos stayed with Carlin through *Apt. 2C*, the comic's ill-fated HBO pilot, in 1985.

On the road, Carlin and Hamza were "four-walling" theaters, renting out the venues and then promoting the shows themselves. For the rest of his life Carlin continued to do as many as a hundred dates a year, taking home paychecks considerably larger than he might have drawn from a tour promoter. He'd play anywhere, he joked, as long as it had a zip code. When Jim Wiggins resettled in Illinois and revamped an old airline pilot's bar in Palatine called Durty Nelly's, he asked Carlin to come bless the place. Planning a trip to New York, Carlin arranged a layover in Chicago and told Wiggins to book two shows on the night he'd be in town.

Since the comedian had long ago moved off the nightclub scene into theaters, Carlin's booking was big news for Durty Nelly's. The club's big back room, which Wiggins had named the Blarney Stone, held just 180 customers. "I'm sure we stuffed 225 people into each show," says Wiggins. "They were ass-cheek to ass-cheek in that room." He made up special "tickets"—bars of soap wrapped in Day-glo sticky paper—and had the audience surprise Carlin by holding them up the first time he swore. Biff Rose, Carlin's loony old colleague from *The Kraft Summer Music Hall*, opened the shows, with Wiggins introducing. "There's me opening for two of my heroes, two of my kids' godfathers, in a room I had designed and decorated," Wiggins recalls. "It was a highlight of my life." En route to the airport the next day, he gave Carlin a briefcase full of cash. Carlin handed it back to Joan, Wiggins's wife. "That's your money," he said. "I did it as a gift for all you guys"—all the comedians still pounding the club circuit.

The Orwellian year 1984 marked a turning point for Carlin. For one thing, his mother died. She had hovered over him his whole life, and her absence brought a kind of relief. "It was truly like a ton of bricks had been lifted off his shoulders," his daughter, Kelly, once said. Though Mary had been living on the West Coast since the mid-1970s, she hadn't seen her second son much in recent years. Eighty-nine at the time of her death, she'd lived long enough to see Reagan go from baseball announcer to B-movie actor to California governor to the leader of the free world.

Reagan's reelection in 1984 confirmed for Carlin that this wasn't his decade. Though he rarely resorted to political humor—in part because he felt it dated quickly, in part because he was an independent thinker who could mock liberals as deftly as conservatives—Carlin did indulge himself in a few Reagan quickies. "Don't you think it's just a little bit strange that Ronald Reagan had an operation on his asshole and George Bush had an operation on his middle finger?" he joked at the beginning of one of the HBO specials. The tone that Reagan set "just fed your dissatisfaction," he later remembered. And the sense of entitlement adopted by the yuppie generation irked him long after the country had moved on from horn-rimmed glasses and pastel-colored polo shirts with upturned collars.

The period confirmed for Carlin that he was a lifelong outsider, a man who had no interest in being accepted. "Abraham Maslow said the fully realized man does not identify with the local group," he said.

When I saw that, it rang another bell. I thought: bingo! I do not identify with the local group, I do not feel a part of it. I really have never felt like a participant, I've always felt like an observer. Always. I only identified this in retrospect, way after the fact, that I have been on the outside, and I don't like being on the inside. I don't like being in their world. I've never felt comfortable there; I don't belong to that. So, when he says the "local group," I take that as meaning a lot of things: the local social clubs or fraternal orders, or lodges or associations or clubs of any kind, things where you sacrifice your individual identity for the sake of a group, for the sake of the group mind. I've always felt different and outside. Now, I also extended that, once again in retrospect, as I examined my feelings.

I don't really identify with America. I don't really feel like an American or part of the American experience, and I don't really feel like a member of the human race, to tell you the truth. I know I am, but I really don't. All the definitions are there, but I don't really feel a part of it. I think I have found a detached point of view, an ideal emotional detachment from the American experience and culture and the human experience and culture and human choices.

Like Democritus, the ancient Greek known as the "mocker" and the "laughing philosopher," Carlin saw humor and laughter as the only logical response to a crazy world. When concerned townspeople asked Hippocrates about the philosopher, who seemed to be going mad, Hippocrates pronounced him "too sane for his own good." Inside the gatefold of *Class Clown*, Carlin had featured a parable about a country that produced a harvest said to make those who ate it insane. "We must eat the grain to survive," said the king, "but there must be those among us who will remember that we are insane."

In 1983 he had taken his first whack at publishing, writing an oversized, thirty-two-page concert-program-style book called *Sometimes a Little Brain Damage Can Help*. Heavily illustrated and designed like a scrapbook, the book satisfied his chronic urge to categorize and make lists—full pages crammed with pet causes of the Miscellaneous Ailments Foundation ("the creeps . . . the willies . . . the shits") and People I Can Do Without ("people whose kids' names all start with the same initial . . . athletes who give 110%"). Other pages of "miscellaneous bullshit" represented the kind of shameless puns Carlin loved as a kid, reading *Esar's Comic Dictionary*. ("She was an earthy woman, so I treated her like dirt.")

Some of the drawings were by Holly Tucker, wife of Corky Siegel, the bandleader from the Summerfest incident in Milwaukee. The centerpiece, a two-page spread of 209 "impolite" words scrawled in calligraphy above a drawing of a urinal, provided the artist and her husband with an unexpected moment of amusement. When they went to pick up an early draft of the artwork at a printer's shop, there was a little old lady behind the counter. As she was handing the print job to the couple, she leaned in to give it a good read. Siegel and his wife were mortified, until the attendant looked up with a smile. "Oh, this is cute!" she said.

In late 1984 Carlin took another swing at hosting *Saturday Night Live*, which was in the middle of one of its extended periods without creator Lorne Michaels at the helm. After viewing a brief clip of Carlin on the first *SNL* episode nearly a decade earlier ("Does anybody know who that was? He sure had a lot of hair"), he joked about the long gap: "They told me if I did a real good job, they'd have me back. . . . I'm really glad that some people live up to their word." He noted the complaint that NBC had supposedly received from the archbishop's office about his God monologue, then proceeded to bait the current arch-bishop, the newly appointed John Joseph O'Connor, with more material about religion.

This time on *SNL* he was a team player, guest-anchoring the newscast and taking part in a few sketches. He played to type as an Irish fireman, making a guest appearance in Billy Crystal's parody of *The Joe Franklin Show,* and he soloed in a mock infomercial for "Ted's Book of World Records."

By this time Carlin was like a nutty uncle to the emerging generation of comedians. He gave Bob "Bobcat" Goldthwait, a newcomer by way of the Boston and San Francisco scenes who always seemed on the verge of hysterics, a part in the proposed HBO series *Apt. 2C.* Garry Shandling, who had mustered up the nerve to approach Carlin for comedy advice when he was still an electrical engineering student at the University of Arizona in the early 1970s, was now a regular Carson guest host and the cocreator of Showtime's *It's Garry Shandling's Show.* Shandling loved to recount his youthful encounter with Carlin, who was performing at a jazz club in Phoenix when he took the time to read the nervous kid's work.

Carlin's curiosity about the unexamined side of human life was a huge inspiration for Steven Wright, the molasses-paced surrealist whose breakthrough came with his 1985 debut album of comic koans, *I Have a Pony.* "I was amazed how he talked about everyday things," says Wright, "little things people don't usually discuss. He'd make his comedy about these mundane things, and it was hilarious—the speed of light, and coasters, and lint." Wright, who recited routines from *FM & AM* and *Class Clown* (with proper credit) for his public speaking class at Boston's Emerson College, says he instinctively gravitated toward Carlin's "whole approach, like he was an outsider of society, looking in." Over the years he had several opportunities to speak with Carlin, who sought Wright's advice on playing certain venues and told the younger comic he was one of the comedians Carlin had on his iPod. The connection was as meaningful for Wright the last time as the first. "It was a big rush for me that he liked what I did," he says.

The *Carlin on Campus* HBO special, which aired in 1984, was Carlin's best yet. On an eccentric set designed by Brenda—a landscape of oversized geometric shapes—he crafted a kind of comic poetry by blessing the performance with a mock recitation, jumbling lines from the Lord's Prayer with the Pledge of Allegiance ("Give us this day as we forgive those who so proudly we hail"). He also offered an updated, well-polished version of "Baseball and Football" and, in a long hunk about "Cars and Driving," the astute observation that everyone who drives slower than you is an "idiot," whereas those who drive faster are invariably "maniacs." The closing credits were accompanied by a brief taped performance of the star of the show playing an original composition called "Armadillo Blues" on piano while wearing a nun's habit.

The hour was interspersed with several minutes of completed material from the work he had done with animator Bob Kurtz and his staff for *The Illustrated George Carlin*. "It's No Bullshit" was a cartoon parody on amazing-facts features like Ripley's *Believe It or Not*, with fake news items and a compendium of fanciful sporting events, like a blind golf tournament. The music over the end credits was provided by Kurtz's friend Joe Siracusa, a veteran of Spike Jones's anarchic orchestra, who, much to Carlin's delight, improvised a one-man band of cuckoo sounds—bells and whistles and hiccups and washboard percussion.

Kurtz entered the short film, packaged as *Drawing on My Mind*, in several festivals, and it won first prize in its category at an animation festival in Canada. In New York a woman asked the director whether he felt the "Blind Golf" bit was offensive to blind people. "Not anybody who saw it," he replied. At another festival in France, the print with the French translation didn't arrive in time, so the audience watched it in English. Despite the language barrier, "People were laughing so hard they thought they were going to die," Kurtz recalls. "For five days, people would yell at me, 'It's No Bullshit!' We didn't win an award, but it was the hit of the festival."

As had Kurtz, comedian Chris Rush got a call out of the blue to help Carlin work on a script for his proposed HBO series *Apt. 2C*.

Rush, a motor-mouthed, high-IQ Brooklynite whose comedy has always reflected the peculiar mix of his instinctive perversity with his
clinical training as a molecular biologist, says he got started in comedy
while still a toddler, performing ersatz opera with made-up dirty lyrics
at family gatherings. He was Carlin's kind of guy. In fact, though, it
was Brenda who turned her husband on to the shaved-headed, philosophically inquisitive potty-mouth. She was the first of the two to hear
Rush's headlong debut album, *First Rush*, recorded for Atlantic in 1973
while Rush was writing for the fledgling *National Lampoon*. One day
Carlin called his fellow New Yorker and asked him to fly to LA for a
meeting. "It was a stunning fucking thing," says Rush. "Here was a
guy I idolized. . . . He was the guy that softened the beach for the rest
of us."

They hit it off and began writing together. At one point Rush stayed
at Carlin's house in Brentwood for the better part of a week while
Brenda was away. Officially, Carlin was also writing with his good
friend Pat McCormick, a longtime *Tonight Show* contributor whose association with the show went back to the Paar years. McCormick was a
hulking, anything-goes comic presence who had recently starred as Big
Enos in the *Smokey and the Bandit* films. Also involved were the
British-Canadian comedy writing duo of Andrew Nicholls and Darrell
Vickers, who later became Johnny Carson's head writers, until his re-
tirement in 1992. They were introduced to Carlin by his brother Pat,
who met the writing team while all three were working under the table
for Alan Thicke on his short-lived late-night show, *Thicke of the Night*.
(Carlin sometimes helped set up his older brother with writing work,
once calling the office of *Hustler* magazine to get someone to read a
submission from Patrick. Pat Carlin kept an office in the same building
as Carlin's for a while, before quitting Hollywood and moving to up-
state New York with his wife.)

"George was very healthy at this time—bottled water all around
and tofu salads," says Nicholls. "He used to hug everyone when they
got to work and hug them all good-bye at the end of the day. Pretty in-
timidating for us, just down from Canada, only a few years after listening to his albums at night on headphones under the covers."

Prefiguring *Seinfeld*, the premise of *Apt. 2C* featured an apartment-dwelling writer constantly distracted by the shenanigans of his eccentric friends and neighbors, who included McCormick, Goldthwait, stand-up comic Jeff Altman, and Lois Bromfield (whose sister, Valri, had appeared on the first *SNL*). Carlin's daughter, Kelly, played a Girl Scout. Despite the writing talent rounded up for *Apt. 2C*, Rush could tell that the constraint of working with a writing team was unproductive for Carlin. "If you're a gunfighter for twenty-five years, and all of a sudden they ask you to be a group leader in an advertising agency—you're not good at working with people, you know?" says Rush, who had a part in the pilot but backed out. "I told him, 'I see what you're trying to do, but it's falling short.'" At one point an HBO executive gave Carlin some notes on the network's suggestions for improvement, including a recommendation to tone down the four-letter words. Not surprisingly, that pretty much sealed the show's fate. Carlin had wanted to push the network on Rush's own idea for a show, a mind-boggling conceptual thing he called *Innertube*. "After *Apt. 2C* lit a bomb," says Rush, "that was the end of that."

Not long after the pilot disappeared, Carlin called Rush in New York and told him to come by the Ritz-Carlton, where he was staying. After encouraging the younger comic to berate him for not taking his advice—with some reluctance, Rush launched into a private, foul-mouthed, one-man roast of his friend—Carlin, laughing, wrote out a check for $18,000. Write a movie, he said. The script that Rush eventually produced, a gag vehicle called *Strange Days*, went nowhere.

It had been a decade since Carlin had acted in *Car Wash*, nearly two since *With Six You Get Eggroll*. Despite the disappointing experience of the HBO pilot, he was warming to the idea of renewing his acting aspirations. Kelly, too, was thinking about pursuing a career in acting, and father and daughter enrolled together in a workshop class with Hollywood acting coach Stephen Book. "He thought it was time to become knowledgeable as an actor, to have technique and expertise," says Book. Also in the class were the young actors Tate Donovan and Grant Heslov. In one class, Carlin and his daughter partnered to do a scene. Book gave them Somerset Maugham's *Rain*, the story of a prostitute named Sadie Thompson, who arrives on an island in the South Pacific, and the zealous missionary who hopes to reform her. "I thought, This is going to be interesting," says Book with a laugh.

The first acting that Carlin did after starting the class was in the brief noirish set pieces ("The Envelope") at the beginning and end of his next HBO special, *Playin' with Your Head*. The stand-up performance was taped over two nights in May 1986 at the Beverly Theater. Much as Moranis had spoofed Carlin's habit of analyzing common turns of phrase, the real Carlin opened with a bit about the odd and annoying ways we say hello and good-bye to each other. He liked to mash them together, he joked: "Toodle-oo, go with God, and don't take any wooden nickels." He also did material on why there aren't more variations on the notion of a moment of silence for the dearly departed ("How about a moment of muffled conversation for the treated and released?") and, in a hint of the politically incorrect button-pushing that would partly define his later years in comedy, a crass joke about guys who wear earrings. "I'm better than that," he began to apologize, then recanted: "No, I'm not!"

Playin' with Your Head was Carlin's first HBO special with a new director, Rocco Urbisci. Urbisci's first job in Hollywood had been on the staff of Steve Allen's last talk show, locally produced at the KTLA studio in Los Angeles and syndicated to several markets in 1970 and 1971. Urbisci had booked Carlin on Allen's show a number of times during the comic's transformative period, when bookings were uncertain. Later the two worked together on *The Midnight Special*. Although they hadn't seen each other for years when Urbisci showed up backstage at a Carlin set at the Wadsworth Theatre on Wilshire Boulevard, Carlin impulsively asked if the director would like to take on his next HBO project. They collaborated on all of Carlin's original HBO events until his death more than two decades later.

Coincidental to the acting class, Carlin was offered a supporting role in an upcoming comedy featuring Bette Midler and Shelley Long, who was nearing the end of her five years starring on the NBC sitcom *Cheers. Outrageous Fortune* was directed by Hollywood veteran Arthur Hiller, who had directed *Silver Streak* with Pryor and, years earlier, *The*

Out-of-Towners with Jack Lemmon, the man Carlin once suggested was his comic-acting role model. With its title plucked from the famous soliloquy of Shakespeare's *Hamlet,* the slapstick-y movie followed the story of a pair of aspiring actresses who end up dating the same man, who turns out to be an agent for the KGB. In a flat-brimmed cowboy hat and sporting an uncharacteristic tan, Carlin played Frank Madras, an old desert drunk who convinces the women to hire him as a tracker. Comically cranky about letting himself get sucked into his new clients' dangerous escapade, he lends them his clothes as a disguise and spends much of the movie wearing Midler's print skirt and orange sweater. "There were projects that he really busted his ass on," says Book. Though it proved formulaic, *Outrageous Fortune* was one of these.

Carlin brought a bit less desire to *Justin Case,* an NBC movie for which director Blake Edwards hand-picked the comic as the lead. Carlin played the ghost of a private detective trying to learn the circumstances behind his own murder at the hands of a mysterious "Lady in Black." Dead detectives, old rascals, fading hippies, corrupt clergymen, and sage advisors—for the rest of his career, Carlin was nearly always cast to type, usually based on the stock voices he'd been using in his act for years. Even the gratification of being the first choice of Edwards, who'd made not only the *Pink Panther* films but also *Breakfast at Tiffany's,* and (with Lemmon starring) the dramatic *Days of Wine and Roses,* was not quite enough to convince Carlin that this project was more than a paycheck.

He had more fun with 1989's *Bill & Ted's Excellent Adventure,* playing Rufus, the back-from-the-future mentor to the title characters—two clueless, metal-loving dudes, played by Alex Winter and Keanu Reeves, who must pass their history exam in order to save humankind. The future, Rufus reports, is paradise: "Bowling averages are way up. Mini-golf scores are way down. And we have more excellent water slides than any other planet we communicate with." It was a distinctly different attitude than Carlin the comedian would soon take, as his sense of humor grew progressively more apocalyptic.

A *Bill & Ted's* sequel and a made-for-television quickie about two Wall Street janitors, called *Working Tra$h* (costarring a young Ben

Stiller), provided little indication that Carlin would suddenly blossom as an actor. His breakthrough came in the 1991 film version of Pat Conroy's best-selling novel, *The Prince of Tides*. Producer-director Barbra Streisand picked Carlin to play the role of Eddie Detreville, the gay neighbor of one of the movie's main characters, calling him over to her home to audition privately. Carlin worked tirelessly to capture the role, says his acting coach. Taking walks with Book around his LA neighborhood, Carlin stayed in character as the wispy Eddie. According to Book, some of the people Carlin encountered while preparing for the role had no idea they were speaking with the famous comedian: "To this day, my neighbor wants to set him up with her brother, Doug."

Book felt that his acting student reached a peak with his work on *Prince of Tides*—that he might have earned himself an Oscar nomination if he'd only been in another scene or two. The Grammys were more familiar territory. Carlin was nominated for the awards three times during the decade, for *A Place for My Stuff*, *Playin' with Your Head*, and the album version of his sixth HBO special, 1988's *What Am I Doing in New Jersey?* Late bloomer Rodney Dangerfield won the comedy Grammy in 1980, and Carlin contemporaries Pryor and Cosby won in 1982 and 1986, respectively.

By 1988 the outrageous Sam Kinison was the talk of television and the comedy world. With long, frizzy hair sprouting from beneath his ubiquitous beret, the stumpy former evangelist, "discovered" a few years earlier on one of Dangerfield's *Young Comedians* specials for HBO, was all over MTV with his celebrity-studded video cover of the Troggs's "Wild Thing." Kinison's comedy was a volcanic outburst, an eruption of grievances with cheating girlfriends, the hypocritical Catholic Church, and the general idiocies of humankind, not necessarily in that order. Nothing was sacred to Kinison, who could even find fault with the starving faces on late-night ads for hunger relief. As the comedian Bill Hicks later said, "Kinison was the first guy I ever saw go onstage and not ask the audience in any way, shape, or form to like him. I found that highly reassuring."

Carlin evidently did, too, accentuating his exasperation with his fellow Americans in his sixth HBO special in 1988. It opened with a canned segment in which he took a cab from Manhattan to the site of the gig, the Park Theater in Union City. The cab driver was played by Carlin's old friend Bob Altman, who had recently named his daughter Carlen in honor of his former acid-trip companion and philosophical debate partner. When Carlin runs into a bar for directions, Altman hollers over his shoulder, "Ask 'em about what they think of man's role in the universe."

Disgust with the squandered promise of the human race was the overriding theme of the performance, with Carlin adapting for the stage the "People I Can Do Without" concept from the *Brain Damage* book. He also launched a rant about Civil War reenactors ("Use live ammo, assholes!") and, ten years after the Supreme Court case, ripped the FCC, which had "all by itself decided that television and radio are the only two parts of American life not protected by the First Amendment." Going on about the heightened climate of repression of the Reagan eighties, standing on a barbed-wire set designed to look like a threatening back alley, he posed an open question to the Rev. Donald Wildmon, who was then on a crusade against immorality in American culture. He wondered whether the reverend was familiar with the function of the knobs on his radio. After joking that perhaps the reverend was "not comfortable with anything with two knobs," he made a declaration: "I'm pretty sick and tired of all these fuckin' church people." This was the first concrete indication that the comic was developing a more confrontational persona onstage, which would lead even some longtime fans to claim they thought he became "angry" in his later years.

When Kinison died in a car crash in 1992, Carlin sent the biggest floral arrangement to his funeral. "We couldn't get it into the viewing room," says Bill Kinison, the comedian's brother, former manager, and biographer. The two comics had met at the Grammy Awards and crossed paths on occasion at the Comedy Store. Though the emotionally raw Pryor was Kinison's idol, meeting Carlin, his brother says, was a high point for the comic. When Bill Kinison called Carlin to thank him for the flowers, Carlin told him he felt a strange connection to the shooting star. "I feel like Sam is feeding me material from the other side," he said.

Carlin was less impressed with Andrew "Dice" Clay, another eight-ies comedian, who got lumped with Kinison and radio host Howard Stern as the clown princes of the era's in-your-face humor. Though Clay himself noted that his cartoonish act was meant to be "a macho moron . . . juvenile comedy," Carlin told the psychology professor Timothy Jay that Clay was killing his own livelihood. As he began to attract a skinhead crowd that considered the comic's bigotry and chau-vinism as validation, the mainstream of Clay's audience was dropping out, intimidated.

Still, Carlin saw that the culture was changing, and he was chang-ing accordingly. "I realized I had to raise my voice literally and in a fig-urative sense," he recalled, "to raise the stakes a little bit onstage in order to compete with a very noisy culture. There's a lot of din in the culture, and to get attention, you have to raise your voice." Voluble, hotheaded comedians such as Kinison and Bill Hicks felt compelled to address the things that infuriated them. Though other great comedi-ans' moments were yet to come—Jerry Seinfeld and his jeweler's eye for trivialities, Chris Rock's intrepid social surgery, Jon Stewart's in-stantaneous deflation of the hot-air newsmakers of the day, all of them owing a distinct, and routinely acknowledged, debt to Carlin—the late 1980s were the last time the comic, who was entering his autumnal season as the "Grand Old Man of the Counterculture" (as the *New York Times* called him), looked to the current crop to gauge his own place in the field.

10

SQUEAMISH

I'll be watching you, ya prick, so you better be good." That was
how Carlin introduced himself to his new opening act, Dennis
Blair, at a 1988 gig in Omaha. Blair, a Rodney Dangerfield protégé who earned a writing credit and a bit of screen time in Dangerfield's 1983 comedy with Joe Pesci, *Easy Money*, is a daffy musical
comedian in the Steve Martin mold. He first saw Carlin perform in
the early eighties in Atlantic City, where Carlin was opening for
Suzanne Somers. He went with Dangerfield, who admired Carlin's
very different style. The feeling was mutual.

"I know George loved Rodney's humor, and Rodney thought
George was hysterical," Blair recalls. "Rodney really liked guys who
made people uncomfortable." For a few years, after Chandler Travis
and Steve Shook had set aside their own musical comedy act to start a
good-time bar band called the Incredible Casuals, Carlin toured with
an opening act named Glenn Super, a genially cranky club guy in jeans
and suspenders who called himself Mr. Microphone, after his favorite
prop. By 1988 Carlin was ready for a new warm-up act, and he and
Jerry Hamza gave Blair a three-month trial. Blair ended up sharing the
bill with the older comic for nearly two decades.

Over the years Blair came to think of his employer as comedy's version of the Beatles' John Lennon: "He started with goofy three-minute

pop songs, and he ended with 'Cold Turkey,'" he says. "He grew, just like a great musical artist."

Carlin took the place of another Beatle, Ringo Starr, in one of the more unusual roles of his life. When Ringo stepped aside as the voice of the storytelling sprite "Mr. Conductor" on the popular PBS kids' show *Shining Time Station*, featuring Thomas the Tank Engine and his fellow toy trains, Carlin took over the role. (He was, he joked, the "anti-Pete Best," the drummer who lost his place in the Beatles to Ringo.) Searching frantically for a replacement, cocreator Rick Siggelkow played a recording for his partner, Britt Allcroft, without identifying the voice. "The first word I heard, 'stuff,' won me over," Allcroft recalled. New to America—she was born in South Africa and had created the original *Thomas the Tank Engine and Friends* for Children's ITV in the United Kingdom—she was unfamiliar with Carlin's warm grumble. She didn't hear the voice that had nearly blown a gasket on his last cable show: "I get pissed, goddamn it!" "I heard a sound that, for children, could be intimate, lyrical, sometimes spooky, soothing and, most important, kind," she recalled.

Even when he was swearing, Carlin's performing voice "always sounded as if he were trying to amuse a child," Jerry Seinfeld once suggested. "It was like the naughtiest, most fun grown-up you ever met was reading you a bedtime story." For the next few years—by his count, forty-five episodes—Carlin provided the narration for the adventures of Thomas and friends, and he appeared onscreen whenever the miniature Mr. Conductor materialized from inside the station house wall in a burst of pixie dust. Tickled by the irony that the Thomas stories were adapted from a series of children's books written by a clergyman, he also delighted in the opportunity to reveal another side of himself. According to Allcroft, Carlin got over his initial nervousness, which hit on his first day in the sound booth. Realizing he was unaccustomed to having no audience, he brought in a teddy bear to tell the stories to. The stuffed bear stayed by his side throughout his work on the series. Still, he couldn't resist alluding to his better-known image, sending Allcroft a T-shirt printed with the words "Britt Happens."

He was similarly proud of his work on a made-for-television minis-eries adapted from Larry McMurtry's book *Streets of Laredo*, the last in-stallment of the *Lonesome Dove* series. Working for Joseph Sargent, who directed the original New York City subway thriller *The Taking of Pelham One Two Three*, Carlin played Billy Williams, a grizzled old Texas knockabout with a pronounced limp, a fringed jacket, and a thin layer of grime that wouldn't wash off. Billy has a soft spot for Maria Garza, whose estranged son, a ruthless bandit, is sought by the bounty hunter Captain Call, played by James Garner. In a cast that in-cluded Sissy Spacek, Sam Shepard, and Ned Beatty, Carlin played a role he could understand—a free agent, a man born genetically inca-pable of lying down for authority figures. "I despise them lawmen," he says. "I just hate their stinkin' hearts." When a young officer tells him to watch his mouth—"You old-timers got rough tongues"—Billy shoots off the tip of his ear.

Streets of Laredo was Carlin's "favorite project of all, and the one he did the best in," says Stephen Book, his acting coach. "He really hit his stride as an actor in that." Carlin agreed. "I just felt terrific in that role," he said.

When the offer came, Carlin also felt pretty good about the prospect of finally taking on his own sitcom. With a half-dozen or so years of legitimate acting work under his belt since he had started tak-ing roles again, he was intrigued when the upstart Fox network made him an offer. Launched in 1986, the network quickly established a rep-utation for taking chances on comedy. *The Simpsons*, Matt Groening's long-running animated series, was one of Fox's first ratings successes. The sketch show *In Living Color* debuted in 1990, quickly propelling comic actors such as Jamie Foxx and Jim Carrey to stardom. The net-work even tried Kinison in a sitcom in 1991. "They're new on the scene, they're making noise, and they've got this word—*edgy*," Carlin recalled. "I thought, fine, maybe I fit that." He owed it to himself, and to his family, he figured, to give the sitcom a shot. Having suffered a third heart attack in early 1991 while driving to Vegas for a gig, he was thinking seriously about scaling back on the road work. Seinfeld had a show, Rosanne Barr had a show, Newhart had his sitcoms, *The Cosby Show* was a blockbuster. Why not him?

Playing George O'Grady, an underemployed cabbie who gleefully flaunts his ponytail ("It pisses people off," he says in the first episode of *The George Carlin Show*), Carlin holds court at the Moylan, a re-creation of the real-life Morningside Heights watering hole he'd frequented for years. The cast of regulars included Alex Rocco, the veteran actor who had parlayed his purported underworld connections in his native Boston into a tough-guy film and television career, most notably in the role of casino owner Moe Greene in *The Godfather*. The show, as Carlin said on the eve of its debut in January 1994, revolved around "nice, controlled anger. . . . It's a combination of indignance and indifference. Basically, I don't give a fuck about the world. I'm pissed that we've wasted our potential on such moronic things as religion and profit." Not surprisingly, he concluded, "This character shares some of the attitudes and feelings that I have." Despite his dyspepsia, he was optimistic about the show, at least for the moment: "If they said I could never do stand-up again in exchange for ten years of this," he told a reporter, "I'd choose this."

At first Carlin was excited to work with the show's cocreator, Sam Simon, who had written for *Taxi* and *Cheers* and developed *The Simpsons* with Groening and James L. Brooks. Simon was also a fellow dog nut; one of the first plots was about George using his little lap dog as a pawn in his shy courtship of a woman running a neighborhood pet shop. Initially scheduled at 9:30 on Fox's powerhouse Sunday night, which included *The Simpsons* and *Married . . . With Children*—"Get ready for the only guy funny enough to follow Al Bundy," one promo promised—the show earned some respectable, if not exactly enthusiastic, early notice. "Carlin's aging hipster character translates well to the sitcom stage," wrote *Variety*'s reviewer. "This is the comic without much of the acid that frequently flows in his stand-up routines. It's a half-hour that's easy to take, and Carlin fans won't be disappointed." But the reviewer also noted the obvious comparisons to *Cheers*, which was similarly set in a bar, and *Seinfeld*, which was becoming extraordinarily popular with its famously "lightweight" scripts. "Show may require more coddling than Fox is used to giving its other, better comedies," the writer concluded, with some prescience.

Though Carlin got to indulge a few whims (in the second episode, for instance, his character insisted he'd seen a UFO, much as the comic himself was then intrigued by the concept of extraterrestrial activity), he soon realized that Simon, the show's executive producer and occasional director, had the real allegiance of Warner Bros. Television, where the show originated. Though media mogul Les Moonves, then the company's president, made Carlin feel welcome—"He was my kind of guy," Carlin recalled, "seemed like a street guy"—the company, he felt, was more interested in protecting Simon, who was "the property they could count on. Sam will do another show." In the end, Simon and Carlin couldn't work together. "Sam will tell you himself," Carlin said, "his reputation in the business is that he's difficult."

In fact, few in the cast and crew felt comfortable with Simon, who was going through a divorce and suffering from chronic back pain and often brought big, aggressive dogs onto the set. "He used to whip Chinese throwing stars at his office walls during pitch meetings," says one participant. "George used to drop by and the meetings were . . . testy. They were both big personalities and Sam, having come off *The Simpsons*, wasn't used to having to debate dialogue and scene structure with an actor." After twenty-seven episodes spread across parts of two seasons, Carlin couldn't wait to leave. When a Fox executive called him on the set to let him know they'd decided to cancel the show, he had already checked out mentally. He was just glad they hadn't waited until the season ended to make the decision.

The responsibilities of the sitcom brought an end to his streak of delivering a new HBO special every two years. Beginning in 1982, when he had regained his health and hit his stride with the network, he had had an hour or so of new material on the air every other year for a decade. In 1990's *Doin' It Again*, taped in New Brunswick, New Jersey, Carlin focused on language, declaring the performance free of namby-pamby New Age lingo: "I will not *share* anything with you," he said, handling the operative word as if it were a dead mouse he was removing from the stage with a stick. "I will not *relate* to you, and you will not *identify* with me."

For Carlin, political correctness was just another form of oppression and rule-making, inevitably to be disobeyed. This special was one of the few times in his career when he addressed a specific category of potentially offensive words—ethnic and racial slurs. "There is absolutely nothing wrong with any of those words in and of themselves," he said. "They're only words. . . . It's the context." No one flinched when Richard Pryor or Eddie Murphy said *nigger*, he reasoned, "because we know they're not racists. Why? They're niggers!"

In the credits Carlin thanked Rutgers Professor William Lutz, who had recently published a book called *Doublespeak: From "Revenue Enhancement" to "Terminal Living": How Government, Business, Advertisers, and Others Use Language to Deceive You*. The linguist's work had inspired the comic to develop another strain of his humor, which would remain a part of his show until he died (or, rather, *expired*, "like a magazine subscription"). Like a true New Yorker, he couldn't tolerate indirect language. That pet peeve became a part of the act. The CIA no longer kills people, he griped—they "neutralize" them. The attempt to reclassify the handicapped as "handi-capable" sent him off the deep end: "These poor people have been bullshitted by the system into believing that if you change the name of the condition, somehow you'll change the condition," he said. Few comics ever become skilled enough in the art form to make a didactic line like that sound funny. He'd never been much of a punch-line comic, anyway. Now, as he headed toward his sixties, the humor wasn't so much about his observations as his opinions.

"I'm doing my best work," he told interviewer Bob Costas around this time. "I'm thinking better than I ever have." The next HBO show, *Jammin' in New York*, which aired live from the theater at Madison Square Garden (then called the New Paramount), was dedicated to Kinison, who died two weeks before its April 1992 taping. Beginning with an extended riff on the country's militaristic self-image, with the televised spectacle of the first Gulf War still fresh, the set revolved around three long, writerly pieces, including an exhaustive examination of air-travel jargon (such as *final destination*: "All destinations are final—that's what it means!") that should have retired the subject for stand-up comedians forever, and a rant against the voguish Save the Planet movement that he called "The Planet Is Fine" (but "the people are fucked"). Machine-gunning his way through a long list of natural and man-made disasters, he proclaimed his delight in bad news—the more death and destruction, the better. "I enjoy chaos and disorder, and not just because they help me professionally," he said in a ludicrous, hyper-articulated announcer's voice. He'd been "an entropy fan" from the time he had learned the meaning of the word in school.

Although Carlin was still justifiably famous for pushing the limits of acceptable language and making crude jokes about human biology, his stand-up had taken a pronounced leap from blue to black. In *Jammin' in New York*, he came on like an encyclopedia of dark humor, skittering from war, prison, and eating disorders to plane crashes and utter annihilation. In his previous HBO special he had even claimed to prove the point that no subject was out of bounds for comedy by doing a brief bit about rape, which involved Porky Pig and Elmer Fudd.

He was poking with ever-lengthening sticks into the field of land mines. Even fellow comics often had a difficult time with Carlin's turn toward dark comedy. "I think you can point out hypocrisy, but you can't be that pessimistic," says Franklyn Ajaye, who thought of Carlin, Klein, and Pryor as his inspirational trinity. "He became a curmudgeon. And you can contrast that with Robert Klein, who felt just as disgusted as George, but he could still have fun with it."

Others, however, saluted Carlin's chutzpah. "If people are sensitive about something, that makes it compelling," says Louis CK, an admirer who dedicated his stand-up special *Chewed Up* to Carlin. "If your job is to talk about stuff, you'd be irresponsible to stay away from things that upset people. . . . The whole point of comedy is to crash through those things." *Jammin' in New York* was the HBO special that confirmed the whole long haul for Carlin. Working live, with more than 6,000 people in the theater, "I knew I'd found my voice," he said years later. "It felt like I really graduated that night."

For several years he had been augmenting his touring income with an annual commitment to Bally's Las Vegas. Having grudgingly reconciled with the city, admitting its obvious financial benefits and ready-made marketplace for a headlining comedian, he soon bought a condo in Vegas, so he could drive himself in to work and come home to his dogs. He was about as low-maintenance a performer as they come, says Joel Fischman, who was vice president of entertainment at Bally's until leaving for Mandalay Bay in 1998. "He'd have his table set up in his room with his tuna fish, his celery stalks and his carrots, his juices and water. You'd go see him before the show, talk a little baseball, maybe." Carlin stayed without incident until the casino closed its celebrity showroom in the late 1990s. "He was very happy with the audiences," says Fischman. "I think they changed a little as Vegas changed, but he was so consistent. If you didn't know what you were getting when you went to see George Carlin, what were you going to the show for?"

The impact of the HBO specials on his career was apparent. In the waning years of the CableACE awards (1979–1997), cable television's equivalent of the Emmys, Carlin became a regular recipient, winning honors for *Doin' It Again, Jammin' in New York*, and, in 1997, two more for the retrospective *George Carlin: 40 Years of Comedy* (which also earned two Emmy nods). He also won his first Grammy in more than twenty years for the *Jammin' in New York* soundtrack album, beating out a weird field expanded to accommodate audiobooks, including recordings by the humor writers Garrison Keillor and Erma Bombeck and another by the *SNL* alum (and future Minnesota senator) Al Franken.

40 Years of Comedy followed closely on the heels of Carlin's ninth HBO event, *Back in Town*. Taped in March 1996, a few months after he was relieved of his sitcom duties, the show took place at the 2,800-seat Beacon Theatre in New York, a historic former movie palace on Upper Broadway. Before settling on the location, Carlin had called Steven Wright, who had headlined there, to ask about the room. He kicked off the performance by running in off the street through a side door directly onto the stage, tossing aside his jacket. Prowling his turf, shoulders hunched, he wondered why the pro-life movement was ho-mophobic: "Who has less abortions than homosexuals?" If he sounded on the last special as if he'd been taking elocution lessons, this time there was an obvious vocal residue from his George O'Grady charac-ter; he used his salty-cabbie voice throughout the hour.

The *40 Years* retrospective aired from the U.S. Comedy Arts Festi-val in Aspen, Colorado. The show featured an onstage interview with Carlin, looking uncharacteristically formal with newly shorn hair and a black cashmere jacket, conducted by a young admirer in a leather jacket named Jon Stewart. The hour also featured a package of clips dating back to Carlin's earliest days on television, as well as an abbrevi-ated stand-up performance by the honoree, anchored by a new piece called "American Bullshit." Befitting the nostalgic format of the trib-ute, Carlin explained what his success in comedy meant to him by equating it with the education he had left behind. Because the nuns gave no grades at Corpus Christi, he told Stewart, resorting to one of his old lines, "the only *A*'s I got, and this is a little corny—I got their attention, I got their approval, their admiration, their approbation, and their applause. And those are the only *A*'s I wanted, and I got 'em," he said. Stewart, looking awestruck, called him sir.

"I'm gonna keep doing this as long as I can," Carlin told old friend John Moffitt, who, along with his fellow executive producers of the festival, Stu Smiley and Pat Tourk Lee, served as executive producers of the show with Brenda and Hamza. "I'm gonna look pretty funny, but I'm still gonna be out there."

Constantly looming HBO deadlines had forced the comedian to write new material with the rigor of an athlete in training. "He really was a workaholic," says Moffitt. "I think it kept his mind sharp as he got older." Just as Joe Monroe had advised him back in Shreveport, he'd been collecting and categorizing his ideas from the start, at first in folders and on index cards, later on a word processor, and then on laptop computers. Lenny Bruce sometimes scribbled down a few notes in his hotel room, but more often than not he treated his gigs as though he were jumping off a ledge into his own brain soup. "Just be-fore he went on, he'd say, 'Not now, baby, I'm thinking,'" recalls Paul

Krassner. Very much unlike his role model, Carlin wrote, rewrote, and self-edited, perpetually calibrating his act to dial up a maximum level of impact.

Chris Rush liked to tease Carlin that he wasn't actually Irish—that they'd "found him in a diaper with a swastika on the side. He had the work habits of a commandant, a middle-echelon guy from the Nazi party who was under direct observation." Rush, as impulsive a comic as Carlin was studious, once watched his friend in his hotel room, walking on a treadmill while working on his laptop. When he needled the older comic about it, Carlin shot back, "Fuck you. You rap out two years of an average comedian's material in one hour backstage. I write the shit out. I'm not an ad-libber."

With the burden of the Fox sitcom lifted, Carlin suddenly landed on a project he'd been preparing for for years. Books by comedians were becoming trendy in the publishing world. Seinfeld's *Seinlanguage* was a number 1 *New York Times* best seller; Cosby and *Mad About You* star Paul Reiser were also succeeding on the shelves, both with popular titles about marriage and parenting. And Ray Romano, the star of *Everybody Loves Raymond*, was about to land a seven-figure book deal for his own debut humor collection.

Carlin's first crack at publishing, 1983's *Brain Damage*, had been a novelty, equal parts *Mad* magazine and concert program. The new book, *Brain Droppings*, published in May 1997, was a legitimate transferal of Carlin's stage act to the page. Opening with expressions of gratitude to his brother Patrick ("who was kind enough to teach me attitude"), his manager and best friend Hamza (whose "inner maniac is even weirder than mine"), and Joe Monroe, he found a corker of an epigraph, credited to Kahlil Gibran: "We shall never understand one another until we reduce the language to seven words."

Brain Droppings was a crash course in the singular worldview of the grown kid from White Harlem. Besides written versions of signature hunks such as "Stuff" and a revision of "The Indian Sergeant" set in primitive times, there were copious random musings, characteristically heavy on the punning and gripes about poorly considered clichés ("If you've seen one, you've seen one"). The book sold briskly through strong word of mouth, staying on the *Times* best-seller list for eighteen weeks. Three years after publication, the audiobook version earned Carlin his third Grammy award. The new wing of his comedy empire eventually grew to include two more best-selling books, 2001's *Napalm & Silly Putty* (another Grammy winner in audiobook form) and 2004's *When Will Jesus Bring the Pork Chops?*, the cover of which—a parody of "The Last Supper," resulted in the title being banned at Wal-Mart, much to Carlin's amusement.

But excitement over his first real book publication was sadly fleeting. On Mother's Day, one day before Carlin's sixtieth birthday, Brenda died of complications from liver cancer. She was fifty-seven; they'd been married thirty-six years.

The length of Brenda's illness had prepared Carlin for life without her. "I'm very much a realist and a practical person," he said.

> But it was not pleasant by any means. She had been stabilized with chemotherapy, but then things took a rapid turn. They kept her alive an extra twelve or eighteen hours, apparently just for me to get back in from the road. And by the time I got there it was gruesome. So it was no picnic, but my tears were fairly contained. . . . I had kind of rehearsed it in my mind.

Fellow comedians sometimes speculate that Carlin grew darker, more pessimistic, after Brenda's death. The truth, however, is that he had already been exploring the limits of dark humor for several years. A month later he was on *The Late Show with David Letterman*, promoting the book. Sitting with the host, he joked about trying to come up with a classified ad that would be guaranteed not to generate any response: "Elderly, accident-prone, severely depressed, alcoholic coal-miner interested in Canadian food and Norwegian folk dancing seeks wealthy, attractive, sexually starved, well-built woman in her late teens. Must be non-smoker."

He could joke, but he missed Brenda's enthusiastic laughter. After her death, he touched his wedding ring a few times during each of his shows, to remind himself of her presence.

He kept himself busy, appearing on talk shows with Tom Snyder, Dennis Miller, and Roseanne Barr to plug the book. He told Snyder he had an autobiography in the works with the comic writer Tony Hendra, who, with performing partner Nick Ullett, had been the support act for Lenny Bruce at Café Au Go Go the week of Bruce's New York busts. Hendra was also a founding editor of *National Lampoon* and the author of *Going Too Far,* a history of subversive comedy.

When director Kevin Smith approached Carlin with a role envisioned expressly for him, he took it. Smith's micro-budget 1994 debut comedy *Clerks* had helped jump-start the film industry's rush toward independent directors. His fourth movie, *Dogma,* was a heavy-handed satire of the Catholic Church, with Matt Damon and Ben Affleck playing fallen angels and Chris Rock as Christ's forgotten thirteenth apostle, Rufus. Carlin played Cardinal Ignatius Glick, a crass commercializer of the church who replaces the symbolic crucifix with a smiling, thumbs-up "Buddy Christ."

Smith was a Carlin disciple. After devouring the HBO specials as a teenager, he began traveling to see his comic hero perform, beginning with a 1988 set at Fairleigh Dickinson University in his home state, New Jersey. "Carlin replaced Catholicism as my religion," he recalled. The comedian became an honorary member of Smith's New Jerseyite universe, making a cameo appearance as a hitchhiker in *Jay and Silent Bob Strike Back* (2001) and playing a major role as Affleck's father, a public works employee with a heart of gold, in *Jersey Girl* (2004). "Listen to the mouth on this one!" he says when he first meets the Affleck character's bride-to-be, played by Jennifer Lopez. The movie took some lumps, but reviewers were generally impressed with Carlin's "convincingly gruff and blue-collar" portrayal, which Smith had written for him based on the director's own father. The comedian's performance was "so understated and devoid of sentimentality," said one writer, "that it comes off as the most deeply emotional one in the movie." Commercial television reruns of the film are notable for the opportunity to see Carlin, liberator of four-letter words, speaking lines overdubbed with euphemistic *gosh darn*s and *dirtball*s.

On *Back in Town*, he had joked about the preponderance of ads for telephone services from MCI, AT&T, and others in the wake of phone industry deregulation: "Are people really breaking their balls to save nine cents on a fuckin' phone call?" Now, around the time of the *Dogma* release, some of Carlin's fans were disappointed to see him in a commercial for an MCI calling plan. As he had a decade earlier, when he did a series of short ads for Fuji videocassettes, the comic renowned for his relentless antiestablishment attitude found himself obliged to address the issue of "selling out." (Carlin also once filmed an unused commercial for Jell-O, a gig that Cosby would eventually make famous.) The complaints, he noted, probably came from a guy wearing "a Gucci shirt or a McDonald's hat. . . . He doesn't live in the woods and eat bark and make his own clothing out of vines. So no one is really pure." Everything in modern life is a kind of compromise, he believed: "Even Ted Kaczynski, who hated technology, used a typewriter to type his manifesto." Carlin's own decision to do the phone ad, besides the fact that MCI (as had Fuji before it) let him gently lampoon his pitchman role with what amounted to a miniature stand-up routine, was based on his understandable desire to retire the remainder of his IRS debt.

The reason: He was committed to a new live-in relationship. The comic who had kicked off his sitcom by scoffing at optimism—"Hope sucks"—had found romance with a woman named Sally Wade. She was a comedy writer who had worked on several episodes of the 1970s sitcom *What's Happening*. They met at a bookstore. "He and Sally had their first date at our house," says Orson Bean, the veteran television personality, who was Wade's neighbor near Venice Beach. "We invited her to a party. She said, 'Can I bring a date?' and it turned out to be George." Carlin soon moved into Sally's home, where he and Bean would swap jokes when they met in the alley, taking out the trash. Though they apparently never took out a marriage license, Carlin was with his second "wife" for ten years, until the end of his life. "I think Sally kind of saved him," says Dennis Blair. "The first thing he'd do after the show every night was call her."

Carlin had been a career loner. The old delicatessen guys, the Dangerfield protegés, and the Comedy Store regulars typically lived for the camaraderie, the one-upmanship, and the old war stories. Carlin was content to travel light, with his laptop and his reading material. When he wanted to air out some new jokes, he usually drove south, to the Comedy and Magic club in Hermosa Beach, where the crowd was less saturated with agents, talent scouts, and other guest-list types than the rooms in LA.

Having hit sixty, however, he was beginning to appreciate his place in the comic pantheon. He joined Robert Klein, Alan King, Jay Leno, Paul Reiser, and others to film a mock opening sequence for Jerry Seinfeld's HBO special *I'm Telling You for the Last Time*, in which the comedian holds a funeral for his old routines. Carlin was honored for lifetime achievement at the American Comedy Awards, and Comedy Central ranked him the second-greatest stand-up comedian of all time, behind Richard Pryor. Though he was flattered, "It was a little embarrassing to be placed ahead of Lenny Bruce," he admitted.

At the American Comedy Awards, Carlin posed for a photo with Pryor and Robert Klein. Klein leaned down to Pryor, in a wheelchair due to his battle with multiple sclerosis, and whispered in his ear, "You were the best I ever saw." When they walked away, Carlin said out of the corner of his mouth, "That guy's fucked up!"

"I knew he wasn't meaning to be cruel," says Klein. "George was sardonic about it. He actually made me laugh." Even in the most dispiriting situations, for Carlin there was no such thing as no laughing matter.

Together with Hamza, he agreed to join the founders of a new comedy venture, Laugh.com, as a limited business partner. Marshall Berle, Milton's nephew, who went from managing Spirit to handling pop metal acts such as Van Halen and Ratt, launched the Laugh.com Web site in the mid-1990s as an outlet for his uncle's vast archive of Friars Club roasts. "I sold one to a guy named Bob Kohn, who lived in Pebble Beach," says Berle. "He turns out to be the guy who comes in and saves the company." Kohn was an Internet entrepreneur who founded the subscription download site eMusic. Together the two men enlisted a who's who of comedy legends, including Red Buttons, Bill Dana, Jonathan Winters, Phyllis Diller, Shelley Berman, Norm Crosby, and Rich Little, as founding partners. Besides Kohn, another of Berle's earliest customers was one Rev. Warren Debenham, a comedy historian from the Bay Area who donated a sizable portion of his massive collection to the San Francisco Public Library. After lending his name to the company, Carlin often called Berle with special requests from the Debenham collection, looking for obscure recordings by the Two Black Crows, an old blackface vaudeville act, or the Canadian duo Wayne and Shuster. "He'd come up with guys I never heard of," says Berle.

Carlin had always looked to the farthest frontiers of comedy. Some of his earliest routines with Jack Burns deliberately trampled the line marking the no-man's land of tastelessness. The "Seven Words," of course, were a direct challenge to commonly accepted notions of propriety. As he reached what he felt was his pinnacle as a writer and performer, however, Carlin pushed harder than ever to make his audience contemplate the verboten. "I find out where they draw the line, then I deliberately step across it," he said. "I try to bring them with me, and make them happy they came."

"Our Last Best Angry Man Takes on God, Children, and Testosterone," read the sticker on the CD version of Carlin's next HBO special, the charmingly titled *You Are All Diseased*. He had looked around and decided that children were the last sacred topic in America, and he directed his attention accordingly. Kids are overprotected, overscheduled, and overrated, he fulminated, when they're really just like other people—"a few winners, a whole lotta losers." He quickly dispensed with any potential criticism: "I know what you're thinking—you say, 'Jesus, he's not gonna attack children, is he?' Yes, he is. And remember, this is Mr. Conductor talking. I know what I'm talking about."

One segment of the "Kids and Parents" bit featured Carlin's rant about school shootings and the grief counseling that follows. Two months after *You Are All Diseased* had its HBO premier, two students at Columbine High School in suburban Colorado went on a shooting spree, killing thirteen and injuring twenty-one before committing suicide, in the deadliest such incident in an American high school.

E-mail in-boxes were soon filled with forwarded messages attributed to Carlin (or, alternately, to a Columbine student who witnessed the attack). On first glance, "The Paradox of Our Time" read like it could have been Carlin, with its rhythmic reliance on juxtapositions: "We have taller buildings, but shorter tempers; wider freeways, but narrower viewpoints. . . . We've added years to life, not life to years." But Carlin had nothing to do with it. The homily was eventually revealed to have been written by a Christian pastor from Seattle named Dr. Bob Moorehead, who was subsequently dismissed from his post in the wake of sexual assault allegations. Carlin, who had concluded his latest performance with a long diatribe about the awesome bullshit propagated by organized religion, was vehement in denying his connection to the Internet chain letters, which spread exponentially. For one thing, he pointed out in a post on his Web site, he was emotionally divorced from the future of mankind. Besides, he wrote, "It's not only bad prose and poetry, it's weak philosophy."

For some time Carlin's name remained an Internet sensation, with anonymous e-mailers attributing various jokes and lists to him. One hoax involved an inane manifesto from "a BAD American . . . George Carlin." Misleading information about Carlin on the Internet was understandable for one very good reason: He had earned a reputation, and not just among devoted fans, for profundity. Even in his thirties and forties, he had been comedy's wise man. Now, officially entering his senior years, his white hair and beard made him seem that much more a comic philosopher. "Life is a festival only to the wise," wrote Emerson. Carlin saw his country as a never-ending festival for his own amusement. When you're born, you get a ticket to the freak show, he said. "If you're born in America, you get a front-row seat. And some of us get to write about it and talk about it."

Carlin "had an instinctive knowledge of how persuasion, propaganda, and influence work, from all directions, by all parties," says Jello Biafra, former frontman for the punk-rock group Dead Kennedys. The comedian's punk attitude—his insistence on telling his audience the truth as he saw it, regardless of its popularity—was ahead of its time, says Biafra, who was a candidate for the Green Party's presidential nomination in 2000 and has since campaigned vigorously on behalf of Ralph Nader.

Though Carlin was occasionally asked whether he would ever consider a third-party candidacy, his response was always the same. He had no faith in the voting process. He hadn't voted in a presidential election since 1972, when he voted for George McGovern; he had volunteered in 1970 on behalf of gubernatorial candidate Jesse Unruh, the California Democrat who opposed incumbent Ronald Reagan, but found the experience discouraging. It was senseless to blame the politicians, he said on one of the specials: "If you have selfish, ignorant citizens, then you're gonna get selfish, ignorant politicians."

Not only did he distrust liberals as much as conservatives—he wasn't interested in third parties, either. The "fashionable" and "faintly dangerous"–sounding Libertarianism was, for him, "just one more bullshit political philosophy." He sided only with H. L. Mencken, who declared, "I belong to no party: I am my own party."

Carlin's extensive history of expressing his distrust of religion made him an unofficial spokesman for nonbelievers. "When it comes to God's existence," he joked in *When Will Jesus Bring the Pork Chops?*, "I'm not an atheist and I'm not an agnostic. I'm an acrostic. The whole thing puzzles me." Science, logic, and reason were his religion. Despite his disdain for New Age ideas, he told one magazine that he felt like a "star child."

> I read somewhere that every atom in us—because we're all made mostly of heavier elements—came from the inside of a star. Had to be. Couldn't come from any other place. So we're all star children, and we're all identical in that sense. We have identical atoms. And they're just rearranged differently. You're the same thing as a Coke machine down the hall in your office, and a cigarette butt in the Buffalo airport.

He sincerely tried to believe in God, Carlin said at the end of *You Are All Diseased*. But there were these nagging little clues to the contrary, such as "war, disease, death, destruction, hunger, filth, poverty, torture, crime, corruption and the Ice Capades. . . . If this is the best God can do," he said, "I am not impressed."

If God was the cause of so much catastrophe and cataclysm, he was happy for the spectacle. His working title for the next HBO special was *I Kinda Like It When a Lot of People Die*. For the cover of the compact disc, he began working with the San Francisco punk collage artist Winston Smith, who has done artwork for *Playboy* and the bands Green Day and Dead Kennedys. A man with an apocalyptic vision of American folly, who took his assumed name from the protagonist of Orwell's *1984* and still wears a fedora, Smith is another example of Carlin's kind of guy. When Carlin explained his idea for the cover art, Smith knew they were simpatico. Among the reams of images from old magazines he clips and saves for his work, "I've got volcanoes, earthquakes, you name it—I've got all kinds of disasters," he says.

The HBO show date was set for November 2001, with the CD to come out a month later. Smith was fast approaching his deadline for the cover art when, on the morning of September 11, he got a call from Carlin. Both men were watching the live footage of the collapse of New York's two World Trade Center towers. "He was hastily getting me to get our stories straight," says Smith, who was not surprised when Carlin said he'd have to change the name of the show. (Carlin eventually settled on *Complaints and Grievances*.) "I thought, under the circumstances, that was probably a wise decision," says Smith. "His reaction was, 'Yeah, the record company—they got no balls.'"

For weeks after the 9/11 attacks, the country was paralyzed by a collective sense of disbelief, and humor seemed to many commentators like an unacceptable extravagance. Comedians fretted publicly about their role at a time when few felt like laughing. A teary David Letterman told his audience, "I don't trust my judgment at a time like this." When Bill Maher agreed with a guest's contention that the Al Qaeda hijackers who flew the planes into the World Trade Center could not reasonably be called "cowards," as President George W. Bush had suggested, the host of ABC's *Politically Incorrect* was widely denounced. Declining advertising support soon led to the show's cancellation.

A little over two months after the 9/11 attacks, Carlin took the stage at the Beacon Theatre for his third HBO special there. After acknowledging the unavoidable topic—the "turd in the punch bowl"—he vowed to plow ahead with the job he was paid to do, ensuring that his audience had fun. "Otherwise, the terrorists win," he said, sucking on the words like expired milk. "Don't you love that stuff? It's our latest mindless cliché." Having trimmed nearly ten minutes of material that applied to the old working title, he did a segment of gross-out humor on scabs and "lip crud" and a lengthy bit about rubbernecking at traffic accidents that he'd done as a warm-up on a recent *Tonight Show*. The centerpiece, however, was a long list of "People Who Oughta Be Killed," including those who use credit cards for small purchases and "guys named Todd." He ended by resurrecting an old idea, a carefully reasoned explanation of how to pare the Ten Commandments down to two. Coveting thy neighbor's wife, he argued, is really just harmless fantasizing; without it, "what's a guy gonna think about when he's waxing his carrot?" The dirty old man was not about to temper his audacity according to the terrorism alerts—though he did show solidarity with his hometown by pulling on a New York City T-shirt as the end credits ran, to the carnivalesque tune "The Sidewalks of New York."

Shortly after Winston Smith finished his work on the *Complaints and Grievances* album art, he was invited to see Carlin perform at his new venue in Vegas, the MGM Grand, where several patrons mistook the white-bearded collage artist for the headlining comedian as he made his way through the casino. Midway through the show, Carlin grew frustrated with a woman who was talking loudly to her companion, ignoring the performer. "Lady, would you shut the fuck up?" Carlin finally blurted, followed by "other, much ruder things," according to Smith. "People realized he wasn't kidding. Suddenly the laughter kind of died down."

It was by no means Carlin's only incident at the MGM, where he'd been performing since finishing his decade-long run at Bally's. For four years he stuck to his contract at the MGM Grand, but it was a mutually disagreeable association. He'd been inciting walkouts for years—one reviewer of a show in Topeka described a scene including "picketers and counter-picketers" outside the theater and "perhaps a dozen folks" who walked out during the performance. At the MGM, Carlin perfected the art of driving faint-hearted ticket holders toward the exits. The constant complaint was that the show was too dark. "Riffs included suicide and beheadings," wrote one local reviewer. At the end of the run, Carlin took the opportunity to renew his contempt for the city and the mindless escapism it stood for: "People who go to Las Vegas, you've got to question their fuckin' intellect to start with," he said. "Traveling hundreds and thousands of miles to essentially give your money to a large corporation is kind of fuckin' moronic." A woman in the audience reportedly yelled, "Stop degrading us!"

Facetiously, Carlin thanked her, indicating he hadn't actually heard what she said. "I hope it was positive. If not, well, blow me," he said.

Just after leaving the MGM in late 2004, Carlin announced that he was voluntarily checking himself into an exclusive rehab facility for an addiction to the pain killer Vicodin, which, compounded with his taste for fine wine, was becoming a problem. He'd never been in rehab before, as he took care to mention, quitting cocaine completely on his own and cutting down his pot smoking to an occasional hit or two (mostly to "punch up the writing," as he told *High Times* magazine).

He started with the Vicodin, he said, before Brenda died, when he dipped into the prescription she had been given for fibromyalgia, a mysterious, possibly stress-related condition characterized by extreme fatigue and sensitivity to pain. He felt "almost unworthy" in the program, he later said, with his self-described habit of a bottle or more of wine and four or five Vicodin per day: "Some of the guys in there were taking fifty Vikes a day and burning down their houses and backing into police vans and shit."

Even if they didn't know about his Vicodin habit, Carlin's friends were well aware that he'd become a wine connoisseur. When Carlin quietly put up five figures of his own money to support Chris Rush's existential one-man show, *Laughter Is the Sound of Bliss*, he took the less-known comic to a fancy dinner. Rush wondered how his friend could justify ordering a $200 bottle of red wine. Then he tried it. "I had two sips, and I started rapping like I was on a mix of acid and Scopo-lamine," says the former molecular biologist. Carlin looked at Rush and said, "Now you know why all those counts fought over vineyards."

His previous habits earned the comedian a voice-over role in the an-imated Pixar film *Cars*. Carlin's character, fittingly, is an aging, daisy-painted Volkswagen minibus named Fillmore, who lives in a Day-glo geodesic dome and talks up the benefits of his "homemade organic fuel." The character was based on Bob Waldmire, a real-life hippie throwback who travels Route 66, where much of the movie is set, in a VW bus, drawing postcards and maps of the historic road's icons.

Carlin's rehab was timed to give him a clean bill of health before starting a new Vegas engagement, at the Stardust, in early 2005. He and Hamza knew Terry Jenkins, entertainment director for the Stardust's parent company, Boyd Gaming, which owned a resort in Tunica, Mis-sissippi, where Carlin had performed. Taking over for Wayne Newton, he stayed at the Stardust Theater until it closed in late 2006, in antici-pation of demolition. The gaming company then brought the come-dian over to the Orleans. He checked it out beforehand by asking Tommy Smothers, who had headlined there with his brother. "Proba-bly the best comedy room in Vegas," Smothers told him. Situated sev-eral blocks off the Las Vegas Strip on Tropicana Avenue, the Mardi Gras–themed Orleans was a welcome change for Carlin, who appreci-ated the fact that audiences needed to make an effort to find him there.

Yet he still had plenty of healthy contempt for the town. Vegas, Carlin said not long after the move, remained for him "the most dispiriting, soul-deadening city on earth." But he couldn't deny the benefit of working out new material in front of an ever-changing audi-ence, unlike the fixed number of devoted fans he could count on dur-ing his periodic visits to medium-sized markets around the country. Though the Vegas audience continually replenished itself, he said, it came with a cost—he couldn't assume the crowds would be his from the outset. "In Pittsburgh I get the hardcore fans who know what I am about. In Las Vegas often I get people who saw me on Leno or got a coupon. . . . Each night I have to find out how they are going to be and I have to train them." The Orleans, he knew, was as apt a fit as he was likely to find in Sin City. "He loved it here," says Jenkins. "Almost every night, George would ask me what percent of the tickets were paid [not comped]. That would always give us an indication about how many people were making that trip from the Strip." He'd also take note of the cab lines outside after the show. More cabs meant more guests specifically there to see Carlin.

Jenkins and his colleagues watched the comic prepare for his last two HBO specials at Boyd's Las Vegas properties. The title of *Life Is Worth Losing*, Carlin's fourth show in a row (and last) from the Beacon Theatre, was a parody of *Life Is Worth Living*, Archbishop Fulton J. Sheen's inspirational prime-time program from the early days of network television. Carlin's thirteenth HBO concert, recorded less than a year after his rehab, was relentlessly bleak, the one special that most supports the notion that he grew darker in his final years. Even the stage was designed like a snowy city cemetery at night. After his opening rap, a jargon-filled verse he called "Modern Man" ("I'm a hands-on, footloose, knee-jerk head case, prematurely post-traumatic, and I've got a love child that sends me hate mail"), Carlin unleashed a cavalcade of black thoughts, a conversational, almost punch-line-free tour through every macabre subject he could think of, from suicide, genocide, torture, and necrophilia to the beheadings that were recently in the news about Iraq. Such behavior doesn't say much for the species, he noted drily. For a finale, he imagined "an apocalypse that is part Stephen King, part Quentin Tarantino, and part George Romero," as one reviewer put it. "In the end, the world is consumed in a mighty conflagration. Only hedonistic New York, Carlin's birthplace, is spared."

His harshest show was a gleeful phantasmagoria. Like dreams, jokes originate in the unconscious, said Sigmund Freud. Both "try to outwit the inner censor." If Carlin were a painter, this would have been his deliberately ugly period. "There are a lot of comics working forty years who might have added ten jokes to their act over that time," comedian Richard Lewis told the *New York Times*. "Carlin treats every HBO special like a gallery opening."

Having taken Lenny Bruce's radical moral reassessments to an extreme in *Life Is Worth Losing*, the next special, *It's Bad for Ya*, was Carlin's nod to the other comic revolutionary of the 1950s, Mort Sahl. Aired live from the arts center in Santa Rosa, California, a stiffer, puffier Carlin, now seventy, padded carefully around a cluttered set designed to look like a cozy den and office, with a thick dictionary on a stand given a place of prominence at center stage. A memorable bit on removing the names of deceased friends from your address book segued into thoughts on the excessive culture of child worship, the misplaced use of the word "pride" ("Being Irish isn't a skill. You wouldn't say you're proud to be five-eleven"), and the "delusional thinking" behind religious and patriotic customs, such as swearing on the Bible and removing your hat for the singing of "God Bless America." In what would prove to be the last recorded hunk George Carlin ever performed, in what has to be the single most impressive body of solo material ever assembled by an American comedian, he went out, fittingly, with an analysis of the existence of individual rights. There are none, he claimed, breaking the bad news to fans who had come to see him as a beacon of American freedom: "We made 'em up." And if they can be taken away, they're not rights: "They're privileges."

Between the last two specials, Carlin took part in a tribute to Sahl at the Wadsworth Theatre in Brentwood. After the show he made out a big check to his predecessor, who, eighty years old and still performing, was having some financial trouble. Sahl had watched Carlin's career closely, and the cantankerous elder comic admits he didn't agree with all of it. "Stuff about white guys playing golf is like throwing fish to a seal," he says, and he never liked the swearing: "The only time I've ever cursed onstage is when I read from the Watergate transcripts." Still, Carlin was one of the only comedians who followed Lenny and Mort who took the job of social critic seriously. "America has been dying for several years," says Sahl. "Would you know it from the comedians?" Watching Carlin's final few HBO shows, you'd have no doubt.

Five years after receiving the Free Speech in Comedy Award at the 2002 U.S. Comedy Arts Festival, Carlin returned to Aspen for his last appearance there. Backstage, he casually told John Moffitt he was suffering from heart failure, that he'd recently been in and out of the hospital. "He was so much shorter and frailer. I was really worried about him," says Moffitt, who pleaded with his old friend to use the oxygen tank the festival had on hand for performers suffering adverse reactions to the altitude. Carlin waved him off, saying he'd resort to it if he needed it. He went onstage with his notes for the upcoming HBO show—working title, *The Parade of Useless Bullshit*—and he did nearly an hour and a half without a break. The crowd gave him a standing ovation.

"He was a tough little guy," says Moffitt. "The good news is that he was working until the very end."

In June 2008 the Kennedy Center announced that Carlin would receive its eleventh annual Mark Twain Prize for American Humor. That it took eleven tries for him to get it was nearly as shocking as the first time he said *cocksucker* in Milwaukee. Richard Pryor accepted the first Twain Prize in 1998, followed by Jonathan Winters, Bob Newhart, Lily Tomlin, and Steve Martin, among others. If he felt it was about time, Carlin kept it to himself. He seemed genuinely pleased with the honor. "Thank you, Mr. Twain," he said in a statement. "Have your people call my people."

Five days later he was admitted to St. John's Hospital in Santa Monica with chest pain. He died late that afternoon, June 22. He had performed the week before at the Orleans, where he was already beginning to organize his thoughts for his next HBO special. In interviews he had been telling a favorite story about the master cellist Pablo Casals, who continued to rehearse three hours a day well into his nineties. Asked why, Casals once replied, "Well, I'm beginning to notice some improvement."

Bum ticker and all, Carlin made it to seventy-one, defining a half-century in American comedy. "There's always hope for comedians," he said near the end. "You notice how long fucking George Burns, Groucho Marx, Milton Berle, and all these cocksuckers lived? I think it's because comedy gives you a way of renewing life energy. There's something about the release of tension that comes from being a comic, having a comic mind, that makes you live forever."

His daughter and his brother spread Carlin's ashes outside a few New York nightclubs and then at Spofford Lake, site of his early performing triumph at Camp Notre Dame. Fittingly, the family announced that the Thomas Jefferson Center for the Protection of Free Expression, along with the American Heart Association, would be the recipients of donations.

Shortly after his death Carlin's partner, Sally Wade, received a proclamation from the U.S. Congress. It accompanied the flag that flew over the Capitol the day after the comedian's death. He would have been supremely amused: Flags, he once said, are only symbols, "and I leave symbols to the symbol-minded."

KICKER

IN LATE 2003 California Representative Doug Ose introduced a bill into Congress that was intended, once and for all, to make broadcast use of George Carlin's "Seven Words You Can Never Say on Television" punishable by law. Ose's bill identified as profane "the words 'shit,' 'piss,' 'fuck,' 'cunt,' 'asshole,' and the phrases 'cock sucker,' 'mother fucker,' and 'ass hole' [*sic*]." Ironically, writes the cognitive scientist Steven Pinker, the Clean Airwaves Act was "the filthiest piece of legislation ever considered by Congress." Once again, Carlin's instincts had been validated. Substituting *asshole* for *tits*, the "Milwaukee Seven" were, in fact, the words you couldn't say.

The Congressman's bill was a response to conservative outrage over the FCC's decision not to fine NBC for its live broadcast of the Golden Globe Awards, during which the rock singer Bono said, "This is really, really fucking brilliant." The FCC had been maddeningly inconsistent on the issue, slapping a small PBS affiliate in the San Francisco area with a fine for indecent words heard in the Martin Scorsese documentary series *The Blues*. The Bono episode and others, including a notorious example of "visual indecency"—Janet Jackson's "wardrobe malfunction" at the 2004 Super Bowl, when one of her breasts was momentarily exposed on national television (for which CBS was fined $550,000, since overturned)—gave the culture the enduring concept of the "fleeting expletive": a one-time instance of profanity, indecency, or obscenity that occurs during live programming.

Given the rise of cable television, satellite media, and the Internet, taboo words about sex acts and bodily functions are more widespread than ever, as Pinker points out in *The Stuff of Thought*. Yet the government continues to hold radio stations and broadcast television networks accountable to another standard. Comically, the author notes, another piece of legislation, the Broadcast Decency Enforcement Act, was passed on the same day that Vice President Dick Cheney told Senator Patrick Leahy on the Senate floor "to be fruitful and multiply, but not in those words."

Upon Carlin's death, reporters took the opportunity to examine all the ways their newspapers continued to dance around the seven words that apparently will still infect your soul and curve your spine. Carlin's "heavy seven" were conspicuously incessant (if bleeped) on Comedy Central's *South Park* and *The Daily Show with Jon Stewart*. They were half the dialogue on HBO's *The Sopranos*, and they were permitted unchecked on broadcast networks in a documentary, *9/11*, and the commercial television debut of *Saving Private Ryan*. Even *The Today Show* let slip with "the word that's probably the Queen Mother of all obscenities, an unflattering reference to female nether regions," when guest Jane Fonda uttered it. "NBC apologized, to be sure," wrote one TV critic, "but the sky didn't fall."

In April 2009 the Supreme Court once again heard a case involving the FCC's jurisdiction over Carlin's magic words. By another 5–4 vote, the court upheld the commission's sanctions against "fleeting expletives." The case featured the spectacle of the conservative Justice Antonin Scalia providing a dramatic, expurgated reenactment of the singer Cher's acceptance of a lifetime achievement honor at the 2002 Billboard Music Awards, seen live on Fox: "People have been telling me I'm on the way out every year, right? So *f-word* 'em." Legal scholars pointed out that the decision sidestepped the First Amendment issue, and they predicted further litigation. That would ensure that Carlin's lexical evangelism—Lenny Bruce's legacy—would have still more days in court.

"What can I say about George Carlin that hasn't already been argued in front of the Supreme Court?" joked Bill Maher when he kicked off the Kennedy Center's posthumous tribute for the Mark Twain Prize. The late comedian's friend Lily Tomlin, his fellow Greenwich Village alum Joan Rivers, and next-generation devotees Jon Stewart and Lewis Black were among those on hand to celebrate the life and career of the comic wordsmith.

In his lifetime, Twain had much to say about censorship and taboo. "Nature knows no indecencies," he wrote. "Man invents them."

At the end of his own life, George Carlin was working on a one-man show he was planning for Broadway. One of his working titles was *Watch My Language*.

NOTES

All direct quotes attributed in the present tense have been drawn from author interviews. Quotes from television appearances are identified in the text, except where noted.

Warm-up

1 "a lawless element": Constance Rourke, *American Humor: A Study of the National Character* (Harcourt, Brace, 1931), 9.

1-2 "a scofflaw . . . who could be charged with breaking and entering": Barry Sanders, *Sudden Glory: Laughter as Subversive History* (Beacon Press, 1995), 252–53.

2 "If you're clothed, you have clothes": George Carlin, *Brain Droppings*, (Hyperion, 1997), 13.

2 "Every comedian does a little George": Jerry Seinfeld, "Dying Is Hard. Comedy Is Harder," *New York Times*, June 24, 2008.

2 "kids, pets, driving, the stores": Charles Taylor, "Dirty Old Man: George Carlin on Obscenity in the Age of Ashcroft," *Salon*, April 3, 2004.

3 "The comic comes into being": Quoted in Rourke, *American Humor*, 22.

4 "I found out that it was an honest craft": Appearance at the National Press Club (C-SPAN), 1999.

4 "I prefer seeing things the way they are": National Press Club, 1999.

5 "No matter how you care to define it": Carlin, *Brain Droppings*, xii.

5 "How he stood above and apart": Terry Teachout, *The Skeptic: A Life of H.L. Mencken* (Perennial/HarperCollins, 2002), 35.

5 "the privilege of the dead": Mark Twain, quoted in "The Privilege of the Grave," *The New Yorker*, December 22, 2008.

1. Heavy Mysteries

8   He "hid behind the government": Taylor, "Dirty Old Man: George Carlin on Obscenity in the Age of Ashcroft."

9   "He had a real line of shit, boy": Interview, Archive of American Television December 17, 2007.

10   "Let's get out of here, Pat": Interview, Archive of American Television

10   "The Irish call it the curse": Interview, Archive of American Television

10   "We ran for four years": Interview, Archive of American Television

11   "all these *A*s that I never got in school": *Carlin on Comedy* (audio recording), Laugh.com, 2002.

11   "The thing is, I never really had issues": T. J. English, "George Carlin Is Still Tossing Out the Good Stuff," *Irish America* (June/July 2006).

11   "I had to fight her off": Interview, Archive of American Television

12   "a man's salary": "What I've Learned: George Carlin," *Esquire* (January 2002).

12   "wonderfully alive and vibrant": Interview, Archive of American Television

12   "Home alone after school": "Proust Questionnaire: George Carlin," *Vanity Fair* (May 2001).

13   "a man bored with sinning": Evan Esar, *Esar's Comic Dictionary* (Harvest House, 1943), 69, 100, 113.

13   *Mad* "was magical, objective proof to kids": Tony Hiss and Jeff Lewis, "The 'Mad' Generation," *New York Times Magazine*, July 31, 1977.

13   "a way of thinking about a world": Robert Boyd, "Born Under a *Mad* Sign," *Los Angeles Times*, March 24, 2007.

14   "That was my family": Interview, Archive of American Television.

14   "There aren't any Huck Finns in radio": Gerald Nachman, *Raised on Radio* (University of California Press, 2000), 212.

15   "You can count on the thumb of one hand": Nachman, *Raised on Radio*, 98.

15   "Fifty percent of what I write": Nachman, *Raised on Radio*, 105.

16   "Our original premise": Nachman, *Raised on Radio*,125.

16   "I was a hip kid": Carlin, *Brain Droppings*, 224.

16   "They took things that were nice and decent": Interview by Marc Cooper, *The Progressive* (July 2001).

16-17   "that one really got my attention": Interview, Archive of American Television

17   "like a flower [to] the sun": Interview, Archive of American Television

17   "I was impressed, not that he was an admiral": *A&E Biography: George Carlin: More Than 7 Words* (2000).

18   "To laugh was to mock heaven": Barry Sanders, *Sudden Glory: Laughter as Subversive History*, (Beacon Press, 1995), 129.

20   "That was her big thing": *A&E Biography: George Carlin.*

21   "It was called 'How Do You Spend Your Leisure Time?'": Sam Merrill, "*Playboy* Interview: George Carlin," *Playboy* (January 1982).

22   "The older I got, the more apparent it became": Merrill, "*Playboy* Interview."

2. Class Clown

25   "I'd make fun of the authority figures": Interview, Archive of American Television.

26   "fly over the area": Appearance on *Dennis Miller Live* (HBO), January 13, 1997.

27   "a voluntary nigger": Mark Goodman, "George Carlin Feels Funny," *Esquire* (December 1974).

27   "They would plant cultures": Tony Hendra, *Going Too Far: The Rise and Demise of Sick, Gross, Black, Sophomoric, Weirdo, Pinko, Anarchist, Underground, Anti-Establishment Humor*, (Dolphin/Doubleday, 1987), 161–62.

28   "colorful, reachable, human": George Carlin, "An Old Underdog Finds Himself on Top," *New York Times*, October 12, 1986.

28   "When my tech sergeant expressed his displeasure": Merrill, "*Playboy* Interview."

29   "I left my gun on the ground": Merrill, "*Playboy* Interview."

31   "I grew up with real rhythm and blues": "George Carlin: How Radio Changed My Life," *Harp* (September/October 2007).

31   "nothing short of a revolution": Hendra, *Going Too Far*, 169.

32   "I had to play that": Dean Johnson, "At 55, Carlin's Sharp Wit Keeps on Cutting," *Boston Herald*, December 11, 1992.

33   "I was staying at the Hotel Nacional de Cuba": Dick Lochte, "Natty and the Beanbag: Burns and Schreiber Owe a Lot to a Taxicab," *TV Guide*, August 18–24, 1973.

35   "one last chance at me": Interview, Archive of American Television.

36   "the most successful of the new sickniks": "The Sickniks," *Time*, July 13, 1959.

36   "Shelley Berman couldn't do Mort Sahl's act": Interview, Archive of American Television.

37   "In my home Westbrook Pegler": Hendra, *Going Too Far*, 163.

37   "At that time George was fairly conservative": Richard Zoglin, *Comedy at the Edge: How Stand-up in the 1970s Changed America*, (Bloomsbury, 2008), 22.

38   "How did you two meet?": Interview, Archive of American Television.

39   "no troublemakers, no queers": Joe Nick Patoski, "The King of Clubs," *Texas Monthly* (April 2000).

40   "We became very inventive and creative": Interview, Archive of American Television.

41   "We're not gonna park cars": Interview, Archive of American Television.

41   "the leading Negro and foreign-language station": John A. Jackson, *Big Beat Heat: Alan Freed and the Early Years of Rock & Roll* (Schirmer Books, 1991), 296.

41   "trying anybody and everybody": Jackson, *Big Beat Heat*, 296–97.

42   "We were insane": Goodman, "George Carlin Feels Funny."

43   "We took positions": *George on George* (interview program), 2003.

44   "He didn't have a lot of connections": Archive of American Television interview.

46   "a duo of hip wits": Hendra, *Going Too Far,* 163.

47   "We didn't know the legendary quality": Hendra, *Going Too Far,* 163.

47   "We felt that was an omen": Interview, Archive of American Television.

48   "Brenda and I clicked on all levels": Merrill, "*Playboy* Interview."

48   "a night light to the bathroom": Jack Paar, *P.S. Jack Paar: An Entertainment* (Doubleday, 1983), 100.

3. Attracting Attention

52   "My mother would say": Interview, Archive of American Television.

52   "Some really great toilets": Phil Berger, *The Last Laugh: The World of the Stand-Up Comics* (Morrow, 1975; Limelight Editions, 1985), 138.

54   "We didn't work very hard": Merrill, "*Playboy* Interview."

56   "I can remember doing the supper show": Interview, Archive of American Television.

56   "Since I have always been able to detect": Steve Allen, *More Funny People* (Stein and Day, 1982), 104.

57   "I was good and juiced": Sound recording included in Ronald K. L. Collins and David M. Skover, *The Trials of Lenny Bruce: The Fall and Rise of an American Icon* (Sourcebooks, Inc., 2002).

57   "sorta grabbed me by the collar": Collins and Skover, *Trials of Lenny Bruce,* 147.

58   "Someday everybody's going to know your name": Appearance on *20/20* (ABC), February 5, 1999.

59   "an extravaganza of patchwork": Bob Dylan, *Chronicles: Volume One,* (Simon & Schuster, 2005), 10–12.

60   "What kind of place you running here?" Berger, *Last Laugh,* 142.

60   "In 1963, the Village was alive": Richard Pryor with Todd Gold, *Pryor Convictions and Other Life Sentences* (Pantheon Books, 1995), 70.

61   "You break it down by talking about it": Collins and Skover, *Trials of Lenny Bruce,* 47–51.

62   "It's one of them numbers": Collins and Skover, *Trials of Lenny Bruce,* 203.

64   "The future seems so precarious": "The Sickniks."

64   "I wasn't very well-educated": Goodman, "George Carlin Feels Funny."

65   "Jester and savant must both": Arthur Koestler, *The Act of Creation* (Macmillan, 1964), 28.

65   "spontaneous flash of insight": Koestler, *Act of Creation,* 45.

65   "The jester makes jokes, he's funny": Jay Dixit, "George Carlin's Last Interview," *Psychology Today,* www.psychologytoday.com

67   "Anything that was challenging verbally": Interview, Archive of American Television.

67-68 "It was a standard fish-out-of-water gimmick": Interview, Archive of American Television.

69   "I didn't get a lot of attention": Interview, Archive of American Television.

4. Values
(How Much Is That Dog Crap in the Window?)

77   "There were a couple of monologues they cut": Interview, Archive of American Television.

79   "One last four-letter word": Lenny Bruce, *How to Talk Dirty and Influence People*, (Playboy Press, 1966), 240.

80   "Lenny's perception was magnificent": Judy Stone, "Carlin: Lenny Bruce Was His Idol," *New York Times*, May 28, 1967.

80   "let me know there was a place to go": Appearance on *Make 'Em Laugh* (PBS), 2009.

85   "high-fidelity ear": "Pop of the News," *Newsweek*, January 9, 1967.

85   "were dead. Just dead people": Interview, Archive of American Television.

89   "I became known as a reliable prime-time variety show comedian": Interview, Archive of American Television.

90   "I found out I can't do this shit": Interview, Archive of American Television.

90   "A man who tries to be everything but himself": Esar, *Esar's Comic Dictionary*, 4.

91   "The music was protest": *Unmasked with George Carlin* (XM Radio), 2007.

93   "nearly as admirable for potent simplicity": Paul Krassner, *The Winner of the Slow Bicycle Race: The Satirical Writings of Paul Krassner* (Seven Stories Press, 1996), 15.

94   "rule-bender and lawbreaker since first grade": Quoted in Paul Krassner, "Remembering George Carlin," *Huffington Post*, June 27, 2008.

5. The Confessional

98   "The crime wave is not a subject for levity": George Carlin, FBI file, released January 23, 2009 (per request no. 1123179–001).

98   "an individual named George Carlin": FBI file.

98   "it was obvious that he was using": FBI file.

99   "thinks that the Director is one of the greatest": FBI file.

99   "tonight our mouths fell open": FBI file.

99   "What do we know of Carlin?": FBI file.

100   "*That's* the kind of sick material": Lenny Bruce, "The Tribunal," *The Lenny Bruce Originals Volume 2* (sound recording) (Fantasy, 1991).

100   "I was opening for—try not to smile": Hendra, p. 251.

100   "O.J. Simpson has already received": George Carlin, *When Will Jesus Bring the Pork Chops?*, (Hyperion, 2004), 207.

101   "I was more or less flabbergasted": Hendra, *Going Too Far,* 252.

100-102   "Presumably the local constables wink": "Legit Profanity a Problem to Brit Café Comics," *Variety*, November 4, 1970.

102   "New York's heart-quarters for great stars": Mickey Podell-Raber with Charles Pignone, *The Copa: Jules Podell and the Hottest Club North of Havana* (Collins, 2007), 93.

102   "The Copa was a tough room": Nachman, *Raised on Radio,* 26.

102   "If Jules wanted attention": Podell-Raber with Pignone, *The Copa,* 116.

103   "I hated that fuckin' place": Interview, Archive of American Television.

103   "I'd say, 'I don't know if you're familiar'": *Esquire*

103   "He would never fire me, that fuck": Interview, Archive of American Television.

103   "It was very artistic, very cinematic": Zoglin, *Comedy at the Edge,* 18.

104   "Three weeks I had of that": Berger, *Last Laugh,* 48.

104   "swinging from the chandeliers": Zoglin,*Comedy at the Edge,* 47.

104   "My days of pretending to be as slick": Pryor and Gold, *Pryor Convictions,* 93–94.

105   "dazzling states of heightened awareness": "LSD," *Time,* June 17, 1966

105   "It opened my eyes": Martin A. Lee and Bruce Shalin, *Acid Dreams: The Complete Social History of LSD: The CIA, the Sixties, and Beyond* (Grove Weidenfeld, 1985), 181.

106   "Those drugs served their purpose": Merrill, "*Playboy* Interview."

106   "He has the ability to couch them in jargon": *Variety*, July 29, 1970.

107   "come up a modish contemporary fellow": *Variety*, September 9, 1970.

107   "I'd wake up in the morning": Merrill, "*Playboy* Interview."

108   "Virginia Graham was a real shit-stirrer": Interview, Archive of American Television.

108   "They did the job for me": Interview, Archive of American Television.

108   "I never went over to Don Adams's house": Stu Werbin, "How George Carlin Showed His Hair," *Rolling Stone,* August 17, 1972.

109   "I sold grass in the mailroom on the side": David Rensin, *The Mailroom: Hollywood History from the Bottom Up* (Ballantine, 2003), 113.

112   "George made a gesture": Berger, *Last Laugh,* 205.

112   "I've only had three people walk offstage": Dan Plutchak, "George Carlin's First and Last Show in Lake Geneva," *Walworth County Today,* July 15, 2008.

112   "where they walk *toward* you": Nachman, *Raised on Radio,* 404.

112   "Hefner is saying to me": Werbin, "How George Carlin Showed His Hair."

113   "routine about materialism in American society": "Comic George Carlin Much Too Successful in 'Arousing' Audience," *Variety*, December 2, 1970.

113   "it never occurred to me": Diahann Carroll with Ross Firestone, *Diahann! An Autobiography* (Little, Brown, 1986), 60.

115   "Everyone had come there to see George Carlin": Berger, *Last Laugh,* 206–7.

116   "a nice, new, mainstream car": Interview, Archive of American Television.

116   "You were just talking to him": Donald Liebenson, "David Brenner at Zanies: 'This Is What Comedy Was Meant to Do,'" *Huffington Post,* November 20, 2008.

118   "Oddest censorship I ever experienced": *Unmasked with George Carlin.*

118   "sloppy and hippy character": Berger, *Last Laugh,* 222.

119   "just trying to make it less fearsome": Appearance on *The Mike Douglas Show* (syndicated), May 15, 1971.

120   "I'd never done a real college-audience-in-the-Sixties kind of thing": Interview, Archive of American Television.

120   "I killed": Interview, Archive of American Television.

6. Special Dispensation

123   "trying to cash in on the hippie craze": Interview, Archive of American Television.

124   "now being thought of as hokey": Interview, Archive of American Television.

125   "They weren't on my side totally": Interview, Archive of American Television.

125   "It's natural for people to distrust": Werbin, "How George Carlin Showed His Hair."

126   "They'd heard about it in show business": Interview, Archive of American Television.

126   "I went over to explain to him": Zoglin, *Comedy at the Edge,* 32.

126   "It's an opportunity for George": Appearance on *The Tonight Show Starring Johnny Carson* (NBC), February 29, 1972.

127   "I don't know about 'better'": Appearance on *The Mike Douglas Show* (syndicated), Feburary 18, 1972.

128   "After twenty years of that": Werbin, "How George Carlin Showed His Hair."

129   "That was really the capper": Werbin, "How George Carlin Showed His Hair."

130   "She didn't know it had reached this level": Interview, Archive of American Television.

131   "He takes seven expletives": Henry Edwards, "Their Satire Is Kid Stuff," *New York Times,* April 28, 1974.

132   "marijuana smoke was so thick in the area": Dave Tianen, "Summerfest: Gig Has Had Many High Notes," *Milwaukee Journal Sentinel,* June 28, 2007.

133   "I couldn't believe my ears": Jim Stingl, "Carlin's Naughty Words Still Ring in Officer's Ears," *Milwaukee Journal Sentinel*, July 1, 2007.

134   "No one said to me, you know": Appearance on *20/20*.

134   "Brenda and I laid off of everything": Werbin, "How George Carlin Showed His Hair."

134-135   "had no idea he was like that": Quoted in Dave Tianen, "Summerfest: The Big 40," *Milwaukee Journal Sentinel*, June 24, 2007.

135   "I find it kind of funny": *Milwaukee Journal Sentinel*, June 28, 2007.

137   "Jeepers creepers, you can imagine": *Milwaukee Journal Sentinel*, June 28, 2007.

142   "use of obscene language is very simple": Stone, "Carlin."

142   "was the first one to make language an issue": *Carlin on Comedy*.

7. Seven Words You Can Never Say on Television

143   "She'd gotten the imprimatur": Interview, Archive of American Television.

144   "Let's face it": Arthur Unger, "The Nonconforming George Carlin," *Christian Science Monitor*, July 23, 1973.

145   "I take a perverse delight": Werbin, "How George Carlin Showed His Hair."

145   "and a number of others just stormed out": Berger, *Last Laugh,* 226–28.

146   "Cocaine was different": Merrill, "*Playboy* Interview."

147   "I 'peed' a long time on him," Berger, *Last Laugh,* 229.

147   "*Shit* has saved my life": Berger, *Last Laugh,* 232.

148   "One man's vulgarity": Anthony Lewis, *Freedom for the Thought That We Hate: A Biography of the First Amendment* (Basic Books, 2007), 42–43, 131–32.

148   "was doing great damage to words": *The Carlin Case*, WBAI, March 30, 1978.

150   "He played all kinds of records": Jesse Walker, *Rebels on the Air: An Alternative History of Radio in America* (New York University Press, 2001), 73.

150   "Whereas I can perhaps understand": *The Carlin Case*.

154   "Obnoxious, gutter language": Marjorie Heins, *Not in Front of the Children: "Indecency," Censorship, and the Innocence of Youth* (Hill and Wang, 2001), 99.

154   "simply as a matter of taste": Matthew Lasar, *Pacifica Radio: The Rise of an Alternative Network* (Temple University Press, 1999), 141.

160   "biggest regret": David Hochman, "*Playboy* Interview: George Carlin," *Playboy* (October 2005).

162   "the first show in the history of television": Tom Shales and James Andrew Miller, *Live from New York: An Uncensored History of Saturday Night Live,* (Back Bay Books, 2002), 22.

163   "punctual, and he fills out forms well": Doug Hill and Jeff Weingrad, *Saturday Night: A Backstage History of Saturday Night Live* (Beech Tree Books/William Morrow, 1986), 84.

163   "I kept praying, 'I hope George Carlin'": Shales and Miller, *Live from New York*, 33.

163   "the major focus of the night": Shales/Miller, *Live from New York*, 62.

165   "I probably didn't have the nerve": Shales/Miller, *Live from New York*, 56.

8. Wasted Time

168   "It is said that every successful business": George Mair, *Inside HBO: The Billion Dollar War Between HBO, Hollywood and the Home Video Revolution* (Dodd, Mead, 1988), 14.

169   "Comedians' Bill of Rights": Appearance on *20 Years of Comedy on HBO*, 1995.

171   "I was never quite sure of it": Tony Orlando and Patsi Bale Cox, *Halfway to Paradise* (St. Martin's Griffin 2003), 153.

171   "You can't be the hot new guy": Interview, Archive of American Television.

172-173 "It would seem to be an American Negro invention": Ashley Montagu, *The Anatomy of Swearing* (Macmillan, 1967), 313.

173-174 "a classic case of burning the house": Heins, *Not in Front of the Children*, 101.

174   "because it is neither a sexual nor excretory organ": Heins, *Not in Front of the Children*, 102.

175   "would risk fine or lose its license": *The Carlin Case*.

175   "of nothing but farting": Lasar, *Pacifica Radio*, 224.

176   "constitutionally sound but not very politically prudent": Heins, *Not in Front of the Children*, 103.

177   "that's as far as I go": Merrill, "*Playboy* Interview."

177   "locked up in school taking sex education courses": Nicholas von Hoffman, "Seven Dirty Words: A Cute Form of Censorship," *Washington Post*, July 29, 1978.

177   "a good deal of street talk": Les Brown, "Court's Decision on Language Stirs Broadcasters," *New York Times*, July 10, 1978.

178   "If you don't like it": Heins, *Not in Front of the Children*, 109.

178   "those transgressions suddenly seemed like small potatoes": Merrill, "*Playboy* Interview."

180   "a trip to the cemetery": Appearance on *Inside the Actors Studio* (Bravo), 2004.

181   "There'll be a lot of concert footage": "George Carlin's Coming of Age," *Harvard Crimson*, July 25, 1978.

183   "Frankly, I feel dated": "George Carlin's Coming of Age."

183   "It was like a breathing-in period": *Carlin on Comedy*.

184   "By the time 1980 arrived": Steve LaBate, "George Carlin On . . . ," *Paste*, September 25, 2007.

184   "My album career had faded": Interview, Archive of American Television.

186   "If you were in Birmingham, Alabama": Betsy Borns, *Comic Lives: Inside the World of American Stand-Up Comedy* (Fireside, 1987), 47.

9. America the Beautiful

192   "The orchestra chairs are piled": Tom Shales, "'Carlin at Carnegie,' A Cherishable Touch," *Washington Post*, January 8, 1983.

192   "HBO didn't kick in for me until": Interview, Archive of American Television.

193   "It was truly like a ton of bricks": *A&E Biography: George Carlin*.

194   "just fed your dissatisfaction": *A&E Biography: George Carlin*.

194   "Abraham Maslow said the fully realized man": Dixit, "George Carlin's Last Interview."

195   "too sane for his own good": Robert R. Provine, *Laughter: A Scientific Investigation* (Viking, 2000), 171.

202   "Kinison was the first guy I ever saw": Cynthia True, *American Scream: The Bill Hicks Story* (HarperEntertainment, 2002), 40.

204   "I realized I had to raise my voice": The Onion A.V. Club and Stephen Thompson, eds., *The Tenacity of the Cockroach: Conversations with Entertainment's Most Enduring Outsiders* (Three Rivers Press, 2002), 24–25.

10. Squeamish

206   "I heard a sound that, for children": Britt Allcroft, "The George Carlin I Knew," *Los Angeles Times*, June 26, 2008.

206   "always sounded as if he were": Seinfeld, "Dying Is Hard."

207   "I just felt terrific in that role": Interview, Archive of American Television.

208   "nice, controlled anger": Jefferson Graham, "Carlin Swaps Stand-Up for Sitcom," *USA Today*, January 13, 1994.

208   "Carlin's aging hipster character": Todd Everett, "Unexpected Things Happen to George," *Daily Variety*, January 14, 1994.

209   "He was my kind of guy": Interview, Archive of American Television.

210   "I'm doing my best work": Ronald L. Smith, *Who's Who in Comedy* (Facts on File, 1992), 92.

211   "I knew I'd found my voice": Interview, Archive of American Television.

215   "I'm very much a realist and a practical person": Hochman, "*Playboy* Interview."

216   "Carlin replaced Catholicism": Kevin Smith, A God Who Cussed," *Newsweek*, June 23, 2008.

216   "convincingly gruff and blue-collar portrayal": Mick LaSalle, "Down and Out in New Jersey, Without Jennifer Lopez By His Side," *San Francisco Chronicle*, March 26, 2004.

216   "so understated and devoid of sentimentality": Stephanie Zacharek, "Jersey Girl," *Salon*, March 26, 2004.

217   "a Gucci shirt or a McDonald's hat": Onion Club and Thompson, *Tenacity of the Cockroach*, 23–24.

218   "it was a little embarrassing to be placed ahead of Lenny Bruce": Joseph P. Kahn, "From 7 Words to Endless Ideas," *Boston Globe*, July 20, 2006.

219   "I find out where they draw the line": *Make 'Em Laugh*.

220   "it's not only bad prose and poetry": www.georgecarlin.com.

220   "If you're born in America": Appearance on *Tavis Smiley* (PBS), April 8, 2004.

221   "just one more bullshit political philosophy": George Carlin, *Napalm & Silly Putty* (Hyperion, 2001), 261.

221   "I belong to no party": Teachout, *The Skeptic*, 236.

221   "I read somewhere that every atom in us": James A. Haught, "God, Life, and Avocado-Colored Kitchen Appliances: A Chat with George Carlin," *Free Inquiry* (Summer 1999).

224   "picketers and counter-picketers": Phil Grecian, "Carlin's Complaints Not Shocking, for Him," *Topeka Capital-Journal*, October 5, 2001.

224   "Riffs included suicide": Norm Clarke, "Dark Carlin," *Las Vegas Review-Journal*, December 4, 2004.

224   "punch up the writing": Richard Cusick, "High Times Interview: The Clown's Dark Genius," *High Times*, November 1997.

224   "Some of the guys in there": Hochman, "*Playboy* Interview."

225   "the most dispiriting, soul-deadening city on earth": Richard Abowitz, "George Carlin Hates Vegas," *Los Angeles Times*, August 13, 2007.

226   "an apocalypse that is part Steven King": Joshua David Mann, "The Complete Carlin: What You Can Learn by Watching 800 Minutes of George Carlin," *Slate*, June 26, 2008.

226   "try to outwit the inner censor": Jim Holt, *Stop Me If You've Heard This: A History and Philosophy of Jokes* (W.W. Norton, 2008), 70.

226   "There are a lot of comics working forty years": Jacques Steinberg, "Refusing to Coast on 7 Infamous Words," *New York Times*, November 4, 2005.

228   "Thank you, Mr. Twain": Paul Harris, "George Carlin to Take Twain Prize," *Variety*, June 18, 2008.

228   "There's always hope for comedians": Hochman, "*Playboy* Interview."

Kicker

231   "the filthiest piece of legislation": Steven Pinker *The Stuff of Thought: Language As a Window into Human Nature* (Penguin Books, 2007), 360.

232   "to be fruitful and multiply": Pinker, *Stuff of Thought,* 20.

232   "the word that's probably the Queen Mother": Glenn Garvin, "Carlin May Be Gone, But the Flap Over His Seven Words Isn't," *Miami Herald,* June 24, 2008.

232   "People have been telling me": Joan Biskupic, "Supreme Court Ruling Bans Broadcast 'Fleeting Expletives,'" *USA Today,* April 28, 2009.

233   "What can I say about George Carlin": *The Eleventh Annual Kennedy Center Mark Twain Prize* (PBS), 2009.

ACKNOWLEDGMENTS

◇　◇　◇　◇　◇　◇　◇

The one thing George Carlin took seriously was refusing to take anything seriously. In making a case for his comic philosophy, I am indebted to the many friends and acquaintances who shared their memories of him with me. Particular thanks to Jenni Matz, Ken Harris, Nick Zaino, David Tillotson, Trevon Blondet, and John Lewis Puff for their help with source materials.

Thanks to Paul Bresnick, my agent, for helping me cast a wide net. Thanks to Ben Schafer, my editor, for his enthusiasm and encouragement. Thanks again to Billie Porter for her keen eye.

I would like to thank Kelly Carlin-McCall for her kindness and willingness to make some room on the shelf.

Much like standup comedy, writing is a solitary pursuit, but I've been blessed with many funny people to brighten my life. In particular, old friends David Marmer and Jay Ablondi have always been comedians without going pro. My friend Jeremy Cowan carries a big shtick. And Rick D'Elia is, in fact, the coolest cousin-in-law.

My father, Al Sullivan, who was born five years to the day before Carlin, still loves to say that he raised an R-rated kid. More importantly, he gave me a critical survival skill: a cracked sense of humor. And my wonderful wife, Monica, and our three beautiful boys—Sam, Will, and Owen—remind me every day that nothing beats a smile and a laugh.

INDEX